First World War
and Army of Occupation
War Diary
France, Belgium and Germany

2 DIVISION
Divisional Troops
41 and 44 Brigade Royal Field Artillery
4 August 1914 - 30 April 1916

WO95/1327

The Naval & Military Press Ltd
www.nmarchive.com
Published in association with The National Archives

Published by

The Naval & Military Press Ltd

Unit 10 Ridgewood Industrial Park,

Uckfield, East Sussex,

TN22 5QE England

Tel: +44 (0) 1825 749494

www.naval-military-press.com

www.nmarchive.com

This diary has been reprinted in facsimile from the original. Any imperfections are inevitably reproduced and the quality may fall short of modern type and cartographic standards.

© **Crown Copyright**
Images reproduced by permission of The National Archives, London, England, 2015.

Contents

Document type	Place/Title	Date From	Date To
Heading	2 Division. Troops. 41 Brigade R.F.A. 1917 Jan To 1918 Dec. 44 Brigade R.F.A. 1914 Aug To 1916 Apr.		
Heading	2 Division. Troops. 41 Brigade R.F.A. 1917 Jan To 1918 Dec. 44 Brigade R.F.A. 1914 Aug To 1916 Apr		
Heading	2nd Division Royal Artillery 41st Brigade R.F.A. Jan-Dec 1917		
Heading	2nd Divisional Artillery 41st Brigade R.F.A. January 1917		
War Diary	Bealcourt	01/01/1917	01/01/1917
War Diary	Gezaincourt	02/01/1917	02/01/1917
War Diary	Sarton	03/01/1917	03/01/1917
War Diary	Bouzincourt	04/01/1917	04/01/1917
War Diary	Mouquet	05/01/1917	05/01/1917
War Diary	Taun Courcellette	06/01/1917	11/01/1917
War Diary	Mouquet Farm Courcellette	12/01/1917	31/01/1917
Heading	2nd Divisional Artillery 41st Brigade R.F.A. February 1917		
War Diary	Monquet Farm Corcellette	01/02/1917	10/02/1917
War Diary	Mouquet Farm	10/02/1917	28/02/1917
Heading	2nd Divisional Artillery. 41st Brigade R.F.A. March 1917		
War Diary	Le Sars	01/03/1917	13/03/1917
War Diary	Loupart Wood	14/03/1917	20/03/1917
War Diary	Bouzincourt Alient Waggonlines	21/02/1917	23/02/1917
War Diary	Starts March	24/03/1917	30/03/1917
War Diary	Carency	31/03/1917	31/03/1917
Heading	2nd Divisional Artillery. 41st Brigade R.F.A. April 1917		
War Diary	Carenchy	01/04/1917	14/04/1917
War Diary	Carenchy Ecoivres	15/04/1917	15/04/1917
War Diary	Ecoivres	16/04/1917	16/04/1917
War Diary	Bailleul	17/04/1917	30/04/1917
Heading	2nd Divisional Artillery 41st Brigade R.F.A. May 1917		
War Diary	Bailleul	01/05/1917	31/05/1917
Heading	2nd Divisional Artillery 41st Brigade R.F.A. June 1917		
War Diary	Bailleul	01/06/1917	30/06/1917
Heading	2nd Divisional Artillery 41st Brigade R.F.A. July 1917		
War Diary	Arras	01/07/1917	02/07/1917
War Diary	Givenchy Festubert	03/07/1917	31/07/1917
Operation(al) Order(s)	Operation Order No 21 by Lieut. Colonel J.G. Dooner, R.F.A. Commanding Left Group, 2nd D.A.	24/07/1917	24/07/1917
Map	Reference		
Heading	2nd Divisional Artillery 41st Brigade R.F.A. August 1917		
War Diary	Givenchy-Festubert	01/08/1917	31/08/1917
Heading	2nd Divisional Artillery 41st Brigade R.F.A. September 1917		
War Diary	Festubert Givenchy	01/09/1917	30/09/1917
Heading	2nd Divisional Artillery 41st Brigade R.F.A. October 1917		

War Diary	Givenchy Festubert	01/10/1917	16/10/1917
War Diary	Thiennes	17/10/1917	18/10/1917
War Diary	St. Julien	19/10/1917	31/10/1917
Heading	2nd Divisional Artillery 41st Brigade R.F.A. November 1917		
War Diary	Ypres	01/11/1917	20/11/1917
War Diary	Watou	21/11/1917	25/11/1917
War Diary	Haplincourt	26/11/1917	26/11/1917
War Diary	Moeuvres	27/11/1917	30/11/1917
Heading	2nd Divisional Artillery 41st Brigade R.F.A. December 1917		
War Diary	Moeuvres	01/12/1917	04/12/1917
War Diary	Hermies	05/12/1917	31/12/1917
Heading	2nd Division 41st Brigade R.F.A. Jan-Dec 1918		
Heading	2nd Divisional Artillery 41st Brigade R.F.A. January 1918		
War Diary	Hermies	01/01/1918	04/01/1918
War Diary	Haplincourt	05/01/1918	19/01/1918
War Diary	Trescault	20/01/1918	31/01/1918
Heading	2nd Divisional Artillery 41st Brigade R.F.A. February 1918		
War Diary	Beaucamp	01/02/1918	28/02/1918
Heading	2nd Divisional Artillery 41st Brigade Royal Field Artillery March 1918		
War Diary	Beaucamp	01/03/1918	23/03/1918
War Diary	Rocquigny	24/03/1918	24/03/1918
War Diary	Le Transloy	24/03/1918	24/03/1918
War Diary	Les Boeufs	24/03/1918	24/03/1918
War Diary	Gueudecourt	24/03/1918	24/03/1918
War Diary	Le Sars	24/03/1918	24/03/1918
War Diary	Contalmaison	25/03/1918	25/03/1918
War Diary	Aveluy Albert	26/03/1918	26/03/1918
War Diary	Bouzincourt	27/03/1918	27/03/1918
War Diary	Varennes	28/03/1918	28/03/1918
War Diary	Varennes Bouzincourt	29/03/1918	31/03/1918
Heading	2nd Divisional Artillery 41st Brigade R.F.A. April 1918		
War Diary	Bouzincourt	01/04/1918	01/04/1918
War Diary	Varennes	02/04/1918	04/04/1918
War Diary	Grouches	05/04/1918	05/04/1918
War Diary	Roziere	06/04/1918	08/04/1918
War Diary	Frevin Capelle	09/04/1918	09/04/1918
War Diary	Blangy	10/04/1918	30/04/1918
Heading	2nd Divisional Artillery 41st Brigade R.F.A. May 1918		
War Diary	Blangy	01/05/1918	31/05/1918
Heading	2nd Divisional Artillery 41st Brigade R.F.A. June 1918		
War Diary	Blangy	01/06/1918	21/06/1918
War Diary	St. Amand	22/06/1918	22/06/1918
War Diary	Monchy	23/06/1918	30/06/1918
Heading	2nd Divisional Artillery 41st Brigade R.F.A. July 1918		
War Diary	Monchy	01/07/1918	31/07/1918
Heading	2nd Divisional Artillery 41st Brigade R.F.A. August 1918		
War Diary	Monchy-Au-Bois And Adinfer	01/08/1918	23/08/1918
War Diary	Courcelles-Le-Comte	23/08/1918	25/08/1918
War Diary	Gomiecourt	25/08/1918	30/08/1918
War Diary	Behagnies	30/08/1918	31/08/1918

Heading	2nd Divisional Artillery 41st Brigade R.F.A. September 1918		
War Diary	Behagnies	01/09/1918	02/09/1918
War Diary	Vaulx-Vraucourt	03/09/1918	03/09/1918
War Diary	Beaumetz-Les-Cambrai	03/09/1918	12/09/1918
War Diary	Hernies	14/09/1918	15/09/1918
War Diary	Louverval	16/09/1918	26/09/1918
War Diary	Demicourt	26/09/1918	27/09/1918
War Diary	Graincourt	27/09/1918	27/09/1918
War Diary	Flesquieres	27/09/1918	28/09/1918
War Diary	Premy Chapel	28/09/1918	28/09/1918
War Diary	Noyelles	29/09/1918	30/09/1918
Heading	2nd Divisional Artillery. 41st Brigade R.F.A. October 1918		
War Diary	Noyelles (Cambrai)	01/10/1918	04/10/1918
War Diary	Noyelles	05/10/1918	07/10/1918
War Diary	Rumilly	08/10/1918	09/10/1918
War Diary	Noyelles	10/10/1918	18/10/1918
War Diary	St. Vaast	19/10/1918	20/10/1918
War Diary	Haussy	21/10/1918	23/10/1918
War Diary	Vertain	24/10/1918	24/10/1918
War Diary	Capelle	25/10/1918	31/10/1918
Heading	2nd Divisional Artillery 41st Brigade R.F.A. November 1918		
War Diary	Capelle	01/11/1918	03/11/1918
War Diary	Villers-Pol	04/11/1918	06/11/1918
War Diary	Preux-Au-Sart	07/11/1918	07/11/1918
War Diary	Audignies	08/11/1918	19/11/1918
War Diary	Meuberge	20/11/1918	23/11/1918
War Diary	Estinne-Au-Mont	24/11/1918	24/11/1918
War Diary	Fontaine L'Eveque	25/11/1918	28/11/1918
War Diary	Pregles	29/11/1918	30/11/1918
Heading	2nd Divisional Artillery 41st Brigade R.F.A. December 1918		
War Diary	Presles	01/12/1918	03/12/1918
War Diary	Malonne	04/12/1918	04/12/1918
War Diary	Nameche	05/12/1918	05/12/1918
War Diary	Huy	06/12/1918	06/12/1918
War Diary	Warzee	07/12/1918	07/12/1918
War Diary	Harze	08/12/1918	09/12/1918
War Diary	Cheneaux Monteau	10/12/1918	10/12/1918
War Diary	Malmedy (Germany)	11/12/1918	11/12/1918
War Diary	Elsenborn	12/12/1918	12/12/1918
War Diary	Montjoie	13/12/1918	13/12/1918
War Diary	Kesternich	14/12/1918	15/12/1918
War Diary	Gey	16/12/1918	20/12/1918
War Diary	Langerwehe	20/12/1918	31/12/1918
War Diary	Langerwehe Germany	01/01/1919	31/01/1919
War Diary	Langerwehe	01/02/1919	28/02/1919
Heading	2nd Division 44th Bde R.F.A. B.H.Q. 44th (How) Bty R.F.A. 56th Battery R.F.A. 60th Battery R.F.A. 2nd Divl Ammn Column Aug-Dec 1914		
Heading	2nd Division 44th Bde R.F.A. 2nd Divl. Ammn Column Aug-Dec 1914		
Diagram etc	Steel Framework Parts.		

Heading	War Diary 2nd Divisional Ammunition Column 5-31-8-14		
War Diary	Preston	05/08/1914	05/08/1914
War Diary	Aldershot	06/08/1914	18/08/1914
War Diary	Southampton	18/08/1914	18/08/1914
War Diary	Havre	19/08/1914	19/08/1914
War Diary	Rouen	19/08/1914	22/08/1914
War Diary	Varcoun	23/08/1914	31/08/1914
Heading	War Diary Ammun Column 2nd Division Volume II 1-30.9.14		
War Diary		01/09/1914	22/09/1914
War Diary	Varcoun	23/09/1914	30/09/1914
Miscellaneous	H.Q. 2 Div.	30/09/1914	30/09/1914
Miscellaneous	Greslines	30/09/1914	30/09/1914
Miscellaneous	R.A. 2nd Division	30/09/1914	30/09/1914
Miscellaneous	2nd Division		
Miscellaneous	O C 47th Battery	30/09/1914	30/09/1914
Miscellaneous	Report On Trenches		
Diagram etc	Rough Sketch		
Diagram etc	Germans		
Heading	2nd Divisional Artillery 2nd Divisional Ammunition Column R.F.A. October 1914		
War Diary	W. Courcelles	01/10/1914	15/10/1914
War Diary	St Omer	16/10/1914	16/10/1914
War Diary	Renescure	17/10/1914	17/10/1914
War Diary	Wallon Cappel	18/10/1914	19/10/1914
War Diary	Eeke	20/10/1914	20/10/1914
War Diary	Reninghelst	21/10/1914	23/10/1914
War Diary	Vlamertinge	24/10/1914	30/10/1914
War Diary	Reningholst Pupperinge	31/10/1914	31/10/1914
Heading	2nd Divisional Artillery 2nd Divisional Ammunition Column R.F.A. November 1914		
War Diary	Reningholst Popperinge	01/11/1914	11/11/1914
War Diary	Reninghelst	12/11/1914	18/11/1914
War Diary	Rouge Croix	19/11/1914	30/11/1914
Heading	2nd Divisional Artillery 2nd Divisional Ammunition Column R.F.A. December 1914		
War Diary	Rouge Croix	01/12/1914	25/12/1914
War Diary	Boheme	26/12/1914	30/12/1914
War Diary	Robex	31/12/1914	31/12/1914
Miscellaneous	2nd Division Ammunition Column		
Miscellaneous	A.A.G. Base		
Miscellaneous	2nd Divnl Ammunition. Column August 1914		
Miscellaneous	Major Desmond G. Trouton's Experience In The Early Fighting Of 1914		
Heading	2nd Division 44th Bde R.F.A. 56th Battery R.F.A. Aug-Dec 1914		
Diagram etc	Steel Framework Parts		
Heading	2nd Division War Diary 56th Battery R.F.A. August 1914		
War Diary		18/08/1914	31/08/1914
Heading	2nd Division War Diary 56th Battery R.F.A. September 1914		
War Diary	Bargny	01/09/1914	01/09/1914
War Diary	Meaux	02/09/1914	02/09/1914
War Diary	Grand Bilbarteru	03/09/1914	03/09/1914

Type	Location	Start	End
War Diary	Mouroux	04/09/1914	04/09/1914
War Diary	Chateau-Le-Vivier	05/09/1914	05/09/1914
War Diary	Chateau De-La-Fortelle	06/09/1914	06/09/1914
War Diary	St Simeon	07/09/1914	07/09/1914
War Diary	Boitrom Right Section Under Lt. Tidmarsh In Action At La Pretoire	08/09/1914	08/09/1914
War Diary	Dompton	09/09/1914	09/09/1914
War Diary	Bussiares Chevillon South of Monnes	10/09/1914	10/09/1914
War Diary	Oulchy Le Chateau	11/09/1914	11/09/1914
War Diary	Courcelles	12/09/1914	12/09/1914
War Diary	Dheuzel	13/09/1914	13/09/1914
War Diary	Grossel River Aisne And Come Into Action At Verneuil.	14/09/1914	14/09/1914
War Diary		14/09/1914	15/09/1914
War Diary	Verneuil	16/09/1914	30/09/1914
Heading	2nd Div War Diary 56th Battery R.F.A. October 1914		
War Diary	Verneuil	29/09/1914	05/10/1914
War Diary		06/10/1914	07/10/1914
War Diary	About One Mile NE of Chassemy	11/10/1914	11/10/1914
War Diary	Mont Hussart Farm	12/10/1914	12/10/1914
War Diary	Arcy	13/10/1914	13/10/1914
War Diary		14/10/1914	14/10/1914
War Diary		15/10/1914	15/10/1914
War Diary	Blaringhem	16/10/1914	16/10/1914
War Diary	Eecke	17/10/1914	19/10/1914
War Diary	Ypres	20/10/1914	20/10/1914
War Diary	St Julien	21/10/1914	21/10/1914
War Diary	Frezenberg	22/10/1914	24/10/1914
War Diary	Gheluvelt	25/10/1914	26/10/1914
War Diary	Hooge	27/10/1914	31/10/1914
Heading	2nd Div. War Diary 56th Battery R.F.A. November 1914		
War Diary	Hooge	01/11/1914	02/11/1914
War Diary	Battery	03/11/1914	03/11/1914
War Diary	Esternest	04/11/1914	04/11/1914
War Diary	Marched To Dickebusche	05/11/1914	05/11/1914
War Diary	Marched To Hazebroucke	06/11/1914	06/11/1914
War Diary	Haze Broucke	07/11/1914	17/11/1914
War Diary	Fletre	18/11/1914	26/11/1914
War Diary	Les Harisoirs	21/11/1914	30/11/1914
Heading	2nd Divisional Artillery 56th Battery R.F.A. December 1914		
War Diary	Les Harisons	01/12/1914	03/12/1914
War Diary	Le Touret Burbure	04/12/1914	11/12/1914
War Diary	Le Touret	12/12/1914	26/12/1914
War Diary	Lespesses	27/12/1914	31/12/1914
Heading	2nd Division 44th Bde R.F.A. B.H.Q. Aug-Dec 1914		
Diagram etc	Steel Framework Parts		
Heading	2nd Division War Diary XLIV Brigade R.F.A. August 1914		
War Diary		04/08/1914	31/08/1914
Heading	2nd Division War Diary XLIV Brigade R.F.A. September 1914		
War Diary		01/09/1914	30/09/1914
Heading	2nd Division War Diary XLIV Brigade R.F.A. October 1914		

War Diary		01/10/1914	31/10/1914
Heading	2nd Division War Diary XLIV Brigade R.F.A. November 1914		
War Diary		01/11/1914	30/11/1914
Heading	2nd Division War Diary XLIV Brigade R.F.A. December 1914		
War Diary	Fletre	01/12/1914	21/12/1914
War Diary	Vendin	22/12/1914	26/12/1914
War Diary	Le Touret	27/12/1914	31/12/1914
Heading	2nd Division 44th Bde R.F.A. 47th (How) Battery R.F.A. Aug-Nov 1914		
Diagram etc	Steel Framework Parts		
Heading	2nd Division 44th Bde. R.F.A. War Diary 47th (How) Battery R.F.A. August 1914		
War Diary		17/08/1914	31/08/1914
Heading	War Diary 47th Battery R.F.A.		
Heading	2nd Division 44th Bde. R.F. 47th (How) Battery R.F.A. September 1914		
War Diary		01/09/1914	30/09/1914
Heading	2nd Division 44th Bde. R.F.A. War Diary 47th (How) Battery R.F.A. October 1914		
War Diary		01/10/1914	31/10/1914
Heading	2nd Division 44th Bde. R.F.A. 47th (How) Battery R.F.A. November 1914		
War Diary		01/11/1914	30/11/1914
Heading	2nd Division 44th Bde. R.F.A. 60th Battery R.F.A. Aug-Nov 1914		
Diagram etc	Steel Framework Parts.		
Heading	2nd Division War Diary 60th Battery R.F.A. August 1914		
War Diary		04/08/1914	31/08/1914
Heading	2nd Division War Diary 60th Battery R.F.A. September 1914		
War Diary		01/09/1914	21/09/1914
Heading	2nd Division War Diary 60th Battery R.F.A. October 1914		
War Diary		01/10/1914	30/10/1914
Heading	2nd Division War Diary 60th Battery R.F.A. November 1914		
War Diary		01/11/1914	30/11/1914
Heading	2nd Division Royal Artillery H.Q. 44th Brigade R.F.A. 56th Batty R.F.A. 1915 Jan-1915 Dec		
Heading	2nd Divisional Artillery 44th Brigade R.F.A, 56th Battery R.F.A. February 1915		
War Diary	Croix Barbee	01/02/1915	05/02/1915
War Diary	Richebourg St Vast	06/02/1915	18/02/1915
War Diary	Les Harisoirs	19/02/1915	26/02/1915
War Diary	Cambrin	27/02/1915	28/02/1915
Heading	44th Brigade R.F.A. 2nd Divisional Artillery 56th Battery R.F.A. April 1915		
War Diary	Cambrin	01/04/1915	30/04/1915
Heading	44th Brigade R.F.A. 2nd Divisional Artillery 56th Battery R.F.A. May 1915		
War Diary	Cambrin	01/05/1915	31/05/1915
Heading	44 Brigade. R.F.A. 2nd Divisional Artillery 56th Battery R.F.A. June 1915		

War Diary	Cambrin	01/06/1915	19/06/1915
War Diary	Bethune	20/06/1915	28/06/1915
War Diary	Cambrin	29/06/1915	30/06/1915
Heading	44th Brigade R.F.A. 2nd Divisional Artillery. 56th Battery R.F.A. July 1915		
War Diary	Cambrin	01/07/1915	31/07/1915
Heading	44th Brigade R.F.A. 2nd Divisional Artillery. 56th Battery R.F.A. August 1915		
War Diary	Cambrin	01/08/1915	30/08/1915
Heading	2nd Divisional Artillery. 44th Brigade R.F.A. January 1915		
War Diary	Le Touret	01/01/1915	31/01/1915
Heading	2nd Divisional Artillery. 44th Brigade R.F.A. February 1915		
War Diary	Le Touret	01/02/1915	07/02/1915
War Diary	Le Quesnoy	08/02/1915	28/02/1915
Heading	2nd Divisional Artillery. 44th Brigade R.F.A. March 1915		
War Diary	Le Quesnoy	01/03/1915	30/03/1915
Heading	2nd Divisional Artillery. 44th Brigade R.F.A. April 1915		
War Diary	Le Quesnoy	01/04/1915	30/04/1915
Heading	2nd Divisional Artillery. 44th Brigade R.F.A. May 1915		
War Diary		01/05/1915	31/05/1915
Heading	2nd Divisional Artillery. 44th Brigade R.F.A. June 1915		
War Diary		01/06/1915	12/06/1915
War Diary	Vebmelles Cambrin	13/06/1915	13/06/1915
War Diary	Toubbiebes	14/06/1915	30/06/1915
Heading	2nd Divisional Artillery. 44th Brigade R.F.A. July 1915		
War Diary		01/07/1915	31/07/1915
Heading	2nd Divisional Divisional Artillery. 44th Brigade R.F.A. August 1915		
War Diary	Bethune	01/08/1915	31/08/1915
Heading	War Diary Headquarters 44th Brigade R.F.A. (2nd Division) September 1915		
War Diary	Bethune	08/09/1915	19/09/1915
War Diary	Le Preol	21/09/1915	30/09/1915
War Diary	Le Quesnoy	30/09/1915	30/09/1915
Heading	2nd Divisional Artillery. 44th Brigade R.F.A. October 1915		
War Diary	Le Quesnoy	01/10/1915	23/10/1915
War Diary	Bethune	24/10/1915	31/10/1915
War Diary		05/10/1915	15/10/1915
Heading	2nd Divisional Artillery. 44th Brigade R.F.A. November 1915		
War Diary	Bethune	01/11/1915	30/11/1915
Heading	2nd Divisional Artillery. 44th Brigade R.F.A. December 1915		
War Diary	Bethune	01/12/1915	28/12/1915
Heading	2nd Divl Artillery. 44th Brigade R.F.A. Jan-Apl 1916		
Heading	2nd Divisional Artillery 44th Brigade R.F.A. January 1916		
War Diary		01/01/1916	31/01/1916
Heading	2nd Divisional Artillery. 44th Brigade R.F.A. February 1916		
War Diary		01/02/1916	29/02/1916

Heading	2nd Divisional Artillery. 44th Brigade R.F.A. March 1916		
War Diary		01/03/1916	31/03/1916
Heading	2nd Divisional Artillery. 44th Brigade R.F.A. April 1916		
War Diary		01/04/1916	30/04/1916

2 DIVISION. TROOPS.

41 BRIGADE R.F.A.

1917 JAN TO 1918 DEC.

44 BRIGADE R.F.A.

1914 AUG TO 1916 APR.

2 DIVISION. TROOPS.

41 BRIGADE R.F.A.

1917 JAN TO 1918 DEC.

44 BRIGADE R.F.A.

1914 AUG TO 1916 APR.

1327

**2ND DIVISION
ROYAL ARTILLERY**

41ST BRIGADE R.F.A.

JAN-DEC 1917

2nd Divisional Artillery

41st BRIGADE R.F.A. ::: JANUARY 1917

WAR DIARY
or
INTELLIGENCE SUMMARY.

(Erase heading not required.)

41st Brigade R.F.A. Form C. 2118.

January 1917.

Vol 28

Place	Date	Hour	Summary of Events and Information	Remarks and references to Appendices
BERTACOURT	1st		Rests at BERTACOURT.	
GEZAINCOURT	2nd		Marched to GEZAINCOURT.	
SARTON	3rd		Marched SARTON. Battery commanders went forward to reconnoitre their future positions.	
BOUZINCOURT	4th		Marched to Camp at BOUZINCOURT – AVELUY road.	
MOUQUET FARM	5th		Relieved 257th Bde R.F.A. 9th, 16th & 15th heads MOUQUET Farm	
nr COURCELETTE	6th		We relieved A/260 nr COURCELETTE.	
ditto	6th		Lieut J.P. Wilson 16th Battery awarded Military Cross. Capt W.G. Dyson 4th Bde ba to Military Cross	
ditto	7th		Observation practically impossible.	
ditto	8th		Observation possible for a short time & registration was carried out.	
ditto	9th		"X" day. light very bad. Roads etc were searched in battery zones.	
ditto	10th		"Y" day fired as ordered. Enemy's retaliation to our barrages was feeble.	
ditto	11th		"Z" day. fired barrage to assist a raid by 61st Divn. Observation impossible.	

Army Form C. 2118.

WAR DIARY
or
INTELLIGENCE SUMMARY.
(Erase heading not required.)

Instructions regarding War Diaries and Intelligence Summaries are contained in F. S. Regs., Part II. and the Staff Manual respectively. Title pages will be prepared in manuscript.

Place	Date	Hour	Summary of Events and Information	Remarks and references to Appendices
MOUQUET FARM & COURCELETTE	15th to 16th	—	Lightning bad — Map firing carried out as ordered in programme —	
ditto.	17th	—	Fired a faint barrage. 47th Battery fired gas shells into MIRAUMONT.	
ditto.	18th	—	Light bad. Fired salvoes as ordered. Lt. Col. GOSCHEN & 36th Bde.R.H.A. took over command of the front	
ditto.	19th	—	Light bad, fired salvoes as ordered & fired on communications. Lt.Col. DOONER went on leave.	
ditto.	20th	—	Light bad, fired Dump Salvoes. 16th Battery had a G.S. wagon & team hit at TULLOCH CORNER, & men killed & 2 wounded	
ditto.	21st 22nd	—	Light bad — Fired dump salvoes —	
ditto.	23rd 24th	—	Enemy's Artillery & aeroplanes were active — fired dump salvoes —	

WAR DIARY
or
INTELLIGENCE SUMMARY
(Erase heading not required.)

Army Form C. 2118

Instructions regarding War Diaries and Intelligence Summaries are contained in F.S. Regs., Part II. and the Staff Manual respectively. Title pages will be prepared in manuscript.

Place	Date	Hour	Summary of Events and Information	Remarks and references to Appendices
MOUQUET FARM & COURCELLETTE	25th		Sub Sect relieved. ½ D/34 joined 47th Battery. Capt. Cadew & 2/Lieut Reid Walker posted to 47th Battery RFA, 2/Lieut S. Atterbank to 76th Battery RFA.	
ditto	26th		Fired as ordered. Enemy shelled TULLOCH CORNER.	
ditto	27th		Light fire. 47th Battery fired 70 rounds sniping. 47th Bty replied on PYS.	
ditto	28th		76 RFA fired 70 rounds sniping. 47th Battery fired 150 rounds on enemy's front in R11 d.	
ditto	29th		Fired as ordered.	
ditto	30th		47 Bty fired on enemy.	
ditto	31st		Light Cood. registration carried out. 47th Btÿ fired on front line.	

R.D. Baxter
Lt Col. comdg A/7?
Bdes R.F.A.

2nd Divisional Artillery.

41st BRIGADE R.F.A. ::: FEBRUARY 1917.

H/1st Brigade R.F.A.

WAR DIARY
or
INTELLIGENCE SUMMARY.
(Erase heading not required.)

Army Form C. 2118.

Vol 29

February 1917

Place	Date	Hour	Summary of Events and Information	Remarks and references to Appendices
Marquet Farm Courcelette	1st		Frost continued — All Batteries fired on Brigade Targets, all registered points — 17th Battery did good shooting at Aeroplane & kept losses on a min —	
			carrying flare, to rise and driving them off —	
Ditto	2nd		Batteries fired at wire and trenches —	
"	3rd		63rd Division attacked Puisieux & River Trench 17th Battery acting in Barrage —	
"	4th		17th Battery came under the command of Colonel Parry 34th Brigade for barrage in support of a raid by 1st Royal Berks on a strong point —	
"	5th		1st Berks attack — Zero hour 3 a.m. Brigade co-operates with 18th Division — attack successful — Fires in retaliation to hostile fire at 8 p.m.	
"	6th		Fires in retaliation to hostile shelling & reliefs —	
"	7th		Thick haze — observation impossible —	
"	8th		Quiet on our front — Patrols on left occupies GRANDCOURT —	
"	9th		Quiet on Front — Major Sloan reconnoitred SOUTH MIRAUMONT Trench —	
"	10		Light poor — Batteries assisted raid by 17th Royal Fusiliers — Six prisoners taken	

Army Form C. 2118.

WAR DIARY
or
INTELLIGENCE SUMMARY.
(Erase heading not required.)

Instructions regarding War Diaries and Intelligence Summaries are contained in F. S. Regs., Part II. and the Staff Manual respectively. Title pages will be prepared in manuscript.

Place	Date	Hour	Summary of Events and Information	Remarks and references to Appendices
MOUQUET FARM	10th		Lieut C.S. DEAR M.G. Battery goes to S.A.A. Section	
	11th		All Quiet - light very poor -	
	12th		Visibility poor - About 70 Germans raided our Trenches between Posts 9 & 70 - Raid was expected - and guns opened fire the moment the Germans Bombardment Started - very few Germans got back to their lines -	
	13th		Hostile Artillery very active - Infantry called six times for Retaliation during the night - Major QUILLER-COUCH M.C. left for B.C. course in England - Captain L.G. SANDFORD took command of the G.T.B.N. in his place -	
	14th		Batteries carried out WIRE CUTTING & REGISTERED new zone - 17th B.G. cut wire N. of PYS road - Hostile artillery very active between 6.30 & 7.30 pm Batteries retaliated very heavily on S.O.S. lines and Tracks -	
	15th		Fired on WIRE and tracks	
	16th		Fired on WIRE enlarging all gaps through the day & night -	
	17th		Fired heavy BARRAGE - While the 18th Div. attacked between E. Miraumont Rd and the River ANCRE	

WAR DIARY
or
INTELLIGENCE SUMMARY.

Army Form C. 2118.

Place	Date	Hour	Summary of Events and Information	Remarks and references to Appendices
MONQUET FARM	18th		VERY FOGGY — Fired on protective BARRAGE lines and Enemy's tracks —	
	19th		" ditto "	
	20th		Rain — Fired on back communications day & night —	
	21st		Batteries re-registered on new Zone — Light very bad. The Zone new & the night of [ ] no good correctly CURCELETTE & P y S —	
			Prisoners Taken state that the Germans in fair tactic back on line LOUPART WOOD — ACHIET — LE — PETIT — BUCQUOY —	
	22nd		Batteries fired on new Zone — THICK MIST	
	23rd		MIST still bad — Batteries fire protective barrages	
	24th		Enemy falling back = Petit MIRAUMONT occupied by 18th Division. 2nd Division patrols entered Serre trenches on their front — Brigade received orders to get all guns out of position and prepare to advance	
	25th		Batteries worked all night and made fair progress —	
	26th		Major SLOAN — Dr DAWSON & Capt CAREY went forward to reconnoitre for German wheatworks — They never returned to 17th Bty and were reported to missing — believed to be Prisoners German — Lieut R.T. BAXTER from 47. Bty. 2nd Lieut CW de GRUMEAU became Adjutant — from 9 E. Bty.	

WAR DIARY
or
INTELLIGENCE SUMMARY.
(Erase heading not required.)

Army Form C. 2118

Place	Date	Hour	Summary of Events and Information	Remarks and references to Appendices
MOUQUET FARM	26th		Position reconnoitred — Guns & Ammunition moved to Courcelette — Captain Cardon left 47th B[ty]	
	27th			
	28th		Lieut Reeves returned from France & took command of 17th B/5. Reconnoitred for new battery positions near LE SARS — Aqueduct Road —	

2nd Divisional Artillery.

41st BRIGADE R.F.A. ::: MARCH 1917.

41st Bde R.F.A.
Vol 29

WAR DIARY
or
INTELLIGENCE SUMMARY. 3rd Div.

Army Form C. 2118

Place	Date	Hour	Summary of Events and Information	Remarks and references to Appendices
LE SARS	MARCH 1st		Batteries prepared positions just N.W. of LE SARS. Got guns into position and started ammunition dumps during the night	
	2nd		Registered LOUPART WOOD	
	3rd		Light very poor - Batteries improves their positions -	
	4th		Cut wire in front of GRENILLERS TRENCH	
	5th		" " " " "	
	6th		Wire cutting continued, but much interfered with by hostile aeroplanes	
	7th		Light very good - Wire cutting again successful	
	8th		Snow Storm. Wire cutting practically impossible	

Army Form C. 2118.

WAR DIARY
or
INTELLIGENCE SUMMARY.
(Erase heading not required.)

Instructions regarding War Diaries and Intelligence Summaries are contained in F.S. Regs., Part II. and the Staff Manual respectively. Title pages will be prepared in manuscript.

Place	Date	Hour	Summary of Events and Information	Remarks and references to Appendices
LESARS	9th		Batteries active during intervals between snow storms. Positions and fired a Test Barrage on GREVILLERS TRENCH.	
	10th		Cooperated in successful attack by 2nd, 18th & 2nd Australian Division - All objectives were gained (IRLES & GREVILLERS TRENCH) Casualties slight. Attack took place at 5.15 AM. Very foggy - impossible to observe Barrage - lt. Infantry were not phased with it.	
	11th		Cut wire in front of LOUPART WOOD & TRENCH	
	12th		During the night 12/13th - Enemy evacuated LOUPART WOOD & whole LOUPART LINE S.E. of ACHIET-LE-PETIT = 2nd Lieut. Scragg pushed posts to g.r. 13.5	
	13th		Reconnoitred Valley Positions just S.W. of LOUPART WOOD	

Army Form C. 2118.

WAR DIARY
or
INTELLIGENCE SUMMARY.
(Erase heading not required.)

Instructions regarding War Diaries and Intelligence Summaries are contained in F. S. Regs., Part II. and the Staff Manual respectively. Title pages will be prepared in manuscript.

Place	Date	Hour	Summary of Events and Information	Remarks and references to Appendices
LOUPART WOOD	March 14th		Batteries shells new positions and made Ammunition Dumps — as shells brought up by Pack by Sherman Works	
	15th		Continued Dumps and brought up Guns — forward Wagon Line established at Le Sars	
	16th		GERMANS FELL BACK ON HINDENBURG LINE — Evacuating BAPAUME — both ACHIET'S & BIHUCOURT LINE — during night 15/16 enemy shelled Le Sars with Gas Shells, but the damage was done.	
	17th		Bryd's Trench. Trenses found — Gun fires at various targets will enemy was well out of Range —	
	18th		Batteries advanced to G29 Central N. of GREVILLERS — Crossing Loupart line with great difficulty owing to mud & Shell holes. Bivouaced in open — heavy Rain —	
	19th		BATTERIES Reconnoitred Country round Grevillers — Order received that Btys was to withdrew very heavy rain sleet — Batteries in open with no cover —	
	20th		Marched via to Wagon Lines near Albert & BOUZINCOURT — Roads very bad —	

T2134. Wt. W708—776. 500000. 4/15. Sir J. C. & S.

Army Form C. 2118.

WAR DIARY
or
INTELLIGENCE SUMMARY.
(Erase heading not required.)

Instructions regarding War Diaries and Intelligence Summaries are contained in F.S. Regs., Part II. and the Staff Manual respectively. Title pages will be prepared in manuscript.

Place	Date	Hour	Summary of Events and Information	Remarks and references to Appendices
Bouzincourt Albert wagon line	21st		Btn. at Wagon-line Albert-Bouzincourt Area – Overhauled harness – wagons etc.	
	22nd		Horses began to pick up again –	
	23rd			
Starts March	24th		Marched to Puchevillers via Senlis – Warloy, Toutencourt –	
	25th		Rested at Puchevillers	
	26th		Marched to Hem – via Beauquesne, Terramesnil – Mᵗ Bᵗ billetted at Hardinval	
	27th	"	Conchy-Sur-Canche – via Frohen-les-Grand, Wavans, Nedox, Vacqueric –	
	28th		Marched to Anvin via Flers, Heruicourt, St. Pol, Wavrans –	
	29th	"	Rested at Anvin –	
	30th		Marched to Marsnil-les-Ruitz – via Pernes & Camblain Chatelain & Divion	
CARENCY	31st		Reconnoitred Battery positions in front of Vimy Ridge – Batteries marched to Gouy-Servins to established wagon lines – During the night, Batteries moved up to positions South of CARENCY in support of IVᵗʰ Canadian Division. Cw. de Suncan Bt. Adj. 41ˢᵗ Bᵈᵉ R.F.A.	

T2134. Wt. W708—776. 500000. 4/15. Sir J. C. & S.

2nd Divisional Artillery.

41st BRIGADE R.F.A. ::: APRIL 1917.

Army Form C. 2118.

WAR DIARY
or
INTELLIGENCE SUMMARY.
(Erase heading not required.)

YL 30

Summary of Events and Information APRIL 1917 41ST BRIGADE RFA.

Remarks and references to Appendices ①

Place	Date	Hour	Summary of Events and Information
CARENCY	April 1st		Advanced parties from Batteries went forward to new positions (Point Q & Fox Covert for 9th & 16th - The 17th Battery on the Arras Road at S19 B 68.80 - 47th Battery on left of Souchez River -
	2nd		Ammunition at positions cleared and sorted 17th Bty in position without cover relieved some attention from 77 mm pits Squeak B5 - Battery Commanders reconnoitred for O. Pos. and registered guns on points on VIMY RIDGE
	3rd		U DAY - Registering continued - suitable OPs looked for - Positions worked on
	4th		17th Battery brought up their remaining section & registered
	5th		Fired feint barrage at 8 A.M. 16th Howrs threw 2 remaining guns into action - enemy wire very poor on 2nd & 3rd lines
	6th		Fired feint barrage at 1.30 pm - wire-cutting on support lines heavy rain in afternoon - Conference at 36 Bde HQ on communications for coming battle

T2134. Wt. W708—776. 500000. 4/15. Sir J. C. & S.

Army Form C. 2118.

WAR DIARY
or
INTELLIGENCE SUMMARY.
(Erase heading not required.)

Summary of Events and Information APRIL 1917 41st BRIGADE R.F.A.

Instructions regarding War Diaries and Intelligence Summaries are contained in F. S. Regs., Part II. and the Staff Manual respectively. Title pages will be prepared in manuscript.

Place	Date	Hour	Summary of Events and Information	Remarks and references to Appendices
CARENCY	APRIL 7th		Enemy put up fairly heavy barrage on our front line system at 3 am & 5.10 am — Batteries fired on wire in zones — very little remains to cut on front line — Hostile aeroplanes very active — & shelling of Zouave Valley above normal (4.2 & 5.9's)	
	8th		Front line wire-cutting continued — C. of E. service held at 17"R.B" position by List (Rev. Holden) 12.30 pm. — Y day —	
	9th		Z. Day — Canadians attacked Vimy Ridge at 5.30 am. with great success — 4000 prisoners taken — 3rd Army also very successful	
	10th		Snow — Sleet & Rain — very trying day — Fired at Chaudiere — also barrage in conjunction with attack on Cyclist Trench — attack successful 17th Bty bombarded during night by one of our own heavy batteries — which put 40 rounds short into S.13.d. Luckily no damage was caused	

Army Form C. 2118

WAR DIARY
or
INTELLIGENCE SUMMARY.
(Erase heading not required.)

Instructions regarding War Diaries and Intelligence Summaries are contained in F.S. Regs., Part II. and the Staff Manual respectively. Title pages will be prepared in manuscript.

APRIL 1917 41st BRIGADE R.F.A.

Place	Date	Hour	Summary of Events and Information	Remarks and references to Appendices
CARENCY	APRIL 11th		BURSTS OF FIRE ON VIMY VILLAGE & LA CHAUDIERE - HEAVY FALL OF SNOW - LIEUT. COL. J.C. DOOMER VISITED 17½ BATTERY TO EXAMINE HOLES MADE BY THE HEAVY BATTERIES. - THIS GUN WAS AGAIN ACTIVE BETWEEN 11 P.M. & MIDNIGHT, FIRING 30 ROUNDS CLOSE TO ARRAS ROAD AT S14 CENTRAL - 47th 13th FIRED ON GIVENCHY	
	12th		FIRED BARRAGE FOR ATTACK ON "PIMPLE" - ZERO AT 5 AM. - HEAVY BLIZZARD RAGING AT THE TIME - ATTACK WAS A COMPLETE SUCCESS 60 PRISONERS (PRUSSIAN GUARDS) WERE TAKEN - THIS COMPLETED THE CAPTURE OF THE VIMY RIDGE - 47th BATTERY BOMBARDED GIVENCHY	
	13th		INFANTRY OCCUPIED GIVENCHY - THE ENEMY RETIRING TO THE OPPY - VENDIN - MERICOURT LINE AND OUT OF RANGE	
	14th		PREPARED TO MOVE OUT OF ACTION	

Army Form C. 2118.

WAR DIARY
or
INTELLIGENCE SUMMARY.
(Erase heading not required.)

APRIL 1917 41st BRIGADE R.F.A.

Place	Date	Hour	Summary of Events and Information	Remarks and references to Appendices
CARENCY ECOIVRES	APRIL 15th		Brigade went out of action and marched via Mt. St. Eloi to Ecoivres — Billeted in hutments — Heavy rain — Very trying march for horses	
ECOIVRES	16th		Reconnoitred for new positions for batteries — West of Bailleul — Brigade resting at Ecoivres — New wagon-lines near Anzin selected — Just outside Arras	
+ BAILLEUL	17th		Brigade marched to new lines at Anzin — Batteries moved up guns and ammunition during the afternoon to new positions in B.19.d. —	
	18th		Registrations carried out — Batteries right in open — Much delay in bringing up ammunition, material etc. owing to congestion on the roads — which are very bad.	
	19th		More registration and targets engaged were seen.	
	20th		47th Battery cut wire North of OPPY	
	21st		Batteries fired on OPPY and at front line wire 1.30 AM & 4 AM — 47th Cut wire on OPPY Zone	

Army Form C. 2118.

WAR DIARY
or
INTELLIGENCE SUMMARY.
(Erase heading not required.)

Summary of Events and Information APRIL 1917 41st Brigade R.F.A.

Place	Date	Hour	Summary of Events and Information	Remarks and references to Appendices
BAILLEUL	April 22nd		Much hostile aeroplane activity – Captive balloon brought down by German in Red aeroplane marked with across inside 2 rings of red & white – very fast – Battery Positions shelled intermittently from 10 A.M. to 6 P.M. – The 16th having 1 man killed and 1 wounded – 17th 1 wounded – H.5 Hows. cut wire on Zone West of OPPY	
	23rd		Flank barrage fired to assist 63rd Div. attack on GAVRELLE. Zero hour 4.45 A.M. – Attack quite successful and strong counter-attacks beaten off – the Germans losing very heavily – 47th Battery had 2nd Lieut. ARNOLD wounded	
	24th		Fired in reply to S.O.S from 63rd Div. 5.30 A.M. Enemy heavily shelled positions between 9.30 A.M. & 11 A.M. – H.5 Hows cut wire	
	25th		Very good observation – Enemy movement sniped at all day – Wire cutting continued	

T.J134. Wt. W708–776. 500000. 4/15. Sir J. C. & S.

Army Form C. 2118.

WAR DIARY
or
INTELLIGENCE SUMMARY.
(Erase heading not required.)

April 1917 41st Brigade R.F.A.

Place	Date	Hour	Summary of Events and Information	Remarks and references to Appendices
Bailleul	April 26		Battery positions heavily shelled by 5.9s & 8" in afternoon & evening. Majors Walmard & Bailey together with Lieuts. Manifold & Ball all of 36 B'de killed. D.A.O. bringing up ammunition here in grave danger, but got away with the loss of one driver killed.	
	27th		Y day – Positions again shelled & Lieut-Col. I. Dooner commanding 41st Brigade acted as Liaison Officer with 6th Infantry Brigade. 41st B'de H.Q. moved to Infantry Brigade H.Q. 2nd Lieut. Reid-Walker 47th By wounded.	
	28th		Z day Attack on Oppy Line by 6th & 8th Brigades which failed (63rd Div. was held up on right.) Fired frequent S.O.S. barrages etc. Canadians on left captured Arleux. Hostile counter attacks at intervals.	
	29th		Barrage at 4 a.m. in support of attack by 99th Brigade on Oppy Line – attack fairly successful. Fired S.O.S. Much enemy activity. 36th B'de relieved 41st B'de as Liaison.	
	30th		Responded to S.O.S. Call at 4 a.m. – Fired at enemy movement and sniping machine guns in Oppy Wood.	

C.W. de Gruther
Lt. M. Adjt. 41st B'de R.F.A.

2nd Divisional Artillery.

41st BRIGADE R.F.A. ::: M A Y 1917.

Army Form C. 2118

41st Bde RFA

Vol 31

WAR DIARY
or
INTELLIGENCE SUMMARY.
(Erase heading not required.)

Instructions regarding War Diaries and Intelligence Summaries are contained in F. S. Regs., Part II. and the Staff Manual respectively. Title pages will be prepared in manuscript.

Place	Date	Hour	Summary of Events and Information	Remarks and references to Appendices
BAILLEUL	MAY 1st		Batteries registered on new S.O.S. Line : Chinese barrage on Oppy at 9 p.m. Hostile reply fairly heavy.	
"	2nd		Chinese Barrage fired 4 a.m. = Slight retaliation	
"	3rd		Attack by Canadian & XIII Corps - Former captured Fresnoy and the Oppy - Mericourt Line - The Second Division captured the Oppy Line south of Fresnoy to N.W. of Oppy = Attacks south of Oppy were repulsed.	
"	4th		Hun artillery quiet - Batteries checked registration and sniped at enemy movement	
"	5th		Very good observation - much sniping done	
"	6th		Batteries heavily shelled at intervals - much movement observed - particularly work of the line Oppy - Neuvireuil -	

Army Form C. 2118

WAR DIARY
or
INTELLIGENCE SUMMARY.
(Erase heading not required.)

Instructions regarding War Diaries and Intelligence Summaries are contained in F. S. Regs., Part II. and the Staff Manual respectively. Title pages will be prepared in manuscript.

Place	Date	Hour	Summary of Events and Information	Remarks and references to Appendices
BAILLEUL	MAY 7		Battery positions and neighbourhood shelled with gas shells and 5.9 Hows.	
	8		9th Battery heavily shelled during early morning – Sergeant Wilson killed and 2 gunners wounded – Enemy attacked FRESNOY & succeeding in entering Oppy MERCOURT LINE and FRESNOY – Attack was made without heavy artillery barrage –	
	9th		Counter attack on FRESNOY by K.O.S.B. and 16" Warwicks – dubious success –	
	10th		Enemy artillery less active – Large explosion occurred in enemy line E. of FRESNOY – S.O.S. sent up by Boche from FRESNOY to the SCARPE about 7.30 p.m.	
	11th		Large explosion observed near FRESNES and CHEZ-BON-TEMPS –	
	12th		Fired on roads and communications –	
	13		" " " " Light very good –	

T2134. Wt. W708–776. 500000. 4/15. Sir J. C. & S.

Army Form C. 2118

WAR DIARY
or
INTELLIGENCE SUMMARY.
(Erase heading not required.)

Instructions regarding War Diaries and Intelligence Summaries are contained in F. S. Regs., Part II. and the Staff Manual respectively. Title pages will be prepared in manuscript.

Place	Date	Hour	Summary of Events and Information	Remarks and references to Appendices
BAILLEUL	15th		2nd Lt WEATHERED JOINED NINTH BATTERY – OBSERVATION VERY FAT –	
"	16th		2nd Lt GOUGH & SMITH JOINED SEVENTEENTH BATTERY – SEVENTEENTH & SIXTEENTH moved a section forward to B.15.c. new Emplacement	
"	17th		PARIS LEAVE OPENED – Sergeant TAMKIN killed at 17.28.b.3 forward section –	
	18th		Fired barrage at 12.30 A.M. in connection with attack by 31st Div. = Batteries (especially 9th) heavily shelled at intervals by 5.9 + 8" –	
	19th		Fired at 2.30 A.M. on front line in anticipation of an attack – which did not materialise – Batteries heavily shelled during evening – no casualties but 9th had one gun hit to Centre and severely damaged –	
	20th		Quiet day –	
	21st		Enemy shelling very active during night – but the day was quieter –	

Army Form C. 2118

WAR DIARY
or
INTELLIGENCE SUMMARY.
(Erase heading not required.)

Instructions regarding War Diaries and Intelligence Summaries are contained in F.S. Regs., Part II. and the Staff Manual respectively. Title pages will be prepared in manuscript.

Place	Date	Hour	Summary of Events and Information	Remarks and references to Appendices
BAILEUL	May 22"		Quiet day. Enemy cut down the willows running south of OPPY WOOD —	
	23"		O/C 17th Battery tried to establish telephonic communication between front line & battery, but unsuccessful.	
	24th 25th		Light very good. Enemy counter batteries fairly active.	
	26th		O.R.A. visited gun positions in the morning. 9th Battery take over one gun from 49nd Battery.	
	27"		One officer killed & 4 other ranks wounded at 27th Battery. Wagon lines by shell fire. Infantry fire on one of our aeroplanes at dusk.	

WAR DIARY
or
INTELLIGENCE SUMMARY.
(Erase heading not required.)

Army Form C. 2118

Place	Date	Hour	Summary of Events and Information	Remarks and references to Appendices
Bailleul	May 28		47th Battery move one gun forward near Asleux. S.O.S. received at 2.15 a.m. apparently a mistake. Hurricane bombardment at 4.15 p.m.	
do.	29		47th Battery cause 2 explosions in hostile battery at Bas-ru-t. B.S.M. Hunt received commission (17th Battery.) Hurricane bombardment at 2.45 p.m. & 11.5 p.m. 2/Lt. Trapp relieves Lt. de Buiseau (on leave) as Adjutant.	
	30		Very quiet day. Hurricane bombardment at 2.20 p.m. & 3.05 p.m. & 3.45 a.m.	
	31		Hurricane bombardment at 4 a.m., 9.30 a.m., & 1.15 p.m. Enemy bombarded our front line at 4.30 p.m. Night firing was stopped, as enemy was supposed to be withdrawing. This turned out to be incorrect.	

2nd Divisional Artillery.

41st BRIGADE R.F.A. :: JUNE 1917.

Army Form C. 2118.

WAR DIARY
or
INTELLIGENCE SUMMARY.
(Erase heading not required.)

41st Brigade R.F.A.

Place	Date	Hour	Summary of Events and Information	Remarks and references to Appendices
BAILLEUL	June 1st		Batteries fired GO-HELL BARRAGE at 3 AM.	
"	2"	"	HURRICANE BOMBARDMENTS at 4·0 AM - 8.30 - 4 PM	
"	3"		QUIET DAY. Test "L1" Series at 5.30 pm - completed by 5.31 pm	
"	4"		HARASSING BARRAGE fired 3.20 pm & 3.28 pm - Batteries to fire on CRUCIFIX TRENCH at intervals during day & night.	
"	5"		Hurricane Bombardments fired at 11·15 AM - 4·20 pm and 11·0 pm.	
"	6"		" " 4·15 pm and 9 AM - Practice Barrage at 10.35 am	
"	7		Fired in response to Rocket Test at 2·40 AM. Fired Practice Barrage at 3 AM - Hurricane Bombardments at 4·10 AM & 8·40 AM	

WAR DIARY
INTELLIGENCE SUMMARY.
(Erase heading not required.)

Army Form C. 2118.

41$\underline{st}$ B^{de} = R.F.A.

Place	Date	Hour	Summary of Events and Information	Remarks and references to Appendices
BAILLEUL Wd	JUNE	8th	Carried out Special Bombardment of OPPY at 1 A.M. to 1.10 A.M. — Fired Practice Barrage at 3.15 A.M. for 12 minutes — Hostile Batteries Active. 2nd Army Battery Positions from 4 A.M. to 5 A.M. — Fired Practice Barrages at 8.30 P.M. & 11.45 P.M.	
	"	9th	Fired Practice Barrage at 12.50 A.M.	
	"	10th	Quiet day — Observation poor	
	"	11th	S.O.S. Test 11 aroused at 1.45 A.M. — Batteries returned by 1.46 A.M.	
	"	12th	Quiet Day Visibility bad — 2nd Div. Horse Show near MAROEUIL	
	"	13th	G.O.C. 2nd Div. inspects Wagon Lines — Batteries fire Hurricane Bombardment from 5 A.M. to 5.2 A.M.	
	"	14	Hurricane Bombardment of tech areas carried out 11.45 A.M & 3 P.M.	

Army Form C. 2118.

WAR DIARY
or
INTELLIGENCE SUMMARY.

(Erase heading not required.)   41st B⁴ RFA

Instructions regarding War Diaries and Intelligence Summaries are contained in F. S. Regs., Part II. and the Staff Manual respectively. Title pages will be prepared in manuscript.

Place	Date	Hour	Summary of Events and Information	Remarks and references to Appendices
AILLEUX	June 15th		Quiet Day - Programme Shoot at 2.30 pm.	
"	16"		" Very Hot. Programme Shoot 5.0 pm	
"	17"		Programme Shoot at 4.10 A.M.	
"	18"		Very Quiet all day	
"	19"		"	
"	20"		Corps Horse Show held near MONT St ELOI - 9th B⁴⁹ won turn-out event	
"	21"		Batteries fired practice Barrage at 5.50 pm.	
"	22"		Dummy Barrage at 10.20 pm	

Army Form C. 2118.

WAR DIARY
or
INTELLIGENCE SUMMARY.
(Erase heading not required.)

H.Q. 18th Bde R.F.A.

Place	Date	Hour	Summary of Events and Information	Remarks and references to Appendices
BAILLEUL	JUNE 23rd		QUIET DAY	
	24th		47th Battery fired GAS SHELL BOMBARDMENT on BACK AREAS & KEEL	
	25th		Batteries fired in Support of Raid by 14th WARWICKS N. of OPPY WOOD	
	26th		" DUMMY BARRAGE	
	27th		" in support of successful raid by 15th WARWICKS (5 DIV.) S. of OPPY WOOD —	
	28th		Successful attack on OPPY TRENCH by 5th DIV. Batteries fired BARRAGE. 163 prisoners were captured as well as objective taken without trouble. 3 machine guns and several minenwerfer also captured. A7, B7 fired LETHAL & INSPIRATORY shells on communication during night.	

Army Form C. 2118.

WAR DIARY
or
INTELLIGENCE SUMMARY.

A/Lt B:de R.F.A.

(Erase heading not required.)

Place	Date	Hour	Summary of Events and Information	Remarks and references to Appendices
BOUDRAL	June 29th		Forward position of 47 Battery withdrawn from position W. of ABLEUX	
		30th	Batteries went out of action and withdrew to wagon lines at St Catherines ARRAS	

W.A. Bruce
Major
4 L B:de R.F.A.

2nd Divisional Artillery

41st BRIGADE R.F.A. ::: JULY 1917.

Army Form C. 2118.

WAR DIARY
or
INTELLIGENCE SUMMARY.
(Erase heading not required.)

41st Brigade R.F.A.

Vol 33

Place	Date	Hour	Summary of Events and Information	Remarks and references to Appendices
ARRAS	JULY 1st		Brigade rested at Wagon Lines, after heavy BAILLEUL positions, and made preparations for the next days TREK —	
	2nd		At 6AM Brigade marched via HERSIN and NOEUX-LES-MINES to BETHUNE — Battery Commanders reconnoitred new positions at FESTUBERT & GIVENCHY fronts — [struck through]	
GIVENCHY — FESTUBERT	3rd		Battery Commanders relieved sections of 330 Brigade — Between who remained in the evening —	
	4th		Guns were registered and remaining sections brought up to HOSTILE AIRCRAFT.	
	5th		Situation Quiet on Front. Left Group H.Q. at LOISNE. Brigade finished registrations — night firing commenced —	
	6th		Registration checked and guns calibrated —	
	7th		Hostile Trench Mortar active opposite CANADIAN ORCHARD — 47th Bty retaliated and knocked out 3 hostile positions.	
	8th		12.50am S.O.S. from PORTUGUESE on left and by 3 on our front —	

WAR DIARY
or
INTELLIGENCE SUMMARY.
(Erase heading not required.)

Army Form C. 2118.

Place	Date	Hour	Summary of Events and Information	Remarks and references to Appendices
GIVENCHY -FESTUBERT	8th cont'd		Enemy raides Potrijere front line - Artillery Barrage continued until 2.30 A.m. RAID failed -	
	9th		Hostile artillery active - RUE de BOIS - RUE de CRAVATTES and 6" How Position at LOISNE	
	10th		QUIET day	
	11th		" " Hostile Aeroplanes active	
	12th		" " FESTUBERT Cross roads received attention by 4.2 How. at 7 P.M.	
	13th		QUIET DAY	
	14th		" "	

Army Form C. 2118.

WAR DIARY
or
INTELLIGENCE SUMMARY.
(Erase heading not required.)

Instructions regarding War Diaries and Intelligence Summaries are contained in F. S. Regs., Part II. and the Staff Manual respectively. Title pages will be prepared in manuscript.

Place	Date	Hour	Summary of Events and Information	Remarks and references to Appendices
GIVENCHY - FESTUBERT	15th		Quiet Day - Church Service at Battery Positions	
	16th		Enemy T.M.s very active on GIVENCHY - retaliation by our own T.M. bombardment.	
	17th		Quiet Day - much work done on Battery Positions	
	18th		Much rain - Observation impossible	
	19th		Enemy fairly active - shelling GIVENCHY with 4.2" & 77 mm. di The enemy made a raid by the 99th Bde near MAD POINT entered the enemy Trenches without difficulty - Only 5 of the enemy were found and these were killed	
	20th		Stormy day - Observation impossible	

WAR DIARY or INTELLIGENCE SUMMARY.

Army Form C. 2118.

Place	Date	Hour	Summary of Events and Information	Remarks and references to Appendices
GIVENCHY -FESTUBERT	21st		Quiet day - much rain - observation bad -	
	22nd		Hostile artillery very active on Battery positions - 9th and 16th Batteries were shelled by 5.9' & 72 cm gun with aeroplane cooperation - from 8AM until 3PM.	
	23rd		Quiet day	
	24th		" " - Our T.Ms in GIVENCHY chew retaliation which our replies to.	
	25th		Battery fired on enemy wire east of OLD MAN'S CORNER - Enemy started heavy bombardment from trenches by CANADIAN ORCHARD at 5pm with T.Ms - This lasted until 7pm - all batteries retaliated vigorously	

Army Form C. 2118.

WAR DIARY
or
INTELLIGENCE SUMMARY.
(Erase heading not required.)

Instructions regarding War Diaries and Intelligence Summaries are contained in F. S. Regs., Part II. and the Staff Manual respectively. Title pages will be prepared in manuscript.

Place	Date	Hour	Summary of Events and Information	Remarks and references to Appendices
GIVENCHY -FESTUBERT	25th (contd)		1st King's Regt. made an unsuccessful raid on enemy trenches by RED DRAGON CRATER. Barrage was fired by 41st Bde - PORTUGUESE ARTILLERY & 36th Bde gave assistance -	41st Bde OO.No 21 and Barrage Maps attached.
	26th		Quiet in morning - At 5.30 p.m. Hostile shelling of 9th Battery position lasting until 9.30 p.m. - Damage nil - Raid by 5th Infantry Bde on the BRICKSTACKS front.	
	27th		9th Battery was again shelled intermittently from 12 Noon to 5 p.m. and continued from thence until 10.30 p.m. PCs were injured but no real damage was caused to guns or men - The battery responded minus one gun, during the night without any trouble.	
	28		Took guns from 9th hands over to CANADIAN D.A. - other guns G.P.S.	
	29		Moved to NEW positions Okeentein rifle rifle	

A6945 Wt. W11422/M1160 35,000 12/16 D. D. & L. Forms/C/2118/14.

WAR DIARY
or
INTELLIGENCE SUMMARY

(Erase heading not required.)

Place	Date	Hour	Summary of Events and Information	Remarks and references to Appendices

Instructions regarding War Diaries and Intelligence Summaries are contained in F.S. Regs., Part II and the Staff Manual respectively. Title pages will be prepared in manuscript.

Army Form C 2118.

Army Form C. 2118.

WAR DIARY
or
INTELLIGENCE SUMMARY.
(Erase heading not required.)

Instructions regarding War Diaries and Intelligence Summaries are contained in F. S. Regs., Part II. and the Staff Manual respectively. Title pages will be prepared in manuscript.

Place	Date	Hour	Summary of Events and Information	Remarks and references to Appendices
GIVENCHY - FESTUBERT				
	30th		Enemy shells GIVENCHY with 4.2" hows during morning, also 77 mm fire on YELLOW ROAD.	
	31st		Light hoor. Hostile artillery on Portuguese Battery positions in RUE DE L'EPINETTE & ANNEQUIN.	

Signed
4th B? R.F.A.

SECRET

Operation Order No. 21.
by
Lieut. Colonel J.G. Dooner, R.F.A.
Commanding LEFT GROUP, 2nd D.A.

Copy No
issued to
24-7-17

Reference Sheet 36c N.W. Edition 9a 1/10000

1. The 1st Kings regt: will raid the enemy's trenches between A.10.c.00.24 and A.9.d.67.85 on the night of 25/26th with The object of the raid is to secure identifications, kill the enemy, destroy M.G and T.M. emplacements, and bring in any of these weapons if any are found.

2. The following artillery will support the attack:—
   1 Battery, 1st Portuguese Div.
   41st Brigade. R.F.A.
   71st Battery. R.F.A.
           Section, VOSPER Battery
   D/36 Battery. R.F.A.
   X.2 and Z.2 T.M. Battery.
   6th T.M. Battery, 5th T.M. Battery   and 5th
   and 6th M.G. Companies will

3. To support the raid, the enemy's line from A.10.c-00.27 — A.9.d.67.85 will be subjected to a heavy trench mortar bombardment for 2 minutes while the field Arty: will place a barrage E, and N of the objective. This barrage will be continued until the raid is over. All available Heavy Arty: reinforced by 1 Field battery, 1st Portg: Div: will be employed on Counter Battery work. Machine Guns will enfilade all enemy spots from which hostile M.G. fire is likely to be brought to bear and dangerous points behind the craters which cannot be brought under fire of Guns or M.Gs will be subjected to a hail of rifle grenades.

4. The trench mortar bombardment will be carried out by X.2. T.M.B and Z.2.T.M.B. (less 1 gun). These guns will be distributed over the whole front to be bombarded and will fire at the highest possible rate from ZERO to ZERO + 2. The detachments will then be

be withdrawn under cover. NEWTON fuzes will be used.

Stokes mortars will supplement this bombardment and will also fire on known machine gun emplacements West of the objective.

5. 18 pdr Batteries will be divided into Frontal Batteries and Enfilading Batteries.

6. **Frontal Batteries**

(a) 71st Battery, R.F.A. (less 1 gun) Zone - figure enclosed between:-
        A 10 c 3½.½
        A 10 c 2.2
        A 10 c 1½.5½
        Trench running East to A10c 6½.6½
        A 10 c 4½.2½

At Zero, open on Western Edge of this zone
At Zero+2, lift to line:-
    A10c 3½.½ - A10 C 2.2 - A10c 3.3. - A10c 2.5½

(b) 16th Battery R.F.A. (less enfilading Section)
Zone:- figure enclosed between:-
        A 10 c 1½.5½
        A 9 d 9½.9
        Trench running to A10a 3½.½
        CANTELEUX ALLEY NORTH to A10c 8½.8½
        Trench thence back to A10c½.5½

At Zero:- open on Western Edge of this zone.
At Zero+2 lift to Trench line from A10c 2.5½ - A10 c6.9½

(c) 14th Battery, R.F.A. Zone - figure enclosed between:-
        A 9 d 9½.9
        A 9 b 4½.½
        A 9 b 4½.4½
        Along trench running to A10 a 3½.½

At Zero - open on Western Edge of this zone
At Zero+2, lift to line A10c ½.9½ - A9 b 8½.½ - A9 b 4½.½
        A 9 b 7½.4½.

(d) After Zero+2 these batteries will search and sweep so as to cover the whole of their respective zones East of the line on to which they lift at that hour.

7. **Enfilading Batteries**

(a) 1 gun 91st Battery. } Enfilade area allotted to
    Vosper Vermelles Section } 91st Battery R.F.A. in para
                               6 (a) above.

(b) 16th Battery. Enfilading } Enfilade trench
    Section.   } from A10c 2.5½ to
                               A10c 2.9½

(c) 9th Battery. (i) 1 gun enfilade trench from
                     A10c 2.9½ to junction with AUSTRIAN
                     WAY
                 (ii) 1 gun about trench junction
                      A10c 4.3½
                 (iii) 1 gun each enfilade areas
                       allotted to 16th and 14th Batteries
                       in paras 6 (b) & (c) above.

(d) 1 Battery, 1st Portuguese Division
    1 gun will enfilade each of the following trenches:-
    (i)   A10c 4½.2½ - A10c 6½.6½
    (ii) A10c 6½.6½ - A10a 3.½
    (iii) A10c 6½.8½ - A10a 3½.½
    (iv) A10a 3½.½   - A10a ½.3½

(e) None of these Batteries will fire West of
    the line to which the frontal Batteries lift
    at Zero + 2.

8.   1 Medium Trench Mortar, Z.Z. Battery, will fire
continuously about A9 b 6.1 at its most rapid rate
of fire. NEWTON Fuze will NOT be used.

9.   At Zero, Howitzer Batteries will open as follows
and continue on same targets throughout the raid.

(a) D/36. 1 gun on each of the following points:-
    (i)   A10c 5½.½   T.M. emplacement.
    (ii) A10c 8.2   M.G.   "
    (iii) A10c 5½.4½   T.M.   "
    (iv) A10c 8.8   T.M.   "
    (v)   A10c 9.9½   T.M.   "
    (vi) A10a 2.2   Trench junction.

P.T.O.

9 (b) 47th Battery. 1 Gun on each of the following points.
   A 10 a 1.3½   Trench Junction
   A 10 a 2½.2½   T.M. Emplacement.
   A 10 a 3½.5   Trenches.
   A 9 b 9.4   Trench junction & dug-outs.
   A 9 b 7.5   Trench junction & M.G. emplacement.

10. Ammunition

   Frontal Batteries :-   50% H.E. ; 50% Time Shrapnel.
   Flanking   "   :-   All time Shrapnel.

11. Rates of Fire

   Zero   – Zero+5   Intense.
   Zero+5 – Zero+10   Normal.
   Zero+10 – Zero+20   Intense
   Zero+20 – Zero+25   Normal

12. At Zero +55, 18 pdrs and 4.5" will fire 3 rounds gun fire, Howitzers 2 rounds gun fire on the targets on which they ceased firing at Zero +25.
   Medium T.M's will fire one round each on their original targets.

13. A Barrage Sketch will be issued as soon as possible.

14. O.C. 16th Battery will detail a Liaison Officer, to whom special instructions will be issued.

15. Zero hour will be notified later.

16. Watches will be synchronised after 6 pm tomorrow

17. Acknowledge

C.A. de Grineau
Lieut & Adjt
Left Group
R.D.A.

Copy No 1 } 40 D.A. R.o D.W.
       2 }
       3 }
       4 }
       5 } 166th Bde.
       6 }
       7 }
       8 }
       9 }
      10 X/2 T.M.B
      11 - 2/2
      12 - 9th By
      13 - 16 "
      14 - 17 "
      15 - 167

      16 }
      17 } to 36th Bde.
      18 }
      19 }
      20 } to Portuguese
      21 } (Right Grp)
      22 to D.T.M.O.

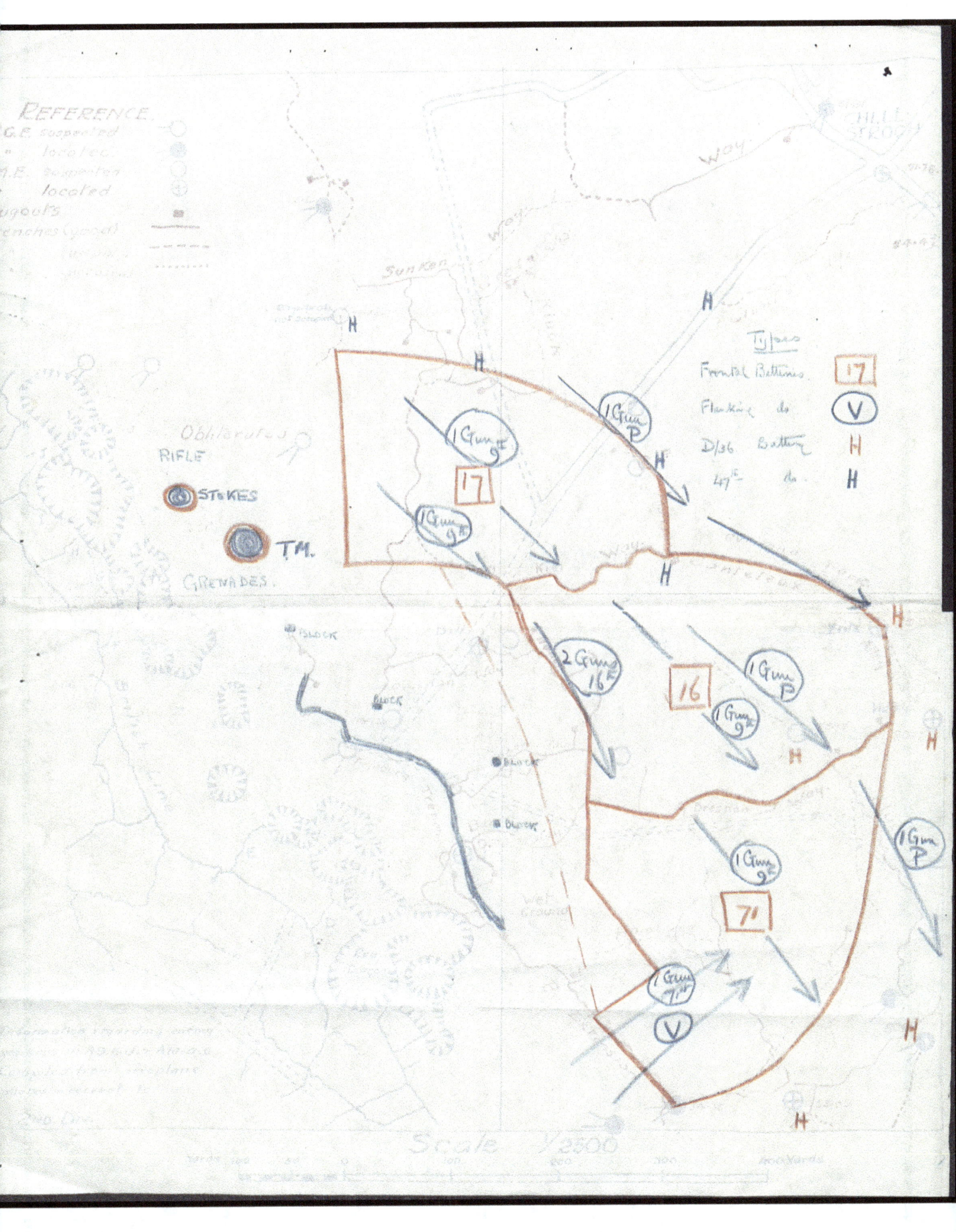

2nd Divisional Artillery

41st BRIGADE R.F.A. ::: AUGUST 1917.

WAR DIARY
or
INTELLIGENCE SUMMARY.
(Erase heading not required.)

Army Form C. 2118.

AUGUST 1917
41st BRIGADE R.F.A.

Vol 34

Place	Date	Hour	Summary of Events and Information	Remarks and references to Appendices
GIVENCHY - FESUBERT	1/8/17		Very wet day – Hostile minnies fairly active on Givenchy lines 3.30-4.30 p.m. some mft guns – 47.05 fired 50 shells on VIOLAINES hostile Battery	
	2/8/17		Very wet – Hostile Artillery active	
	3/8/17		Rain very heavy – day quiet	
	4/8/17		Heavy shower – Hostile Battery – 5"9" – heavily shelled 17" Batty. section putting both guns out of action and falls claiming position near Westwick brige	
	5/8/17		Quiet day. Usual day & nt firing	
	6/8/17	"	"	
	7/8/17	"	" Fires Test S.O.S. 9 p.m.	

Army Form C. 2118.

WAR DIARY
or
INTELLIGENCE SUMMARY.
(Erase heading not required.)

Instructions regarding War Diaries and Intelligence Summaries are contained in F. S. Regs., Part II. and the Staff Manual respectively. Title pages will be prepared in manuscript.

Place	Date	Hour	Summary of Events and Information	Remarks and references to Appendices
GIVENCHY – FESTUBERT	8/9/17		Hostile T.M.s active – Batteries fired in retaliation with good results	
	9/8/17		Active day – Hostile Aircraft persistent – Two brought down + one Hostile Balloon – Cambrai Batteries very active in the Evening Batteries of Concrete emplacements observed near VIOLAINES – heavy TANK GUN emplacement. Enemy trench with abandoned G.S.D5 position – fired over 200 5.9", 4.2" minies – during the day.	
	10/8/17		Usual activity – MIKE CRATER blown (WARLINGHAM) nr GIVENCHY	
	11/8/17		" 9.30 pm. Batteries fired in conjunction with attack by 17th Royal Fusiliers in near lip of new CRATER	
	12/8/17		Very quiet – Artillery retaliated twice for heavy shelling on new CRATERS. 17th Battn engaged Hostile Balloon with shrapnel Evening it the fullest clown.	

Army Form C. 2118.

WAR DIARY
or
INTELLIGENCE SUMMARY.
(Erase heading not required.)

Instructions regarding War Diaries and Intelligence Summaries are contained in F. S. Regs., Part II. and the Staff Manual respectively. Title pages will be prepared in manuscript.

Place	Date	Hour	Summary of Events and Information	Remarks and references to Appendices
GIVENCHY-FESTUBERT				
	13/5/17		Hostile arty did shooting at Hostile Balloon. 17th Battery was heavily shelled all day with 5.9" + 4.2" - position was not badly damaged but one gun was put out of action - One gunner was killed. Between 300 + 400 shells were fired in all - 47th BT retaliated in conjunction with aeroplane observation between 6am and 8.16pm. The bombardment.	
	14/5/17		Very quiet day - some artillery activity	
	15/5/17		Quiet day	
	16/5/17		"	
	17/5/17		" 47th Battery fired on Sap E of New Crater (W.29.d.5.4 to 6.4.22)	
	18/5/17		Enemy artillery fairly active.	

Army Form C. 2118.

WAR DIARY
or
INTELLIGENCE SUMMARY.
(Erase heading not required.)

Instructions regarding War Diaries and Intelligence Summaries are contained in F. S. Regs., Part II. and the Staff Manual respectively. Title pages will be prepared in manuscript.

Place	Date	Hour	Summary of Events and Information	Remarks and references to Appendices
GIVENCHY — FESTUBERT	19/8/17		47th Battery did much counter battery work on hostile positions with good results	
	20/8/17		Hostile T.M's active on Givenchy — fired in retaliation	
	21/8/17		Hostile " " " " Also engaged	
			active hostile batteries	
	22/8/17		47th B'ty carried out destructive shoot on hostile Battery by direct observation from balloon — Gunpits were set on fire and ammunition blown up — 9.2"T bombarded at 9 AM by Sg'ts — about 50 rounds — all very little damage done —	
	23/8/17		Quiet day	
	24/8/17		Quiet day — Major Messervy of 16th Battery received MILITARY CROSS.	
	25/8/17		Enemy Trench Mortars very active on Givenchy, between 4.35 & 9 P.M. Batteries fired heavy retaliation	
	26/8/17		Quiet day	

Army Form C. 2118.

WAR DIARY
or
INTELLIGENCE SUMMARY.
(Erase heading not required.)

Instructions regarding War Diaries and Intelligence Summaries are contained in F. S. Regs., Part II. and the Staff Manual respectively. Title pages will be prepared in manuscript.

Place	Date	Hour	Summary of Events and Information	Remarks and references to Appendices
Givenchy - Festubert	27/8/17		Very Stormy - Quiet day - No firing	
	28/8/17		" " " "	
	29/8/17		Hostile Artillery fairly active -	
	30/8/17		Test S.O.S. (9.1) fires at 11.45 pm. Day Quiet.	
	31/8/17		Quiet day - Hostile T.M. fired a few rounds on Givenchy	

C.W. Duncan Capt. + Adjt -
41st Bde R.F.A.

2nd Divisional Artillery.

41st BRIGADE R.F.A. ::: SEPTEMBER 1917

Army Form C. 2118.

WAR DIARY
or
INTELLIGENCE SUMMARY.
(Erase heading not required.)

4½ B'y 2. R.F.A.

Vol 2 F 25

Place	Date	Hour	Summary of Events and Information	Remarks and references to Appendices
Festubert Givenchy	Sept 1st		Hostile Artillery active - 17th Battery position on Tunis Fort shelled from 10 am to 5 pm after which H.V. 4.2 guns fired intermittently during the rest of the day	
"	2		Quiet day	
"	3		" Batteries registering fresh night Aeroplane co-operation - Our kite Balloons were shelled by H.V. Gun without result.	
"	4th		" Quiet Day -	
"	5th		" During the evening Brigade and Trench Mortars fired on GIVENCHY	
"	6th		Enemy retaliated to the short B'y Artillery with a shelle by 5" Q's and T.M's on our trenches near the CRATERS - a 7.7cm battery also firing on LE PLANTIN.	

Army Form C. 2118.

WAR DIARY
or
INTELLIGENCE SUMMARY.
(Erase heading not required.)

Instructions regarding War Diaries and Intelligence Summaries are contained in F. S. Regs., Part II. and the Staff Manual respectively. Title pages will be prepared in manuscript.

Place	Date	Hour	Summary of Events and Information	Remarks and references to Appendices
Guedecourt	Sept 7th	7ᵗʰ	Very Quiet day – The 6ᵗʰ Infantry Brigade was relieved by the 99 ᵗʰ Bde night	
		8ᵗʰ	Quiet day. Very quiet	
		9ᵗʰ	" " until transfusion – Relieved this morning to the sectors	
		10ᵗʰ	Hostile T.M. ? in action on Factory Post –	
		11ᵗʰ	Batteries fired on S.O.S. Bars 7 – 20. S. 9. 3	
		12ᵗʰ	Quiet day. Light T.M. - Artillery lively on both sides	
		13ᵗʰ	Very hazy – First we tried on the Guenchy sectors at 7.20 am out operations were quite successful –	
		14ᵗʰ	Quiet day	
		15ᵗʰ	" A 4" a Battery Shelled Quinque Rue during the morning	

A6945 Wt. W14422/M1160 35,000 12/16 D.D.&L. Forms/C/2118/14.

WAR DIARY
or
INTELLIGENCE SUMMARY.

(Erase heading not required.)

Army Form C. 2118.

Place	Date	Hour	Summary of Events and Information	Remarks and references to Appendices
Festubert Givenchy	Sept	16"	Hostile 5.9 Battery shelled BARNTON TEE at 4.30 P.M. After which it held attention to SHETLAND ROAD and PIONEER ROAD but stopped when we retaliated. During the night firing on 5.9 reached for the 9" and 17" Batteries on the TUNING FORK firing about 20 rounds in all.	
		17-	Enemy Artillery were active in GIVENCHY about 4.30 to 6.30 pm	
		18"	5.9 Battery shelled 17" Position with 10 rounds - GIVENCHY was shelled intermittently from 1 to 2 pm.	
	"	19"	Abnormally Quiet Day -	
	"	20"	Quiet Day -	

Army Form C. 2118.

WAR DIARY
or
INTELLIGENCE SUMMARY.
(Erase heading not required.)

Instructions regarding War Diaries and Intelligence Summaries are contained in F. S. Regs., Part II. and the Staff Manual respectively. Title pages will be prepared in manuscript.

Place	Date	Hour	Summary of Events and Information	Remarks and references to Appendices
Guenchy tututet	Sept 21st		Quiet Day	
"	22nd		9th Battery slightly shelled with about 10 4.2's - Observers reports much movement near FORGIES and ILLIES -	
"	23rd		9th and 17th Batteries were shelled during evening about 9.10 pm and again at 7 am the following morning - little damage was done -	
"	24th		Enemy opened a heavy Barrage on our Trenches from the BOIS de BIEZ to LA BASSEE CANAL from 5.10 am until 6 AM with T.M.S of all sizes - 77 cm & 4.2 How's. = 5.9's and 4.2 Hows. opened on the Battery positions at the same time. Batteries fired S.O.S. G.1 and ORCHARD and G.3 - The Enemy entered our front line where it crosses the RUE de MARAIS and took one man prisoner. The remainder of the day was quiet	

Army Form C. 2118.

WAR DIARY
or
INTELLIGENCE SUMMARY.
(Erase heading not required.)

Instructions regarding War Diaries and Intelligence Summaries are contained in F. S. Regs., Part II. and the Staff Manual respectively. Title pages will be prepared in manuscript.

Place	Date	Hour	Summary of Events and Information	Remarks and references to Appendices
Giveuchy	Sept 25th	6	Enemy inactive during day. Hostile T.M. fired a few gas bombs during the night, near Givenchy.	
	26th		Quiet day. Usual M.M. fire.	
	27		At 5.30 a.m. Brigade carried out a T.M. Shoot in S28a. It was very successful and little retaliation ensued. Quiet day. Both our Howrs. fired during the night.	
	28th		Quiet day. 9th Battery moved the gun to new position near "Restubert"	
	29th		Quiet day. 7.7cm & 4.2 fired occasionally in Givenchy	
	30th			

C.A. Smoon
Capt. & Adj.
4th Bde R.F.A.

2nd Divisional Artillery.

41st BRIGADE R.F.A. L::: OCTOBER 1917.

Army Form C. 2118.

WAR DIARY
or
INTELLIGENCE SUMMARY.
(Erase heading not required.)

October 1917
41st Brigade RFA

WM 36

Place	Date	Hour	Summary of Events and Information	Remarks and references to Appendices
Givenchy Sector	Oct. 1st		Quiet day - during night enemy blew two mines at Givenchy and occupied the near lip.	
	2nd		Fire covering fire for two raids near CRATERS: One for 1st Kings which was unsuccessful - the other 17th Fusiliers who obtained identification from unknown parcel	
	3rd		Quiet day	
	4th		" " - 112 tons of gas projectiles on AUCHY - HAINES & LA BASSEE	
	5th		GIVENCHY SHELLED during evening probably in retaliation for gas bombardment	
	6th		Quiet day	
	7th		25th Divn Artillery started to relieve Batteries - half completed	

Army Form C. 2118.

WAR DIARY
or
INTELLIGENCE SUMMARY.
(Erase heading not required.)

Instructions regarding War Diaries and Intelligence Summaries are contained in F. S. Regs., Part II. and the Staff Manual respectively. Title pages will be prepared in manuscript.

Place	Date	Hour	Summary of Events and Information	Remarks and references to Appendices
Sunday Perlwest	Oct 8th		Relief completed.	
	"	9th	Brigade marched to AMETTES via BETHUNE and LILLERS	
	"	10		
	"	11		
	"	12		
	"	13	Resting AMETTES	
	"	14		
	"	15		
	"	16		

WAR DIARY
INTELLIGENCE SUMMARY.
(Erase heading not required.)

Army Form C. 2118.

Place	Date	Hour	Summary of Events and Information	Remarks and references to Appendices
THIENNES	6ct 17		Brigade marched to THIENNES	
	18th		" "	
			GOODENAERSVELDE - Brigade and Battery	
			Commanders went forward to Relieve Batteries of 9th Div. at ST JULIEN	
ST JULIEN	19th		Group H.Q. at St Julien of 36th & 41st Brigades which relieved 50th & 51st Brigades R.F.A. During relief shelling of area was intense - 2/Lieut. PHILLIPS 47th Battery wounded -	
	20th		Commenced 48 hours bombardment - heavy retaliation - Capt. Wright 16 Battery A.E.T. wounded	
	21st		Continued Bombardment - intermittent shelling throughout day -	
	22nd		Fired Barrage at 5.35 a.m. - 18th Div. on left captured POELCAPPELLE BREWERY. BEEK and OXFORD HOUSES -, 9th Div. advanced posts 100 x on our front.	
	23rd		Intermittent heavy shelling by hostile artillery throughout day - all calibres	

Army Form C. 2118.

WAR DIARY
INTELLIGENCE SUMMARY
(Erase heading not required.)

Instructions regarding War Diaries and Intelligence Summaries are contained in F. S. Regs., Part II. and the Staff Manual respectively. Title pages will be prepared in manuscript.

Place	Date	Hour	Summary of Events and Information	Remarks and references to Appendices
St. JULIEN Bat.	24th		Commenced another 48 hours bombardment - Quiet our Sector -	
	25th		47th Battery heavily shelled - Lieut. C. GRIEG and 2nd Lieut. A.R. MILLER wounded. Continued 48 hours bombardment. Heavy retaliation all day - MAJOR J.E.W. BROMLEY - 17th Battery - wounded -	
	26th		During night 63rd Div. established post in BERKS HOUSES. Barrage 5. 40 A.M. - Div. on left captured MORAY HOUSES. 63rd Div. on front made an advance of about 500 yards. Canadians captured BELLEVUE on our right. Heavy retaliation, enemy battery suffering. Casualties in men and guns.	
	27th		Intermittent shelling	
	28th	"	2nd Lieut. H.L. PHILLIPS wounded (B.L 53) he remained at duty.	
	29th	"		

Army Form C. 2118.

WAR DIARY
or
INTELLIGENCE SUMMARY.
(Erase heading not required.)

Instructions regarding War Diaries and Intelligence Summaries are contained in F.S. Regs., Part II. and the Staff Manual respectively. Title pages will be prepared in manuscript.

Place	Date	Hour	Summary of Events and Information	Remarks and references to Appendices
ST. JOHEN	Oct. 30	5.40ᵃᵐ	Barrage at 5.40 a.m. 63ʳᵈ Division held up at SOURD FARM and was unable to reach PADDEBEKE	
	31ˢᵗ		Intermittent shelling - Hostile GOTHAS very active and bombed at intervals	

(Sgd) W. A. Snelson
Captain,
4th Brigade NFA.

2nd Divisional Artillery.

41st BRIGADE R.F.A. ::: NOVEMBER 1917.

Army Form C. 2118.

WAR DIARY
INTELLIGENCE SUMMARY.
(Erase heading not required.)

41st BRIGADE RFA   Vol 37

Place	Date	Hour	Summary of Events and Information	Remarks and references to Appendices
YPRES	1/11/17		Arrangement made to relieve 16th Battery by 9th Battery at ST JULIEN as 16th Battery was to be sent to V ARMY School at BAILLY-(ESEC.	
"	2/11/17		Heavy shelling on CANADIAN front on our Right.	
"	3/11/17		Quiet until 4pm when all tracks and roads were heavily shelled. 9th Battery was shelled and gassed during night.	
"	4/11/17		ST JULIEN heavily shelled from 10pm until dusk. Fried poin BARRAGE at 4:40 am. STEENBEKE Valley was also shelled continuously	
"	5/11/17		Roads near St Julien and Steenbeke Valley again shelled throughout day	
	6/11/17		Capture of PASSCHENDAELE by CANADIAN CORPS – Fired fient Barrage in Conjunction with attack.	

WAR DIARY or INTELLIGENCE SUMMARY.

Army Form C. 2118.

(Erase heading not required.)

Instructions regarding War Diaries and Intelligence Summaries are contained in F. S. Regs., Part II. and the Staff Manual respectively. Title pages will be prepared in manuscript.

Place	Date	Hour	Summary of Events and Information	Remarks and references to Appendices
YPRES	5/11/17		Quiet day - Practice Barrage fired in early morning	
	6/11/17		"	
	7/11/17		"	
	8/11/17		" Enemy artillery normal	
	9/11/17		"	
	10/11/17		One Brigade of the 1st Division and the 1st CANADIAN Division attacked N. & N.W. of PASSCHENDAELE at 6 A.M. All objectives were gained but 1st DIV were shelled and counter-attacked with terrific violence and eventually forced to evacuate ridge all ground gained by them. TOURNANT FARM being held. Very heavy rain all day.	
	11/11/17		Quiet day - weather better - Batteries checked registration -	
	12/11/17		Batteries were again heavily shelled by hostile counter batteries.	

WAR DIARY
OF
INTELLIGENCE SUMMARY.
(Erase heading not required.)

Army Form C. 2118.

Place	Date	Hour	Summary of Events and Information	Remarks and references to Appendices
YPRES	13/11/17		At 4.30 pm. Enemy attacked Junction of CANADIANS and 1st Division, but were repulsed by artillery & machine gun fire. Enemy barrage very violent.	
	14/11/17		All Batteries fired in ARMY BARRAGE at 6 A.M. There was also a practice BARRAGE at 3 PM.	
	15/11/17		Practice Barrage at 6 A.M. during which Enemy attacked CANADIANS. S.O.S. was at 6.30 am and batteries immediately shifted to the S.O.S. lines - Enemy completely repulsed. He attacked again at 10 A.M. but with no success.	
	16/11/17		ARMY BARRAGE at 6.50 A.M. - At 5 p.m. 1st CAMERONS. At 7 pm successful attack without Artillery Support - capturing VAT and VEAL COTTAGES as well as several other Strong works. About 700 yards were gained altogether.	

WAR DIARY
or
INTELLIGENCE SUMMARY.
(Erase heading not required.)

Army Form C. 2118.

Place	Date	Hour	Summary of Events and Information	Remarks and references to Appendices
YPRES	16/4/17 (cont.)		Enemy was completely surprised and their artillery were firstly silent. Batteries closed by 1 Bde L.T. were not called upon till 10. There were S.O.S. calls at 7 p.m. - 10.30 p.m. - 2.15 A.m. & 3.30 A.m. Two of them being hostile attacks on our new ground both of which were easily repulsed.	
	17/4/17		Left Group (36th & 41st Brigades) were suddenly relieved by 162nd & 163rd Brigades - while relief being practically completed by 2 p.m. - On completion of relief (32nd Div.) 2nd Divisional Artillery in Thomas & Wagon lines at ESSEX FARM. All guns handed over complete.	
	18/4/17		Bayonets aired at Wagon Lines. ESSEX FARM.	
	19/4/17		" " " " Guns & Equipment drawn from 2nd Corps	
	20/4/17		Marched to WATAU - via POPERINGHE South and JAN-TER-BIEZEN - persistent rumour that Division was off to ITALY!	

WAR DIARY
OR
INTELLIGENCE SUMMARY.
(Erase heading not required.)

Army Form C. 2118.

Place	Date	Hour	Summary of Events and Information	Remarks and references to Appendices
WATOU	24/11/17		Rested at WATOU. Batteries overhauled guns and equipment drawn from Ord Corps all of which were in very bad condition.	
	22/11/17		Rested at WATOU. 10 A.M. inspected guns - Ammunition drawn - mostly mules - horses very indifferent.	
	23/11/17		Division prepared to entrain for BAPAUME AREA. Many rumours proving false - evidently owing to great CAMBRAI battle.	
	24/11/17		Brigade marched to PROVEN to entrain - travelling via HAZEBROUCK LILLERS to MIRAUMONT on the move. 16th Battery rejoined Bde en route.	
	25/11/17		Brigades arrived MIRAUMONT. A.M. marched via ACHIET-LE-GRAND BIHUCOURT - BIEFVILLERS - BAPAUME to HAPLINCOURT	
HAPLINCOURT	26/11/17		Orders to join GUARDS DIV. ARTY. cancelled. Brigade marched to join	

WAR DIARY or INTELLIGENCE SUMMARY

Army Form C. 2118.

Place	Date	Hour	Summary of Events and Information	Remarks and references to Appendices
	26/11/17 (column)		36 R. Div. Arty in action between HERMIES and MEUVRES – Mt BERTINCOURT – RUYAULCOURT MSR – RUYAULCOURT – HERMIES – Very bad march in Blizzard – guides very bad – Battery position near CANAL DU NORD with no shelter reached by rough cross country track – in spite of bad condition all Batteries in before morning with adequate supply of ammunition.	
MŒUVRES	27/11/17		Fighting going on to BOURLON position – Registration gun begun.	
	28/11/17		Batteries continued registration – Quiet day.	
	29/11/17		Enemy patrol took a post a little in BOURLON WOOD – 99th Infantry Bde improved on position between BOURLON & MEUVRES – Remainder of day – Carried out amount Sniping of hostile movement.	
	30/11/17		8.30 A.m. Enemy attacked all along front – principally directed on	

WAR DIARY
OF
INTELLIGENCE SUMMARY.
(Erase heading not required.)

Army Form C. 2118.

Place	Date	Hour	Summary of Events and Information	Remarks and references to Appendices
HIEUVRES	31/12/17 (cont.)		BOURLON WOOD - and left of NEUVES - have fairly continued all day & have fired all day at targets of opportunity, especially when enemy aircraft doing cooperation or against ANNEUX and BOURLON WOOD. Saw no enemy on front against ANNEUX and BOURLON WOOD. At least 5 hostile aeroplanes kept down in air-fighting on our immediate front.	

Cecil Simon
Capt. & Adj.
41st Bde. R.F.A.

2nd Divisional Artillery.

41st BRIGADE R.F.A. ::: DECEMBER 1917.

Army Form C. 2118.

WAR DIARY
or
INTELLIGENCE SUMMARY.
(Erase heading not required.)

41st BRIGADE R.F.A. DECEMBER 1917   VM 38

Place	Date	Hour	Summary of Events and Information	Remarks and references to Appendices
MOEUVRES	1/12/17		After a quiet night the enemy again became active opposite MOEUVRES. On our front, after the furious fighting of the previous day, an line remained without the exception of a few isolated advanced posts. Enemy casualties were estimated at at least 3000 whilst at least four times three hundred were wounded. Batteries fired on enemy troops concentrating N. of MOEUVRES during the morning and helped to repulse an attack on this front during the afternoon. Enemy again suffered heavily and gained nothing. Harassing Fire kept up all through the night.	
"	2/12/17		"Fairly quiet" night and morning, though Enemy were reported to be massing in E.15 at 10 A.M. At 4 p.m. Enemy attacked our positions opposite MOEUVRES and at 5 p.m. made a bombing attack just N. of CANAL DU NORD. Both attacks were repulsed while at the same time our Troops improved our positions considerably just W. of BOURLON WOOD, capturing 60 prisoners. Batteries fired in support of operations and engaged all enemy parties within range. Weather turned very cold.	
"	3/12/17		Enemy Artillery active. All movement was engaged, and aeroplane calls from Ally answered.	

A6945 Wt. W14422/M1160 35,000 12/16 D. D. & L. Forms/C./2118/14.

Army Form C. 2118.

WAR DIARY
or
INTELLIGENCE SUMMARY.
(Erase heading not required.)

Instructions regarding War Diaries and Intelligence Summaries are contained in F. S. Regs., Part II. and the Staff Manual respectively. Title pages will be prepared in manuscript.

Place	Date	Hour	Summary of Events and Information	Remarks and references to Appendices
MOEUVRES	4/12/17		Enemy fairly quiet. Hostile artillery occasionally fires short bursts in neighbourhood of Cantn. Lock 7, and Battery positions. News received that BRITISH were going to evacuate the BOURLON salient owing to the danger it involved in defending it against a serious attack by the enemy and the casualties in holding it. Battery positions near Lyme Copse on W. of CANAL DU NORD were detailed for 2nd Div. Artillery at almost extreme range, and Brigade ordered to retire during night. Owing to wagon lines moving back at same time the withdrawal of Batteries was much affected, and ammunition had to be left in old positions in some cases.	
HERMIES	5/12/17		Brigade withdrew during night 4/5th and Batteries did recuperation during day. Enemy artillery active during afternoon - when their patrols could be seen following up the partial withdrawal of the infantry. 9th Battery Wagons in charge of Captain Lt. REEVES went to the old position during darkness and removed ammunition left-behind.	

A6945 Wt. W1422/M1160 35,000 12/16 D. D. & L. Forms/C./2118/14.

Army Form C. 2118.

3

WAR DIARY
or
INTELLIGENCE SUMMARY.
(Erase heading not required.)

Instructions regarding War Diaries and Intelligence Summaries are contained in F. S. Regs., Part II. and the Staff Manual respectively. Title pages will be prepared in manuscript.

Place	Date	Hour	Summary of Events and Information	Remarks and references to Appendices
HERMIES	5/12/17	(cont)	There was now in front of the infantry and in our rear wire - Dummies were removed safely *	
"	6/12/17		O.Ps reconnoitred and negotiations checked. Some hostile batteries moved forward E. of MOEUVRES. Enemy seen pied GRAINCOURT, cutting off some forward posts on the left of 47th Div. front. Replied to S.O.S. front 4 p.m. and harassed enemy communications during night	
"	7/12/17		Much enemy movement engaged especially on CAMBRAI - BAPAUME road. A good many casualties could be observed.	
"	8/12/17		Quiet day. Much movement seen between BOURLON and LOCK 5. HEAVY ARTILLERY intervened and everything within range of field guns were tackled.	

Army Form C. 2118.
4

WAR DIARY
or
INTELLIGENCE SUMMARY.
(Erase heading not required.)

Instructions regarding War Diaries and Intelligence Summaries are contained in F. S. Regs., Part II. and the Staff Manual respectively. Title pages will be prepared in manuscript.

Place	Date	Hour	Summary of Events and Information	Remarks and references to Appendices
HERMIES	9/12/17		Thick mist all day. Heavy firing heard on our right. Batteries fired bursts on S.O.S. lines and enemy communication trenches in reply to hostile bombardment of our front & support lines.	
"	10/12/17		Light frost. Much aerial activity, mostly hostile. A bombing squadron of 14 machines including 3 GOTHAS bombed area from CANAL in rear of Battery positions to HAVRINCOURT WOOD. No apparent damage or casualties. Later in day one British & one German Aeroplanes fell near MEUVRES. Batteries engaged movement- Calibration and harassed Communications. 57th Div. had successful patrol encounter on our left near BOURSIES capturing 14 prisoners.	
"	11/12/17		Thick mist made observation impossible.	
"	12/12/17		Fine day. Much aerial activity again. Hostile machines bombed HAVRINCOURT WOOD and HERMIES 10:30 A.M. British Balloon brought down 12:30 P.M. and another unsuccessfully attacked 3:30 P.M. Movement slight & usual night firing carried out.	

Army Form C. 2118.

WAR DIARY
or
INTELLIGENCE SUMMARY.
(Erase heading not required.)

Instructions regarding War Diaries and Intelligence Summaries are contained in F.S. Regs., Part II. and the Staff Manual respectively. Title pages will be prepared in manuscript.

Place	Date	Hour	Summary of Events and Information	Remarks and references to Appendices
HERMES	13/12/17		Quiet day - observation impossible owing to mist.	
"	14/12/17		Rain and mist. Quiet day. Wagon lines moved to HAPLIN COURT	
"	15/12/17		Light gale. Checked S.O.S. lines. Hostile artillery shelled N.E. of HAVRIN COURT from 10 am to 12 noon	
"	16/12/17		Very misty - Quiet day.	
"	17/12/17		Much Snow " "	
"	18/12/17		Good light. Enemy working parties fired on at LOCK 6, and bank of CANAL DU NORD. Enemy 77 M.M. battery observed firing from W. outskirts of GRAIN COURT - engaged and silenced by 4.5 hows. and 18 pdrs	
"	19/12/17		Quiet day. Want harassing fire during day & night.	

Army Form C. 2118.

WAR DIARY
or
INTELLIGENCE SUMMARY.
(Erase heading not required.)

Instructions regarding War Diaries and Intelligence Summaries are contained in F.S. Regs., Part II. and the Staff Manual respectively. Title pages will be prepared in manuscript.

Place	Date	Hour	Summary of Events and Information	Remarks and references to Appendices
HERMIES	20/12/17		Heavy frost & ground mist. Enemy shelled HERMIES during afternoon.	
"	21/12/17		Quiet day.	
"	22/12/17		Much snow - Quiet day	
"	23/12/17		Good light - much Enemy movement N.W. of GRAIN COURT - all within range freely fired upon.	
"	24/12/17		Mist. Enemy shelled Battery positions and Bde HQ in burst of about 12 rounds at a time, about 4 times during day. No casualties. At 6.30 pm we discharged gas in large quantities and 12 Stokes fired in conjunction - No retaliation. Espade of.	
"	25/12/17		Christmas day - Very Quiet - Usual harassing fire day & night.	
"	26/12/17		Hostile Observers seen on Top of SPOIL HEAP at K3d 8.3. Salvo fired at them with good effect.	

(A7992). Wt. W12639/M1293. 750,000. 1/17. D.D. & L., Ltd. Forms/C.2118/14

WAR DIARY
or
INTELLIGENCE SUMMARY.
(Erase heading not required.)

Army Form C. 2118.

Instructions regarding War Diaries and Intelligence Summaries are contained in F.S. Regs., Part II. and the Staff Manual respectively. Title pages will be prepared in manuscript.

Place	Date	Hour	Summary of Events and Information	Remarks and references to Appendices
HERMIES	27/12/17		Enemy very active in Trenches in day – We fired in retaliation a matter of times.	
	28/12/17		Enemy again active in Trenches, probably in retaliation for our gun on Christmas Eve. We fired on intervals during day and night in response.	
	29/12/17		Quiet day – much aerial activity. Anti-aircraft guns in confits. area had quite a field day and accounted for a good many hostile machines.	
	30/12/17		Enemy attacked in eighty FLESQUIERES, he was repulsed except for about 400x of Trenches. Enemy losses very heavy – The Barrage started at 6.30 A.M. German attacks about 7.40 A.M. At 10 A.M. front line heavily shelled by enemy – at 11.30 pm enemy started a heavy concentrated shoot of 5.9's, 4.2's, + 77 mm. on certain front of Battalion + 184 H.Q.	

Army Form C. 2118.

WAR DIARY
or
INTELLIGENCE SUMMARY.
(Erase heading not required.)

Place	Date	Hour	Summary of Events and Information	Remarks and references to Appendices
HERMIES	30/12/17		Cont. with concentrated bursts of gas shells in persuant intervals. Very violent for 1½ hours, continuing at a slightly slower rate for another 1½ hours. No casualties inflicted and damage slight. At least 4000 rounds were fired.	
"	31/12/17		Good light — Enemy Neidon HERMIES and railway in front of Batteries during afternoon with 5.9s. About 72 midnight many batteries commenced heavy seeing in the New Year by a burst of fire.	

CHJ Smieren
Capt & Adjt.
41st Bde R.F.A.

2ND DIVISION

41ST BRIGADE R.F.A.
JAN - DEC 1918.

2nd Divisional Artillery.

41st BRIGADE R.F.A. :: JANUARY 1918.

WAR DIARY
or
INTELLIGENCE SUMMARY.
(Erase heading not required.)

Army Form C. 2118.

WA 39 4th Brigade

Place	Date	Hour	Summary of Events and Information	Remarks and references to Appendices
HERMIES	1/1/18		Observation difficult, almost making shooting impossible: very quiet.	
	2/1/18		Light again very poor: battery commanders with brigade commander reconnoitred reserve positions in rear.	
	3/1/18		Commenced relief of Brigade by the 79th Brigade R.F.A. 79th D.A., each battery relieving one section. S.O.S. let up on right battalion front at 4.40 p.m., on account of the enemy making four of our advancing patrols. An hour's bombardment was carried out & the barrage of these Cos posts during the night.	
	4/1/18		Relief of brigade completed, and batteries proceeded to their wagon-lines at HAPLINCOURT for 14 days rest as Reserve Brigade	

Army Form C. 2118.

WAR DIARY
or
INTELLIGENCE SUMMARY.
(Erase heading not required.)

Instructions regarding War Diaries and Intelligence Summaries are contained in F. S. Regs., Part II. and the Staff Manual respectively. Title pages will be prepared in manuscript.

Place	Date	Hour	Summary of Events and Information	Remarks and references to Appendices
HAPLINCOURT	5/1/18	to	Brigade remained at wagon lines during this period, carrying out the usual routine of daily work, cleaning up, and generally preparing for the next coming duty in the line.	
	7/1/18			
	18/1/18		Officers of the Brigade proceeded to the position of 223rd Bde. R.F.A. 63rd. D.A., which the Brigade was shortly going to relieve.	
	19/1/18		One section per battery relieves section of 223rd Bde. in the "LA VACQUERIE" Sector of the CAMBRAI Salient.	
TRESCAULT	20/1/18		Relief completed, Brigade becomes sub-group of left group of 63rd. D.A.	
	21/1/18		Brigade engaged in registration and generally settling in new position.	

WAR DIARY or INTELLIGENCE SUMMARY

Army Form C. 2118.

Place	Date	Hour	Summary of Events and Information	Remarks and references to Appendices
TRESCAULT	22/1/18		Brigade change the past its reference for and becomes Right Group. H.Q's move out relieve H.Q's 77th Army Bde R.F.A. 17th. Battery remain with Left Group. B/77 and C/77 come temporarily under command of group. Forward section of 4) 17. Battery relieved by section of D/77, attacked 19th. D.4; 9th Battery sleeps move to new position at BEAUCAMP. 10th Battery shelled during day.	
	23/1/18		Brigade now covers right Infantry Brigade of 63rd Division and has five batteries in the group; day quiet.	
	24/1/18		Second Division takes over and Infantry relief commenced. 9th Battery completes move to new position at BEAUCAMP. Batteries all carried out registration and harassing fire & night.	

Army Form C. 2118.

WAR DIARY
or
INTELLIGENCE SUMMARY.
(Erase heading not required.)

Instructions regarding War Diaries and Intelligence Summaries are contained in F. S. Regs., Part II. and the Staff Manual respectively. Title pages will be prepared in manuscript.

Place	Date	Hour	Summary of Events and Information	Remarks and references to Appendices
TRESCAULT	25/1/18		Observation fairly good, unual firing by batteries.	
	26/1/18		Thick fog all day, making observation impossible, schemes of fire were kept up a enemy's approaches.	
	27/1/18.		Fog still continued, but very quiet.	
	28/1/18		Light very much better, but still rather hazy. Hostile artillery very quiet indeed.	
	29/1/18		Quiet day, nothing to report.	
	30/1/18		Enemy shelled batteries of brigade from 8.30 a.m. by 7.7cm. in 4th H.F. and gas shell, not much damage done; otherwise all quiet.	
	31/1/18		Observation poor, batteries carried out usual firing.	Maj Jenn: 3 Lt RFA for Act Lt Col Ret. RFA

2nd Divisional Artillery.

41st BRIGADE R.F.A. ::: FEBRUARY 1918.

Army Form C. 2118.

WAR DIARY
or
INTELLIGENCE SUMMARY.
(Erase heading not required.)

41st Brigade RFA.

FEBRUARY 1918

Vol 40

Place	Date	Hour	Summary of Events and Information	Remarks and references to Appendices
BEAUCAMP	1/2/18		1st Royal Berks and 23rd Royal Fusiliers came into the line — Fog all day and very quiet — Batteries worked on positions — Usual night firing on enemy communications.	
	2-2-18		Great aerial activity — Hostile plane brought down near BERTINCOURT.	
	3-2-18		5th Inf. Brigade relieved 99th Brigade — 2nd H.L.I. and 2nd Oxfs & Bucks coming into line — during night 3/4/15 — Sniping at night firing.	
	4/2/18		Enemy fairly active in early morning — Shelling Battery positions at FEUCHY — Our artillery retaliated and situation quietened. Fine day — Movement sniped and usual night firing.	
	5-2-18		Normal day —	
	6-2-18		ditto ditto — 17th Battery position at BOAR COPSE shelled by 5.9 How from 2pm — 4 pm —	
	7-2-18		Hostile artillery active — 17th Battery again shelled by 5.9 How.	
	8-2-18		" " Enemy artillery quiet.	

WAR DIARY or INTELLIGENCE SUMMARY

Army Form C. 2118.

Place	Date	Hour	Summary of Events and Information	Remarks and references to Appendices
BEAUCAMP	9.2.18		Hostile artillery more active -	
	10.2.18		Hostile artillery very active BEAUCAMP. RIBECOURT. BOAR COPSE shelled by 8" How. Lieut. Col. E.J.R. PEEL, C.M.G., D.S.O. assumes temporary command of Brigade	
	11.2.18		Enemy guns a little more quiet	Q.17.d
	12.2.18		GOUZEAUCOURT received attention from 5.9 Hows. during day - Also bombarded with GAS and H.E. Shells in bursts during night - SILENT day on Telephone.	
	13.2.18		Movement round LA VACQUERIE sniped by 18/Mx at 7pm - OBSERVATION good.	
	14.2.18		Raid by 24th R.Fs at 7.30 a.m. - 14/15th inst. Rainy day.	
	15.2.18		Quiet day.	
	16.2.18		Very few lights. - Enemy more active with artillery & aircraft. Back area bombed by GOTHAS during night.	

Army Form C. 2118.

WAR DIARY
or
INTELLIGENCE SUMMARY.
(Erase heading not required.)

Instructions regarding War Diaries and Intelligence Summaries are contained in F. S. Regs., Part II. and the Staff Manual respectively. Title pages will be prepared in manuscript.

Place	Date	Hour	Summary of Events and Information	Remarks and references to Appendices
BEAUCAMP	17.2.18		NORMAL DAY	
	18.2.18		The 17" Battery at BOAR COPSE shelled with 8" and 12" from 9.30 am to 12.30 am. Over 1000 rounds flown up. 9" Battery salved a Motor Lorry about 100m near Battalion H.Q. near VILLERS PLOUICH - Section of 17 Battery moved from BOAR COPSE to new position in Q17c	
	19.2.18		Hostile T.M.s very active on Welsh Ridge - Batteries retaliated - Some rain by 1st R. Berks. at 11 p.m. with a little artillery co-operation - unsuccessful - Remaining guns 9/17" Battery moved to new position.	
	20.2.18		Quiet day - 1st Royal BERKS attempted to raid hostile working party - also unsuccessful - enemy withdrawing before 20:10.	
	21.2.18		Hostile artillery became more active.	
	22.2.18		Quiet day.	

Army Form C. 2118.

WAR DIARY
or
INTELLIGENCE SUMMARY.
(Erase heading not required.)

Instructions regarding War Diaries and Intelligence Summaries are contained in F. S. Regs., Part II. and the Staff Manual respectively. Title pages will be prepared in manuscript.

Place	Date	Hour	Summary of Events and Information	Remarks and references to Appendices
BEAUCAMP	23.2.18		WELSH RIDGE trenches received attention from 4.2s and T.Ms. during morning - evening - vicinity of BOAR COPSE shelled by 8" -	
	24.2.18		Very fine day. Hostile guns shelled BEAUCAMP and VILLERS PLOUICH during morning. Hostile guns fired into S.E. corner of HAVRINCOURT WOOD	
	25.2.18		Quiet day. 2 am. 5 am. ^ 3000 GAS SHELLS were fired into S.E. corner of HAVRINCOURT WOOD	
	26.2.18		2nd DIVISION extended its front nine left. Hostile artillery active. 9th Battery shelled during morning with 5.9 hows. At 5 am & 6.30 a.m. HAVRINCOURT WOOD again shelled with S.A.S.	
	27.2.18		Quiet day - Rear Position nr METZ was unusual. Gassing of HAVRINCOURT WOOD and area continued at 6.30 p.m. to 9 p.m.	
	28.2.18	7.9/16	CHESHIRE REGT of 39th DIV carried out a raid on GONNELIEU, which was very successful - Batteries fired in conjunction with raid.	

Smith Capt & Adjt
45st Brigade R.F.A.

2nd Divisional Artillery.

3

41st BRIGADE ROYAL FIELD ARTILLERY

MARCH 1918.

WAR DIARY
INTELLIGENCE SUMMARY

41st Brigade R.F.A.

MARCH 1918

Army Form C. 2118.

Vol 41

Place	Date	Hour	Summary of Events and Information	Remarks and references to Appendices
BEAUCAMP	1-3-18		Hostile raid on our extreme left, with very heavy T.M. and Artillery Barrage, took place at 5.AM. The TRESCAULT - RIBECOURT and BEAUCAMP valleys were heavily bombarded from 4.30 AM onwards. S.O.S. went up at 5 AM. The hostile artillery was very active throughout the rest of the day - CHARING-CROSS and BEAUCAMP were intermittently shelled with 4.2 + 5.9, - guns carried out a counter Battery shoot with 5.9's using aeroplane observation, on a section of 6" Hows - S.E. edge of BEAUCAMP. Two "Drachenam" - "Strafe" fired on hostile trenches at 4.45 pm and 5-5 pm.	
	2.3.18		Light poor and a quiet day. Aerial shelling of BEAUCAMP and VILLERS-PLOUICH. 1st Batn Kings Regt. attempted silent raid on our front without success.	
	3.3.18		Aeroplane very bad to observation. Quiet day. Back area near HAVRINCOURT shelled intermittently with 4.2, 15E. and 8"s during evening.	
	4.3.18		Observation poor. Batteries near HAVRINCOURT WOOD shelled from 9 am to 2 pm with 4" Gun - attempt to DEcauville our lines - no serious damage.	

Army Form C. 2118.

WAR DIARY
or
INTELLIGENCE SUMMARY.
(Erase heading not required.)

Instructions regarding War Diaries and Intelligence Summaries are contained in F. S. Regs., Part II. and the Staff Manual respectively. Title pages will be prepared in manuscript.

Place	Date	Hour	Summary of Events and Information	Remarks and references to Appendices
BEAUCAMP	5-3-18		BEAUCAMP and Valley heavily BEAUCAMP shelled during day with 77mm + 4.2 How. Otherwise unimportant. Considerable night firing on both sides on roads and back areas.	
	6-3-18		Enemy shelled TRESCAULT SPUR with 8" for 3 hours firing about 9 rounds in all during the morning. Considerable movement seen from F.O.O. and hostile were shelling at intervals all day. Lt. Colonel P. BARTON D.S.O. took command of 4th Brigade - hostile shelling of BEAUCAMP with 4.2 - incident registration; TRESCAULT SPUR shelling with 8" continued front near our VILLERS - PLOUCH shelling intermittent not in excessive - BEAUCAMP Battery positions received some gas shelling.	
	7-3-18		Enemy active upon BEAUCAMP village and Valley, also VILLERS-PLOUCH with 77 M.M. and 4.2 How. during morning. Enemy working parties seen at FRANKS near SONNET FARM were fired on with good results -	

Army Form C. 2118.

WAR DIARY
or
INTELLIGENCE SUMMARY.
(Erase heading not required.)

Instructions regarding War Diaries and Intelligence Summaries are contained in F. S. Regs., Part II. and the Staff Manual respectively. Title pages will be prepared in manuscript.

Place	Date	Hour	Summary of Events and Information	Remarks and references to Appendices
BEAUCAMP	9.3.18		Visibility good — Enemy Aircraft very active — AA Aircraft section near BEAUCAMP got a direct hit on one plane — bring it down N.E. of VILLERS PLUICH. Enemy shelling very heavy during night.	
	10.3.18		Hostile Aeroplane put down at noon near RIBECOURT but our front was quiet — Nothing materialized — rest of day quiet.	
	11.3.18		Quiet day. Observation poor and no unusual occurrences.	
	12.3.18		Fired COUNTER PREPARATION at dawn — Enemy very active in his registration of BEAUCAMP FACTORY. all Calibres. At 12 midnight heavy gas shelling of 9.5", 4.7" and D/say positions near BEAUCAMP. Counter Preparation from 1 a.m. to 6.25 a.m. on 12/13" gas very intense and batteries fired in their masks.	
	13.3.18		Enemy fired occasionally — area near BEAUCAMP full of gas.	

Army Form C. 2118.

WAR DIARY
or
INTELLIGENCE SUMMARY.
(Erase heading not required.)

Place	Date	Hour	Summary of Events and Information	Remarks and references to Appendices
BEAUCAMP	14/3/18		16th Battery exchanged positions with 95 Battery - owing to gas casualties and We went to rest of the battn. Gas shelling of neighbourhood of BEAUCAMP resumed from 8pm to midnight - heavy concentration. Night firing very active. 47th and D/87 much affected by the gas, which does not clear.	
	15.3.18		Gas shelling during night again resumed - our night firing also very active. Preparation fired at dawn.	
	16.3.18		11 a.m. Brigade cooperation in raid by 1st KINGS. on German post. Very successful BARRAGE, and an identification officer. No prisoners taken but 70 Germans killed.	
	17.3.18		16th Battery (late 95) position S.W. corner of BEAUCAMP. Shelled with 4.2" A.A. in a few S.G.s from 11 am to 1.35 pm - about 400 rounds. One gun damaged, no ammunition destroyed - no casualties. Also about 30 rounds ammunition destroyed - no casualties.	

Army Form C. 2118.

WAR DIARY
or
INTELLIGENCE SUMMARY.

(Erase heading not required.)

Place	Date	Hour	Summary of Events and Information	Remarks and references to Appendices
BEAVCAMP	18.3.18		1st Battery position again shelled - with 5.9, 8" rounds - and 4.2" 30 rounds during the morning. NO CASUALTIES. but a few more rounds of ammunition destroyed. Cooperated in unsuccessful raid by 17th Royal FUSILIERS who gained identification and killed 10 Germans, in CORNER TRENCH, 400 yards N.E. of LA VACQUERIE, wire was successfully cut by 47th Battery. identification obtained enemy to be 88th R.I.R. 21st Div. relieve 88th Brigade. Received orders that 41st Brigade would relieve 88th Brigade.	
	19.3.18		All quiet. Some gas shells (S) both ways during night. On 20th/22nd inst. TRESCAULT	
	20.3.18		47th Div. infantry relieved 2nd Div. Infantry in LA VACQUERIE front on 19/20 - and 20/R.E. Hostile Artillery very quiet. Received intelligence German offensive expected.	
	21.3.18		All quiet until 4 A.M. when enemy opened bombardment with GAS SHELLS on Battery area. At 4.40 A.M. intense bombardment opened on whole of 3rd and 5th Army fronts with minenwerfer and all calibres. Back areas very heavily shelled by H.V. guns. On 47th Div. front the bombardment was all quick to intense but enemy infantry got into our outpost line during the morning. local counter	

Army Form C. 2118.

WAR DIARY
or
INTELLIGENCE SUMMARY.
(Erase heading not required.)

Instructions regarding War Diaries and Intelligence Summaries are contained in F. S. Regs., Part II. and the Staff Manual respectively. Title pages will be prepared in manuscript.

Place	Date	Hour	Summary of Events and Information	Remarks and references to Appendices
BEAUCAMP	21.3.18		attacks were made but enemy to gained situation at 9 p.m. infantry retired to HIGHLAND RIDGE with H'rs on CAMBRAI – ST QUENTIN railway. The Brigade was engaged all day firing at good targets and did fine work. Barrage on S.O.S. lines at the break up pursuit of the attacking parties. The 165 and 17th Batteries near BEAUCAMP were in kaleis during the opening of the attack with gas, 4.2", 5.9"- Both batteries fired for over 4½ hours in their gas masks. The 165 suffering several casualties. During the night 21st/22nd The forward batteries retired to the METZ positions covering HIGHLAND RIDGE Line.	
	22.3.18		Misty morning – During a considerable force advance from MARCOING came under very heavy artillery fire and many casualties were inflicted in them. Infantry retired to TRESCAULT – HERMIES LINE.	
	23.3.18		During early morning Brigade moved to positions 2.W. of NEUVILLE and former retirement of 142 Inf Brigade. At 2 p.m. Brigade relieved to position S of BUS. Enemy pressed on and occupied YTRES and LECHELLE AERODROME. After engaging hostile infantry Brigade fell back to ROCQUIGNY at dusk, taking up position N.E. of the village. Enemy captured BUS during the night – [Lieut MacINTYRE (18th Bat(oo)) wounded. Destroyed ANTI-TANK GUN on HIGHLAND RIDGE before moving.	

Army Form C. 2118.

WAR DIARY
or
INTELLIGENCE SUMMARY.
(Erase heading not required.)

Instructions regarding War Diaries and Intelligence Summaries are contained in F.S. Regs., Part II. and the Staff Manual respectively. Title pages will be prepared in manuscript.

Place	Date	Hour	Summary of Events and Information	Remarks and references to Appendices
ROCQUIGNY LE TRANSLOY LES BOEUFS GUEUDECOURT LE SARS.	24.3.18		Engaged enemy advancing on ROCQUIGNY in early morning but then retired via LE TRANSLOY where position was again in action for a short period - Thence to N.Y GUEUDECOURT. At 2 p.m. enemy advanced from MORVAL and occupied LES BOEUFS, his advance was then checked by section of 9th 10th and 17th Battalions with a expensive Infantry line was being formed. Then retired through very congested road through GUEUDECOURT and round to EAUCOURT L'ABBAYE eventually halting at LE SARS (DESTREMONT FARM) during afternoon. Brig-Gen. BAYLEY and Staff 141 Inf. Bde was captured by mounted Germans between HIGH WOOD and MARTINPUICH - M/87 and A/186 Brigade captured also. Patrol found BARKER on road dying of wounds - he was killed by M.V. there a few minutes after we passed.	
CONTALMAISON	25.3.18		Moved at dawn to positions West of CONTALMAISON via POZIERES and LABOISSELLE. Engaged enemy attacking BAZENTIN-LE-PETIT and covered the ate line retirement. Remained in position until 1.30 a.m. and then retired via ALBERT to AVELUY, enemy having occupied POZIERES about 10.30 p.m. Lieut. Lieut. SCROGGIE with an Infantry patrol up to PATRIERES at 11 p.m. They found no Germans there. Eventually POZIERES DUMP	

WAR DIARY or INTELLIGENCE SUMMARY

Army Form C. 2118.

Place	Date	Hour	Summary of Events and Information	Remarks and references to Appendices
AVELUY and ALBERT	26.3.18		Batteries moved from position in river bank at AVELUY to position between AVELUY and BOUZINCOURT about 9 A.M. Shelled enemy advancing in mass at about 11.15 A.M. in direction AVELUY - ALBERT. Very good. Observation was possible and enemy suffered many casualties but they eventually occupied ALBERT and part of AVELUY. Brigade retired at dusk to position near BOUZINCOURT. We were supporting 12th DIVISION. Lieutenant J.P. WILSON, 9th Battery, wounded at 11.30 A.M. A very interesting day. 4.45 P.M. Saw 4 Boche-Batteries coming into action along BAPAUME - ALBERT Road near POZIERES - got flank on them. H.Q. Hut Shelled during afternoon every - Lieut K. MADDICKS-JONES - ORDERLY OFFICER wounded and H.Q. eventually burnt. Vacates Hut at 7.30 P.M.	
BOUZINCOURT	27.3.18		Enemy attempts to advance from AVELUY and ALBERT - Batteries fired continuously all day with great effect. The German attack made very slight headway during principal fight. At very 5000 strong - BRIGADIER GEN. BERKELEY VINCENT very appreciative. Germans Shells caused several casualties to teams with ammunition. Brigade was relieved at about 10 P.M. by 77th Army Bde R.F.A. and marched to ENGLEBELMER, where orders were received to go to VARENNES, which was reached at 4 A.M. Troops very tired after long march.	
VARENNES	28.3.18		Our total retirement from LA VACQUERIE to ALBERT, 25 miles between nights 21st/22nd and night 25th/26th. Fighting continuously all the time. Much needed rest at VARENNES.	

Army Form C. 2118.

WAR DIARY
or
INTELLIGENCE SUMMARY.
(Erase heading not required.)

Place	Date	Hour	Summary of Events and Information	Remarks and references to Appendices
VARENNES BOUZINCOURT	29.3.18 (GOOD FRIDAY)		Brigade relieved 77 Army Bugde. R.F.A. in old position near BOUZINCOURT. Occupied old H.Q. in Pretorius Camp in huts 1/2 mile N.W. of BOUZINCOURT. Severe artillery action on back areas, roads E.C.	
	30.3.18		Heavy rain. Much random shelling by enemy on back areas. Batteries fired harassing fire on enemy communications near RUPERT. Moved a section of 16th Battery to "shoot" on cross-roads AVELUY - BOUZINCOURT. Also Div. gun of 17th Frenomi position.	
	31.3.18 (EASTER SUNDAY)		17th and 47th Div. carried out minor operations at 6 A.M. which was not very successful. Batteries cooperated and fired on area generally. Enemy 4.2 How. were active during early morning in retaliation, evidently much annoyed by our TANKS who retired through Battery positions. Lieut. T. Fox of 17th Battery and 2nd Lieut. G. PERRY of 9th Battery were killed by 4.2 which burst close to their mess. 2nd Lieut. CLARK (17th Battery) and 2nd Lieut. SCROGGIE (16 Battery were wounded.) Rest of day was fairly quiet. Brigade H.Q. moved to SENLIS at dusk, alongside 140 INF. BDE	

2nd Divisional Artillery.

41st BRIGADE R. F. A.

APRIL 1918.

Army Form C. 2118.

WAR DIARY
or
INTELLIGENCE SUMMARY
(Erase heading not required.)

41st Brigade R.F.A.

APRIL 1918

Instructions regarding War Diaries and Intelligence Summaries are contained in F.S. Regs., Part II. and the Staff Manual respectively. Title pages will be prepared in manuscript.

Place	Date	Hour	Summary of Events and Information	Remarks and references to Appendices
BOUZINCOURT	1-4-18		Fairly quiet day - The enemy appeared to be held on front - 36th Brigade R.F.A. came up to relieve 41st Brigade R.F.A.. 16th and 47th Batteries withdrew to Varennes but 9th and 17th remained covering front until following day.	
VARENNES	2-4-18		9th and 17th Batteries relief completed about 9 am. These Batteries withdrew to VARENNES and rejoined Brigade resting at wagon lines.	
"	3-4-18		Rested at VARENNES -	
"	4-4-18		" " "	
GROUCHES	5-4-18		2nd Divn. Arty. marched to GROUCHES via LOUVENCOURT, SARTON, and DOULLENS - Good Billets -	
ROZIERE	6-4-18		Received orders during night that 2nd D.A. would join 1st Division in FREVENT area - Brigade marched to ROZIERE, via GRAND RULLECOURT, LIENCOURT, and ESTREE WAMIN - Good Billets for men but horse accommodation very poor -	

(A7092). Wt.W28599/M1293 750,000. 1/17. D.D. & L., Ltd. Forms/C.2118-14.

WAR DIARY
or
INTELLIGENCE SUMMARY.
(Erase heading not required.)

Army Form C. 2118.

2.

Place	Date	Hour	Summary of Events and Information	Remarks and references to Appendices
ROZIERE	7.4.18		Brigade rested at ROZIERES - WET day	
"	8.4.18		"	
FREVIN - CAPELLE	9.4.18		Brigade marched to ACQ area at 9 a.m. via AVESNES-LES-COMTE, AUBIGNY to FREVIN CAPELLE - As the head of the column led by the 36th Brigade entered ACQ the enemy commenced to shell with H.V. long range gun - causing casualties - Brigade halted for some time outside ACQ and eventually billeted for the night in FREVIN - CAPELLE - Receive orders to join 1st CANADIAN DIVISION on ARRAS Front on following day.	
BLANGY	10.4.18		Battery positions near BLANGY reconnoitred in the morning - Brigade going into action later in the day South of the river SCARPE - wagon-lines established at MADAGASCAR Corner. Brigade H.Q in dug-outs in RAILWAY TRIANGLE on the way to FEUCHY. 18pr Batteries all close together in VALLEY S.E. of BLANGY PARK - 47th Battery near twin Bridge under the ARRAS - LENS and ARRAS - DOUAI railway junction.	

Army Form C. 2118.

WAR DIARY
or
INTELLIGENCE SUMMARY.
(Erase heading not required.)

Instructions regarding War Diaries and Intelligence Summaries are contained in F. S. Regs., Part II. and the Staff Manual respectively. Title pages will be prepared in manuscript.

Place	Date	Hour	Summary of Events and Information	Remarks and references to Appendices
BLANGY	11-4-18		Batteries registered on a sniper, enemy movement - carried out a good deal of harassing fire throughout the night. Established Brigade O.P.	
"	12-4-18		Fine day - light excellent for registration. Brigade fired much harassing fire throughout the day and night - Brigade O.P. receives a fair amount of attention from 77 m.m. direction of ORANGE HILL	
"	13-4-18		Quiet day - a good many hostile Jerenemy seen. and sniped at - Harassing fire continued all day and night, firing bursts at intervals.	
"	14-4-18		Quiet day - harassed German communications - very little hostile artillery fire. Brigade O.P. received attention from 4.2 how. and 77 m.m. No damage caused.	

Army Form C. 2118.

WAR DIARY
or
INTELLIGENCE SUMMARY.
(Erase heading not required.)

Instructions regarding War Diaries and Intelligence Summaries are contained in F. S. Regs., Part II. and the Staff Manual respectively. Title pages will be prepared in manuscript.

Place	Date	Hour	Summary of Events and Information	Remarks and references to Appendices
BLANGY	15.4.18		Quiet day – Brigade H.Q. removed from Railway Triangle to BLANGY CHATEAU – Usual harassing programme carried out. Much movement reported in Indian and Italian ravines – private relief – fired on communications at night.	
"	16-4-18		Quiet day – usual harassing fire at night.	
"	17-4-18		9th and 47th Batteries ran single guns forward to old battery positions and fired ammunition from there on likely tender spots – usual harassing fire at night	
"	18-4-18		Routes and new positions reconnoitred. 9th and 17th Batteries exchanged zones. Military Medals from 47th Divn. were awarded to the following N.C.O.s and men.– H.Q. = 2/Corp. BUXTON H.J. Sophr. COOPER V. Gunner CROOKS F. 9/5/85 Sgt. HEPPLE E. Bdr. DUNKERTON J. 16th Bm. OAKEY W.J. 41 Bm. STOKER J. Gnr. RYAN J. 17th Sgt. PRESBURY C. Dvr. BURGIN W. Dvr. HEATH C.	

(A7092) Wt. W12859/M1293 750,000. 1/17. D. D. & L., Ltd. Forms/C.2118/14

Army Form C. 2118.

WAR DIARY
or
INTELLIGENCE SUMMARY.

(Erase heading not required.)

Instructions regarding War Diaries and Intelligence Summaries are contained in F. S. Regs., Part II. and the Staff Manual respectively. Title pages will be prepared in manuscript.

Place	Date	Hour	Summary of Events and Information	Remarks and references to Appendices
BLANGY	19-4-18		Fired on enemy movement and reported new works - usual fire kept up on communications and approaches.	
"	20-4-18		Supported raid at 4.30 a.m. by 3rd CANADIAN INFANTRY. Offensive being ICELAND and IONIAN TRENCHES pulse of FEUCHY. Identification secured.	
"	21-4-18		Hostile 5.9" How fairly active during morning in vicinity of Batteries. Advanced wagon-lines near guns without damage. 6 MADAGASCAR.	
"	22-4-18		Hostile artillery fairly active - 5.9 Battery fires on FRED'S WOOD and on marshy ground between ST NICHOLAS and BLANGY. Checked damage on ICELAND and IONIAN TRENCHES.	
"	23-4-18		Fired in support of a raid by 4th CANADIAN INFANTRY on ICELAND and IONIAN - Infantry successfully entered trenches but enemy had vacated them beforehand - very good barrage.	

Army Form C. 2118.

WAR DIARY
or
INTELLIGENCE SUMMARY.
(Erase heading not required.)

Place	Date	Hour	Summary of Events and Information	Remarks and references to Appendices
BLANGY	24-4-18		Enemy Artillery aggressive in neighbourhood of FEUCHY and BATTERY VALLEY - mainly in retaliation for our fire. 10.15 p.m. S.O.S. went up on Right Front front - the Boche having gun pits just acquired by 15th Div. The enemy were ejected.	
"	25-4-18		Quiet day - usual harassing fire -	
"	26-4-18		Quiet day - usual supplying carried on and communications made unhealthy -	
"	27-4-18		Very quiet day -	
"	28-4-18		G.O.C. R.A. CANADIAN CORPS inspected Battery positions during morning - Studied position for 15 pdr ANTI-TANK gun on ATHIES-FAMPOUX road. G.O.C was very complimentary -	
"	29-4-18		Quiet day - harassed usual communications. Lieut. C. L. GREIG & 17 "B" received Bar to M.C. B.S.M. COOK (18th Battery) received BAR to D.C.M. Bdr McGILL 16th Battery & Gunner WARD, H 9th Battery received M.Ms. from 47th Div.	
"	30-4-18		" " Very wet -	41st Bdy / RFA 2 5-17

2nd Divisional Artillery.

41st BRIGADE R.F.A. ::: M A Y 1918.

WAR DIARY
or
INTELLIGENCE SUMMARY.

Army Form C. 2118.

41st Brigade R.F.A.

Vol 43

MAY. 1918

Place	Date	Hour	Summary of Events and Information	Remarks and references to Appendices
BLANGY	May 1st 1918		Very wet and cold. Quiet day. Brigade carried out normal harassing fire.	
	2nd		Warmer. Hostile artillery more active, and also enemy aeroplanes.	
	3rd		Very fine and warm. Observation good. Batteries engaged enemy movement. Hostile artillery active on back areas. Attempt on front system. Heavy bombardment in night & early morning.	
	4th		Good observation - arranged new Brigade O.P. in CAM AVENUE - much enemy movement round ORANGE HILL and Trenches just south of SCARPE - 15th Div. Infantry relieved 1st CANADIAN DIV. INFANTRY during night.	
	5th		Quiet day - usual harassing fire maintained	
	6th		Quiet day " " "	

Army Form C. 2118.

WAR DIARY
or
INTELLIGENCE SUMMARY.
(Erase heading not required.)

Place	Date	Hour	Summary of Events and Information	Remarks and references to Appendices
BLANGY	MAY 7th		Observation poor - very quiet day - B.C.s conferred at Brigade H.Q. when a possible German offensive in this front.	
	8th		Quiet day - normal harassing fire	
	9th		Quiet day - Preparations made for German offensive rumoured about to commence on 10th. Lieut. C.L. Craig M.C. posted 2/Captain (17th Battery)	
	10th		Fairly quiet. No offensive - BLANGY and Battery positions receives attention from 77 mm at intervals during the day.	
	11th		Quiet day - except for heavy bursts of fire on Western Edge of BLANGY at 4 pm and 7 pm - 5·9s from direction of MONCHY. Brigade Commander and B.C.'s started to reconnoitre rear defence line but owing to an alteration in Defence Scheme did not continue.	

Army Form C. 2118.

WAR DIARY
or
INTELLIGENCE SUMMARY.

(Erase heading not required.)

Instructions regarding War Diaries and Intelligence Summaries are contained in F. S. Regs., Part II. and the Staff Manual respectively. Title pages will be prepared in manuscript.

3

Place	Date	Hour	Summary of Events and Information	Remarks and references to Appendices
BLANGY	May 12th		Quiet day - harassed communications as usual during night. Much rain.	
	13th		Very good observation - Quiet day - hostile artillery very active between 10 pm & 11.30 pm.	
	14th		Hostile artillery very active in BLANGY and St LAURENT areas during day - Little damage done - one gun of 17th Battery put out of action by 77 m.m. shell.	
	15th		Very Hot day - Blangy again received attention from hostile 4.2 Hows - apart from telephone lines no damage done	

Army Form C. 2118.

WAR DIARY
or
INTELLIGENCE SUMMARY.
(Erase heading not required.)

Instructions regarding War Diaries and Intelligence Summaries are contained in F. S. Regs., Part II. and the Staff Manual respectively. Title pages will be prepared in manuscript.

Place	Date	Hour	Summary of Events and Information	Remarks and references to Appendices
BLANGY	May 16th		Assisted in hostile raid near FARBUS which was successful - taking 3 prisoners and inflicting severe casualties on the enemy. C.R.A. visited Wagon lines.	
	17th		Hostile artillery active S. of FRED'S WOOD, SCARPE VALLEY and S.E. edge of ARRAS - also on left towards FARBUS - A.D.V.S. 15th Div. inspected Brigade horses.	
	18th		BLANGY heavily shelled with 5.9 and 4.2 hows. - counter battery shoot on The 8" Hows. there. BLANGY BRIDGE and CROSS ROADS shelled with gas and H.E. from 7.7 M.M. between 9 and 10 P.M. One of our aeroplanes forced to land in ICELAND TRENCH - later in the day it was practically destroyed by 18 M.M.	
	19th		Quiet day. Visibility good. Church parade - collection for R.A. Prisoners of War Fund - very successful	

Army Form C. 2118.

WAR DIARY
or
INTELLIGENCE SUMMARY.
(Erase heading not required.)

Instructions regarding War Diaries and Intelligence Summaries are contained in F. S. Regs., Part II. and the Staff Manual respectively. Title pages will be prepared in manuscript.

Place	Date	Hour	Summary of Events and Information	Remarks and references to Appendices
BLANGY	May 20th		Hostile 4.2s and 77m.m. fairly active in BLANGY AREA. ARRAS shelled with 59's and gas during night. Visibility very good all day, batteries did much sniping.	
	21st		Lamp signalling tested and worked well. All firing on targets by VISUAL. Hostile 77mm very active morning BLANGY in trouble and from 10pm to 11.30pm in BLANGY PARK, St. LAURENT and neighbourhood of RAILWAY. C.R.A. inspected Battery positions during morning.	
	22nd		Quiet day. 17th Battery gun calibrated at PETSWANIA Range. Weather turned thundery hot.	
	23rd		Quiet day. Very strong wind. 92 Battery held shoots at Wagon-lines. Very successful meeting. 4.2 How shelled BLANGY battery positions during afternoon.	

Army Form C. 2118.

WAR DIARY
or
INTELLIGENCE SUMMARY.
(Erase heading not required.)

Place	Date	Hour	Summary of Events and Information	Remarks and references to Appendices
BLANGY	May 24th		Heavy rain all day. Hostile artillery very active. Harassing all roads, especially from St NICHOLAS to BLANGY and St LAURENT. Forward section of 9 E. and Brigade H.Q. had to move back to main Wagon-Lines.	
	May 25th		Hostile artillery about normal; hostile fire on battery positions and surrounding ridges. Roads and exits from ARRAS were all shelling during the day.	
	26–		Abnormal activity remained artillery continued. med chiefly directed on area N. of the SCARPE during the day. There was a heavy concentration on BLANGY morning and afternoon and the evening about 9 p.m. followed by gas-shelling in BLANGY and shelling in VALLEY lying BLUE-CROSS between 2 and 5 a.m. 26th/27th–	

Army Form C. 2118.

WAR DIARY
or
INTELLIGENCE SUMMARY.
(Erase heading not required.)

Instructions regarding War Diaries and Intelligence Summaries are contained in F. S. Regs., Part II. and the Staff Manual respectively. Title pages will be prepared in manuscript.

6

Place	Date	Hour	Summary of Events and Information	Remarks and references to Appendices
BLANGY	May 27th	7 A.M.	At 7 A.M. a large mine between TILLOY and ST LAURENT received a bombardment of yellow-cross gas, which lasted about 4.30 a.m. Owing the strong wind and mine men engaged the concentration was not very strong. Rest of day quiet except for a burst fire on BLANGY during the morning, and occasional gas shells round 17th Battery in Early morning. One or two bursts H.V. 2 Hour very near same battery during the day on ST LAURENT. Normal day - Heavy mine burst 5-9 + 4.2 hour on ST LAURENT	
	28th		BLANGY and ATHIES at 11 a.m. and 1.20 p.m. respectively. Forward areas shelled by 4.2 + 77mm between 10 and 11 p.m. High velocity gun active all day in area round Wagnonlien - MADAGASCAR CORNER and ECURIE - Municipal shelling came from ROEUX and PLOUVAIN areas.	
	29th		Quiet day on front - Hostile artillery put down heavy burst of fire near BLANGY DUMP with 4.8 + H.E. 60 pounder position very heavily shelled. F.G. CH. d'ANZIN. - Major Bromley D.S.O. R.F.A. president. - (1) Battery	

Army Form C. 2118.

WAR DIARY
or
INTELLIGENCE SUMMARY.

(Erase heading not required.)

Instructions regarding War Diaries and Intelligence Summaries are contained in F. S. Regs, Part II. and the Staff Manual respectively. Title pages will be prepared in manuscript.

Place	Date	Hour	Summary of Events and Information	Remarks and references to Appendices
BLANGY	May 30		Hostile shelling more active about BLANGY and RAILWAY - with intermittent bursts on Battery positions. 2 Lieut R.K. REYNOLDS G.S. Battery was killed by a 4.2 which fell at the door of his dug-out. Batteries fired in support of raid by 4"/5" Black Watch N. of RAMPOUK which was unsuccessful.	
	31st		Shelling fairly active around BLANGY - at intervals during day. One gun 17th Battery put on F.Q. action during morning	

W. G. Green Capt R.A.
41st Brigade R.F.A.

2nd Divisional Artillery

41st BRIGADE R.F.A. ::: JUNE 1918.

Army Form C. 2118.

WAR DIARY
or
INTELLIGENCE SUMMARY.
(Erase heading not required.)

41st Brigade RFA

June 1918

Instructions regarding War Diaries and Intelligence Summaries are contained in F. S. Regs., Part II. and the Staff Manual respectively. Title pages will be prepared in manuscript.

Place	Date	Hour	Summary of Events and Information	Remarks and references to Appendices
BLANGY	1-6-18		Assisted in raid by Division on our right. Very successful, 27 prisoners taken and one machine gun. Fine day — observation much below movement seen and harassed.	
"	2-6-18		Fine day — Enemy artillery fairly active on BLANGY	
"	3-6-18		Quiet day — Hostile artillery active on BLANGY between 11.30 am & 4 pm. Rest of front quiet. 2/Lieut LOMAS joined 9th Battery	
"	4-6-18		Quiet day — usual harassing fire and sniping at movement.	
	5-6-18		Hostile Artillery very active area from BLANGY & AKKAS at intervals	
	6-6-18		Enemy artillery active on POINT DU JOUR Ridge, area North of the SCARPE and intermittent bursts on BLANGY.	

WAR DIARY or INTELLIGENCE SUMMARY

Army Form C. 2118.

(2)

Place	Date	Hour	Summary of Events and Information	Remarks and references to Appendices
BLANGY	7-6-18		Hostile artillery quiet until 1.30 P.M. when 77 M.M. Battery fired rounds of fire on BLANGY CHATEAU, and area of 17th Battery. A stray round from a 4.2 Battery which also fired at intervals most unfortunately fell at entrance of 17th Battery mess and killed MAJOR J.E.M. BROMLEY D.S.O commanding the Battery, 2nd Lieut. MAGETH wounded slightly but remained at duty.	
	8-6-18		Quiet day. Major BROMLEY buried at ANZIN cemetery.	
	9-6-18		Enemy front East of FEUCHY raided at 2 A.M. but much increased. At 2.30 A.M. enemy commenced heavy bombardment N. of FAMPOUX, and gun S.O.S. went up 2.36 A.M. on our front. Our shelled Battery area. Artillery retaliated but enemy made a quick raid and captured 4 prisoners. 17th forward section had both guns knocked out. Very quiet day.	
	10-6-18		" " BLANGY shelled 77mm (4 per minute during evening)	
	11-6-18		" " " At 11am at 17th Battery position hit and 4 horses killed, 10 drivers being wounded.	

WAR DIARY
or
INTELLIGENCE SUMMARY.

Army Form C. 2118.

Place	Date	Hour	Summary of Events and Information	Remarks and references to Appendices
BLANGY	12-6-18		Division on right fired practice barrage at 3.15 p.m. Heavy artillery co-operating. Slight retaliation on Battery positions and BLANGY about 4 p.m. otherwise quiet.	
	13-6-18		Very quiet day. Major R T BAKER M.C. took command of 17th Battery – wire D. AUDLAND in Captain – Captain GREIG going to 47th Battery.	
	14-6-18		Enemy fires heavy concentration on South Bank of SCARPE G.24 between 9-10 a.m., doing no damage.	
	15-6-18		BLANGY CHATEAU and CROSS Roads shelled from 9.30 to 10.30 a.m. Rest of day quiet.	
	16-6-18		Very quiet day.	
	17-6-18		Much individual movement seen from O.P.; sniped and knocked everything within range – Warning order of relief by 2nd D.A. received.	

Army Form C. 2118.

WAR DIARY
or
INTELLIGENCE SUMMARY.
(Erase heading not required.)

Instructions regarding War Diaries and Intelligence Summaries are contained in F. S. Regs., Part II. and the Staff Manual respectively. Title pages will be prepared in manuscript.

(4)

Place	Date	Hour	Summary of Events and Information	Remarks and references to Appendices
BLANGY	18-6-18		Quiet day -	
	19-6-18		70th Brigade 15th Div. Artillery relieves positions - and detail (rather small). Quiet day.	
	20-6-18		Quiet day excepting that BLANGY Cross roads much more heavily shelled from 7 - 9 A.M. by 5.9 How. that Batteries relieved by 70th Brigade.	
	21-6-18		Half Battery relief took place and completed the return. 47th Battery fired in raid and landed their guns over. Brigade returning to wagon lines at MADAGASCAR CORNER.	
ST. AMAND	22-6-18		Brigade marched to ST. AMAND via DUISANS - BEAUMETZ - LES LOGES - and LA HELIERE. Section going straight up into action done night relieving 181 Brigade R.F.A. near ADINFER WOOD.	
MONCHY	23-6-18		Relief of 181 Brigade completed and guns registered. Col. Jochem 36th Brigade being group commander of 2nd Div. Artillery - 41st Brigade HQ remaining at wagon lines ST AMAND - 17th Battery is reserve at POMMIER. 41st Brigade Signals going into action apart from rest of Bde HQ.	

Army Form C. 2118.

WAR DIARY
or
INTELLIGENCE SUMMARY.
(Erase heading not required.)

Place	Date	Hour	Summary of Events and Information	Remarks and references to Appendices
MONCHY	24-6-18		Batteries shelled and calibrated guns (Siegmondt?) Forward positions and began work on gun-positions and dug-outs. Influenza epidemic began in Batteries - 16th + 17th + 18th Bty. very much affected	
	25-6-18		Quiet day - Batteries all hard at work improving positions. Batteries fired barrage in support of raid on left which was unsuccessful. Lt. TH ROBINSON joined 92nd Battery. Major P BARTON D.S.O. commanding A51 Brigade went on leave to England.	
	26-6-18		Quiet day - Influenza raging - over 100 cases from 17th Battery alone. Hospital started near Brigade H.Q. and apparent epidemic isolated	
	27-6-18		A wet day.	
	28-6-18		Report xxx 150 cases - besides D/ Battery Grenville who go to C.C.S.	

Army Form C. 2118.

WAR DIARY
or
INTELLIGENCE SUMMARY.
(Erase heading not required.)

Place	Date	Hour	Summary of Events and Information	Remarks and references to Appendices
MONCHY	29-6-18		Battery Commanders Conference - Defensive Position discussed. S.O.S. Barrage fired + demonstrated effect to Infantry.	
	30-6-18		Quiet day - Surplus horses picked from D.A.C. Troops up Battalion - Equipment on reduced establishment - air 18 per Battery first line wagon teams being returned to horse teams. Hospital now has 200 cases but men slowly being returned to units.	

W.A. Green
Capt + Adjt
41st Brigade R.F.A.

2nd Divisional Artillery.

41st BRIGADE R.F.A. ::: JULY 1918.

WAR DIARY
or
INTELLIGENCE SUMMARY.
(Erase heading not required.)

Army Form C. 2118.

July 1918
41st Brigade R.F.A.

Vol 45

2nd Divisional Artillery

Place	Date	Hour	Summary of Events and Information	Remarks and references to Appendices
MONCHY	1.7.18		Quiet day - usual harassing fire carried out	
"	2.7.18		"	
"	3.7.18		Maj. Gen. PEREIRA G.O.C. 2nd Division visited battery positions with Brig. Gen. SANDERS C.R.A.	
"	4.7.18		"	
"	5.7.18		Hostile Artillery gas shells 16th Battery forward section which has been actively sniping movement	
"	6.7.18		Quiet day - Lieut. FARNHILL joined 16th Battery	
"	7.7.18		Usual harassing fire	
"	8.7.18		"	
"	9.7.18		Reinforcements arrived at wagon lines - good stamp of men	

Army Form C. 2118.

2

WAR DIARY
or
INTELLIGENCE SUMMARY.
(Erase heading not required.)

July 1918   41st Brigade R.F.A.

Instructions regarding War Diaries and Intelligence Summaries are contained in F.S. Regs., Part II. and the Staff Manual respectively. Title pages will be prepared in manuscript.

Place	Date	Hour	Summary of Events and Information	Remarks and references to Appendices
Monchy	10.7.18		Hostile Artillery rather active registering with air bursts – usual harassing fire carried out	
	11.7.18		Quiet day – Batteries registered and obtained to evening raid by 1st Kings Regt. Major Queller-Couch M.C. of Battery to Div. H.Q. as 2/A.S.O. 2	
	12.7.18		Very wet. Quiet day.	
	13.7.18		Very Quiet again.	
	14.7.18		16th Battery Right Section moved from Erquinvillers Position for a covering raid, registered as returns – Battalia fired in support gave by 1st Kings Regt. which was very successful 9 prisoners taken.	
	15.7.18		Quiet day. 17th Battery moved from position near HAMEAU FARM. 16th Battery Right Section returned to position. 60th Rifles who carried raid without opposition.	
	16.7.18		Quiet day – Hostile A/R Artillery shelled 16th Battery position MONCHY – ADINFER AREA	
	17.7.18		41st Brigade became CENTRE GROUP under command of Colonel P. Barton D.S.O. covering CENTRE "AYETTE" SECTOR – 6th Infantry Brigade. –	

Army Form C. 2118.

3

WAR DIARY
or
INTELLIGENCE SUMMARY.
(Erase heading not required.)

July, 1918
41st Bnigde R.F.A.

Place	Date	Hour	Summary of Events and Information	Remarks and references to Appendices
Monday	18-7-18		Quiet day – Guns registered and slight movement –	
"	19-7-18		" " Usual harassing fire –	
"	20-7-18		" " Hostile 77 mm fire occasional nomilis on ADINFER WOOD falling on men of 9" Battery.	
"	21-7-18		Trial unsuccessful machine gun raid by 1st Berks. Regt. Quiet day –	
"	22-7-18		Assisted in special shoot by HEAVIES on LOGEAST WOOD & hostile enemy batteries – little retaliation.	
"	23-7-18		12.30 am Successful raid by 1st Berks. Regt. quite successful – 5 Prisoners taken and many enemy killed – 4 dug-outs destroyed.	
"	24-7-18		Quiet day	
"	25-7-18		Very wet day – 163rd Battery shelled by 42 Howr in evening – 2 men killed & 7 wounded	

Army Form C. 2118.
4

WAR DIARY
or
INTELLIGENCE SUMMARY.
(Erase heading not required.)

July 1918   41st Bde L RFA

Instructions regarding War Diaries and Intelligence Summaries are contained in F.S. Regs., Part II. and the Staff Manual respectively. Title pages will be prepared in manuscript.

Place	Date	Hour	Summary of Events and Information	Remarks and references to Appendices
Monday	26-7-18		Quiet day – 9th Battery fired Test S.O.S. – usual harassing fire	
"	27-7-18		Very wet day – Two U.S.A. Officers conducted round Battery positions – usual harassing fire	
"	28-7-18		Arrangements made for relief by 6th Kings Regt. Enemy artillery fired a concentration of 5.9, 4.2 Hows on ADINFER – Driver S. Askwith 9th Battery RFA received Military Medal	
"	29-7-18		Fire in support of Raid by 1st Kings Regt. in front in front of AYETTE. Very successful. Barrage opened & finished well. Zero hour 10.40 pm. 7 Prisoners Taken.	
"	30-7-18		9th Battery fired map – line reference from B6.NE.5 AV.16.015 to BIENVILLERS. Quiet day – Forward positions fired in cooperation with raid by 112th Brigade at night	
"	31-7-18		Hostile aeroplane more active – Hostile 77mm harassed Road A near Monchy during morning – Otherwise quiet – Relief of unit finished	

Owen Sweeney Capt & Adj.
for Lt Col O.W. Sanger, RFA

2nd Divisional Artillery.

41st BRIGADE R.F.A. :: AUGUST 1918.

WAR DIARY
or
INTELLIGENCE SUMMARY
(Erase heading not required.)

Army Form C. 2118.

419th Brigade R.F.A 46

Place	Date	Hour	Summary of Events and Information	Remarks and references to Appendices
MONCHY-au-BOIS and ADINFER	1st August 1918		Uneventful day. SE corner of ADINFER WOOD was heavily shelled for about half an hour at mid-day.	
	6th		Some shelling of neighbourhood of Brigade H.Q. (E5-d) by long range 77m.m. at 7 and 10.15 p.m. Lieut Maurice-Jones, D.S.O. returned to the Brigade and joined the 9th Battery.	
	7th 8th		16th Battery fired competitions for Corps Sports. Winners in Boot Throwing team 16th Battery; Single Jumping 16th Battery; aerial shoot made for raid by the 1st Kings opposite AYETTE. Preliminary arrangements made for raid by the 1st Kings opposite AYETTE.	
	10th		Some shelling of MONCHY during the evening.	
	11th		Final arrangements made for raid by 1st Kings. BERLES-au-BOIS was bombed during the night – reported that 32 Guards were killed.	
	12th 14th		American Platoon (319th Regt) now in trenches in AYETTE sector. 1st Kings raided enemy posts at 2.30 a.m. making 2 companies. 7 prisoners, very light casualties. Prisoners were of II/453 rd I.R – moral. During the day the 1st Kings reoccupied enemy outpost line, 3-400 yards beyond our front line. 319th American Regt. took over from 1st Kings during the night.	
	15th		Active harrassing policy instituted, consequent on enemy withdrawal from their outpost line.	

Army Form C. 2118.

WAR DIARY
or
INTELLIGENCE SUMMARY.
(Erase heading not required.)

Instructions regarding War Diaries and Intelligence Summaries are contained in F.S. Regs., Part II and the Staff Manual respectively. Title pages will be prepared in manuscript.

Place	Date	Hour	Summary of Events and Information	Remarks and references to Appendices
MONCHY-au-BOIS and ADINFER	1916 August 17th		Conference between Brigade Commanders as to future operations. Battery commanders reconnoitred new forward position.	
	19th		Brigade and Battery Commanders of 40th Brigade R.H.A. shown round forward area. Last batteries of 41st Brigade moved to forward position during the night.	
	20th		Brigade H.Q. moved to forward position at Fq C.1.9. Batteries of the Brigade moved into their advanced positions after dark. Whole brigade in action along hedge in Fq.a.	
	21st		Attack by 99th Inf. Brigade on ridge W of COURCELLES-LE-COMTE. Barrage opened at 4.55 a.m. Irish went until 11.30 a.m. No hostile artillery retaliation on batteries area. 3rd Division went through 2nd to beyond COURCELLES.	
	22nd		Brigade withdrew to recure at BIENVILLERS and ST. AMAND.	
COURCELLES-LE-COMTE	23rd		Brigade marched at 12.30 a.m. ½ mile S.W. of AYETTE — and got into action about 9 a.m. underground 3 a.m. in COJEUL VALLEY ¾ of ridge, ½ mile SW of COURCELLES. 47th (How) battery went beyond the ridge into valley, ¾ mile SSW of COURCELLES, it was very boldly handled by Major Dyer, M.C., suffering a good many casualties in personnel and horses but in doing so gave the barrage.	

Army Form C. 2118.

WAR DIARY
or
INTELLIGENCE SUMMARY.
(Erase heading not required.)

Instructions regarding War Diaries and Intelligence Summaries are contained in F. S. Regs., Part II. and the Staff Manual respectively. Title pages will be prepared in manuscript.

Place	Date	Hour	Summary of Events and Information	Remarks and references to Appendices
COURCELLES LE-COMTE	1918 August 23rd (contd)		3rd Division having taken GOMIECOURT, 2nd Division went through, and advanced BEHAGNIES - SAPIGNIES, starting under a barrage at 11 a.m. H.Q. 1000 yds. W.S.W. of COURCELLES.	
	24th	10.30 p.	Brigade Commander was summoned to conference at 5th Infy. Brigade H.Q. to arrange barrage for next day.	
	25th		5th Infy. Brigade attacked BEHAGNIES frontally at 3.30 a.m. under creeping barrage of 7 Artillery brigades, with heavy artillery co-operation; then a battalion swung south and captured SAPIGNIES.	
		4.20 a.m.	Brigade Commander was summoned to 156th Infy. Brigade H.Q. (62nd Division) to arrange barrage. At 9 a.m. the 187th Infy. Brigade attacked under creeping barrage and gained a line about 2,000 yards E of BEHAGNIES - SAPIGNIES.	
GOMIECOURT			Brigade moved to positions about 1200 yards S of GOMIECOURT. Heavy hostile counter-attack broken off about 5 p.m., largely by artillery fire. 17th Battery, in action about 1000 yards ENE of BIHUCOURT, fired the "S.O.S." under heavy shell fire. Brigade H.Q. moved in the evening to pits SW of GOMIECOURT, alongside 186th Infy. Brigade. Attack for following day arranged at 11 p.m.	

Army Form C. 2118.

WAR DIARY
or
~~INTELLIGENCE~~ SUMMARY.
(Erase heading not required.)

Instructions regarding War Diaries and Intelligence
Summaries are contained in F. S. Regs., Part II.
and the Staff Manual respectively. Title pages
will be prepared in manuscript.

Place	Date	Hour	Summary of Events and Information	Remarks and references to Appendices
GOMIECOURT	August 1918 26th		16th Infantry Brigade attacked under creeping barrage at 6 a.m. reaching, practically, BEUGNATRE - ECOUST ST MEIN road, N of VAULX - VRAUCOURT. Brigade moved and came into action just S of SAPIGNIES - 47th (How) Battery just S.E.	
	28th		Brigade moved and got into action in the afternoon 1 mile N of BEUGNATRE. He batteries were rather heavily shelled during the night.	
	29th		A small operation by 16th Infy. Brigade at 2 p.m. to get "Above Line" about H6a S.E. was well supported by 47th (How) Battery entirely on the initiative of its B.C., Major Dyson. At 5.30 p.m. the 186th Infantry Brigade attacked along SAPIGNIES and trenches, running E.S.E. from road in H6c, under creeping barrage. The operation was very successful and objective 1,000 yds. S.S.W. of VAULX - VRAUCOURT was gained.	
	30th		186th Infantry Brigade attacked VAULX - VRAUCOURT and ridge just E of it at 5 a.m. under creeping barrage. Objectives were gained - a few enemy pockets remaining in N end of village on the Brigade on the left were	

Army Form C. 2118.

WAR DIARY
or
INTELLIGENCE SUMMARY.
(Erase heading not required.)

Instructions regarding War Diaries and Intelligence Summaries are contained in F. S. Regs., Part II. and the Staff Manual respectively. Title pages will be prepared in manuscript.

Place	Date	Hour	Summary of Events and Information	Remarks and references to Appendices
BEHAGNIES	1914 August 30th (contd)		not able to reach its final objective. In the afternoon H.Q. moved to 1,500 yds E of BEHAGNIES and the Battalions moved to positions in H5b.	
	31st		No change in the situation.	

C Manskonth
Comdg. 41st Brigade, R.F.A.

2nd Divisional Artillery.

41st BRIGADE R.F.A. ::: SEPTEMBER 1918.

WAR DIARY

INTELLIGENCE SUMMARY
(Erase heading not required)

Army Form C. 2118.

41st Brigade, R.F.A.

Instructions regarding War Diaries and Intelligence Summaries are contained in F.S. Regs. Part II and the Staff Manual respectively. Title pages will be prepared in manuscript.

Place	Date 1918	Hour	Summary of Events and Information	Remarks and references to Appendices
BEHAGNIES	September 1st			
	2nd		Arrangements made to attack by 185th Infantry Brigade. Attack by 185th Infantry Brigade commenced at 5.30 a.m. under barrage. Advanced H.Q. established at 7 a.m. in front of "Three Trees" on BEUGNY-ECOUST road, ¾ mile W of VAULX-VRAUCOURT. Immediately after the battle the 47th Battery moved into position ¼ mile S of VAULX-VRAUCOURT, the other batteries following later in the morning. Conference between B.O.C. and Brigadier-Generals of 2nd Division to arrange operations for next day. 187th Infantry Brigade today reached line of road running NNW from MORCHIES, this made the 5th Division on the right nor the 3rd Division on the left progressed as expected. The 197th Infantry Brigade took 500 prisoners, including about 20 officers.	
VAULX-VRAU-COURT	3rd		2nd Division attacked at 5.20 a.m. and met with practically no opposition. 6th Infantry Brigade took over the whole divisional front after the attack and secured an advance guard and the 41st Brigade were given the task of operating with them. 9th Battery was made "close support" battery, the B.C. being	

Army Form C. 2118.

WAR DIARY
INTELLIGENCE SUMMARY.
(Erase heading not required.)

Instructions regarding War Diaries and Intelligence Summaries are contained in F. S. Regs., Part II. and the Staff Manual respectively. Title pages will be prepared in manuscript.

Place	Date	Hour	Summary of Events and Information	Remarks and references to Appendices
VAULX – VRAUCOURT	1918 September 3rd (contd)		with the Battalion Commanders. 47th Battery began to move up about 9.30.a.m. Joint Headquarters with the 1st Infantry Brigade established temporarily at MARICOURT WOOD about 9.30.a.m. While there cavalry and tanks ("Whippets") came up to co-operate. At 12.30 p.m. Headquarters were advanced to CRUCIFIX cross roads, on	
BEAUMETZ -LES- CAMBRAI			BAPAUME – CAMBRAI road near BEAUMETZ-LES-CAMBRAI. Batteries got into positions of readiness behind BEAUMETZ at 1.30 p.m. Enemy were reported in HERMIES and DEMICOURT at 1.30 p.m. – They were dealt with by "Whippets". Our outpost line was established on the line HERMIES – DEMICOURT – BOURSIES and the main line of resistance DOIGNIES – BOURSIES. H.Q., 1st Batt. Infantry and Artillery, established in German hospital just W. of BEAUMETZ.	

Army Form C. 2118.

WAR DIARY
or
INTELLIGENCE SUMMARY.

(Erase heading not required.)

Instructions regarding War Diaries and Intelligence Summaries are contained in F. S. Regs., Part II. and the Staff Manual respectively. Title pages will be prepared in manuscript.

Place	Date	Hour	Summary of Events and Information	Remarks and references to Appendices
BEAUMETZ-LES-CAMBRAI	1918 September 4th		Batteries all in action between BEAUMETZ and DOIGNIES. 1st Kings attacked April heap at K.20 Central under a barrage at 10 p.m. but without success.	
	5th		Front now held by the 99th Infantry Brigade. During the afternoon H.Q. were moved to dug-out just W. of DOIGNIES, alongside 17th Battery.	
	6th		Batteries came back into reserve positions N. of BAPAUME-CAMBRAI road, just E. of where MORCHIES-BEAUMETZ road crosses it. H.Q. established in bivouac just behind batteries. A good deal of shelling and bombing in this neighbourhood throughout the night.	
	7th		Heavy area shelling in neighbourhood of H.Q. until 11.30 a.m.	
	9th		Forward battery positions reconnoitred.	
	10th		Batteries took up positions in valleys S. of DOIGNIES.	
	11th		5th Infantry Brigade attacked at 6.15 p.m. and made satisfactory progress. The CANAL du NORD was crossed on the night of the attack.	

Army Form C. 2118.

WAR DIARY
INTELLIGENCE SUMMARY.
(Erase heading not required.)

Place	Date	Hour	Summary of Events and Information	Remarks and references to Appendices
BEAUMETZ-"LES"-CAMBRAI	1918 September 12th		5th Infantry Brigade attacked again, nothing down towards of old HINDENBURG front line, in conjunction with attack on HAVRINCOURT by 62nd Division on the right. The attacks were successful.	
HERMIES	14th		H.Q. moved to HERMIES in the evening, alongside the 6th Infantry Brigade.	
	15th		New battery positions selected in valleys between HERMIES and DOIGNIES. Batteries moved up at dusk. There was a good deal of bombing during the night.	
LOUVERVAL	16th		Attached to Guards Division as from 9 p.m. New H.Q. established in trench just N of DOIGNIES-LAGNICOURT road, ½ mile W of LOUVERVAL WOOD, - alongside 2nd Guards Brigade.	
	17th 18th		A lot of shelling of valley near H.Q. in the evening. Enemy counter-attacked strongly at HAVRINCOURT, commencing by shelling battery and back area heavily with high explosive and gas. They got a footing in our trenches W of the canal but were ejected during the night. Later accounts show that the enemy was defeated at all points and suffered considerable losses.	

Army Form C. 2118.

WAR DIARY
—of—
INTELLIGENCE SUMMARY.
(Erase heading not required.)

Instructions regarding War Diaries and Intelligence Summaries are contained in F. S. Regs., Part II. and the Staff Manual respectively. Title pages will be prepared in manuscript.

Place	Date	Hour	Summary of Events and Information	Remarks and references to Appendices
LOUVERVAL	1917 Sept. 19th		Quiet day; no change in situation.	
	20th			
	21st			
	22nd	~~~~~	Quiet day, until the evening when the enemy shelled our trenches W of the canal in K.3.c. He got in, but was turned out again. Batteries put down a considerable amount of SOS fire throughout the night & there was a considerable amount of hostile movement.	
	23rd		Quiet day, but a great deal of harassing of battery and back area during the night. Enemy seemed to be putting down a "counter preparation". Barrages MOEUVRES between 3 and 5.30 a.m. (24th).	
	24th		Quiet both during day & night.	
	25th		The enemy shelled the neighbourhood of MOEUVRES at 6.30 p.m. rather heavily and at 9.30 a.m. put down a barrage on the front held by the Guards. No infantry action developed; the brigade fired in the SOS Area for about 20 minutes at a slow rate.	

Army Form C. 2118.

WAR DIARY
INTELLIGENCE SUMMARY.
(Erase heading not required.)

Place	Date	Hour	Summary of Events and Information	Remarks and references to Appendices
LOUVERVAL	1918 Sept 26th		77m.m. gun very active in harassing round about Brigade H.Q. H.Q. moved in the evening to dugout in trench on ridge between HERMIES and DOIGNIES, 1 m. S.W. of DEMICOURT. Batteries, except 9" which was already there, moved up into battle positions in valley S.S.W. of DEMICOURT.	
DEMICOURT DOIGNIES	27th		Attack by 3rd Army began at 5.20 a.m. - dark, foggy fine. Progress was good, the "Red Line" being taken by 7 a.m. - at 7.30 a.m. the attack was well on the way to the "Brown Line". Preparation to advance commenced at 10.30 a.m. H.Q. established temporarily near SPIN ALLEY (north 1 m. S.W. of GRAINCOURT) 1st and 3rd Canadian Brigades and 6th Infantry Brigade.	
GRAINCOURT			9" Battery and a section of the 47th (under Lieut. ARNOLD) went up into action on the E of the canal. They got into action at 4.40 p.m. and put down a good counter barrage on "GRAINCOURT line" N.E. of ORIVAL WOOD. About 5.30 p.m. Brigade and Battery Commanders reconnoitred for positions + selected them 1 m. N.W. of FLESQUIÈRES. Batteries commenced moving up at once and made preparation for an attack next day. H.Q. established with the 6th Infantry Brigade in dugout in trench 600 yards	
FLESQUIÈRES			W.N.W. of Nord of FLESQUIÈRES	

Army Form C. 2118.

WAR DIARY
of
INTELLIGENCE SUMMARY.
(Erase heading not required.)

Instructions regarding War Diaries and Intelligence Summaries are contained in F. S. Regs., Part II. and the Staff Manual respectively. Title pages will be prepared in manuscript.

Place	Date	Hour	Summary of Events and Information	Remarks and references to Appendices
FLESQUIERES	1918 Septem 28th		6th Infantry Brigade attacked at 5.20 a.m. They got through NINE WOOD and later down to the ESCAUT canal. About 9 a.m. H.Q. were moved to old gun position in the FLESQUIERES —	
PREMY CHAPEL			NOYELLES road, ¾ m. W of PREMY CHAPEL at 10 a.m. 9th Battery had a section in action ½ m. W of PREMY CHAPEL and shot a captured 77 m/m gun firing over them this night. H.Q. were moved into a dugout — CAPTAIN'S SUPPORT just	
NOYELLES	29th		N of FLESQUIERES — NOYELLES road, ¾ m. W.S.W. of NOYELLES. There was a lot of fighting during the night. The 17th Divisions got a few men across the canal. Infantry got over the canal all along during the night, against strong opposition. During the morning batteries were getting good enough targets on high ground S.W. of CAMBRAI: 9th Battery went over the hill into action just N of NOYELLES at 3 p.m., the road being under shell fire.	

Army Form C. 2118.

WAR DIARY
INTELLIGENCE SUMMARY.
(Erase heading not required.)

Instructions regarding War Diaries and Intelligence Summaries are contained in F. S. Regs., Part II. and the Staff Manual respectively. Title pages will be prepared in manuscript.

Place	Date	Hour	Summary of Events and Information	Remarks and references to Appendices
NOYELLES	1918 September 27 (contd)		In the afternoon Brigade and Battery Commanders reconnoitred the crossings of the ESCAUT canal and the area L.E. of it for battery positions. The crossings (pontoon bridges) were under rather heavy fire & were all commanded by shell fire except the no 300 yards S.E of pontoon road bridge. Fire apparently directed by low flying aeroplanes. During the early morning the 16", 17" & 47" Siege Batteries came into action on N-W outskirts of NOYELLES. At NOYELLES the town got an abundant supply of water for the first time since 20th August. 5th Infantry Brigade took over the divisional front. Quiet day	
	28th			

Lieut Col. R.F.A.
Comdg, 41st Brigade, R.F.A.

2nd Divisional Artillery.

41st BRIGADE R.F.A. :: OCTOBER 1918.

Army Form C. 2118.

WAR DIARY
or
INTELLIGENCE SUMMARY.

41st Brigade R.F.A.

October 1918

Place	Date	Hour	Summary of Events and Information	Remarks
NOYELLES (CAMBRAI)	1st		Fired barrage to cover attack by 5th Inf. Brigade at 17.00. Attack successful and 200 prisoners taken. Bout from hostile plane wounded two men of 9th Battery.	
	2nd		Harassed area in front of NIERGNIES - FAUBOURG DE PARIS - CAMBRAI - attacked without much success at 05.00. Trench Mortars put 5.9 How into action alongside 6th Battery and fired in conjunction with 47th Battery. Enemy shelled CANAL crossings very heavily all day with H.V. guns - FAUBOURG-DE-PARIS on fire.	
	3rd		Quiet day. Hostile artillery active on CANAL crossings and back areas. 6th Brigade to move line from 5th Brigade - 1st Kings and South Staffs in the line. Colonel BARTON became O.C. Left Group (14th - 36th - + 41st Brigades) evening front. H.H.Q. liason with 6th Inf. Bde/s H.Q. General WILLAN.	
	4th		H.V. guns still very active - 47th Battery lost 4 ORs killed and 2 wounded. Rumoured Counter-attack by enemy with Tanks did not materialise. Harassing fire carried out vigorously on both sides. 16th Battery had 2 ORs killed and wounded by one shell in wagon line.	

Army Form C. 2118.

WAR DIARY
or
INTELLIGENCE SUMMARY.
(Erase heading not required.)

4^(th) Brigade R.F.A.

Title pages October

Place	Date	Hour	Summary of Events and Information	Remarks and references to Appendices
NOYELLES	5^(th)		Quiet day. Canal still shelled heavily. 16^(th) Battery in duty at O.P. near Quarry ₤ MONT SUR L'OEUVRES had dug-outs badly wounded by shell entering dug-out. Major DYSON - 47^(th) Battery - received 2^(nd) bar to M.C. Lieut. G. SMITH 17^(th) Battery received M.C. B.S.M. FAWLEY (17^(th)) D.C.M. 9^(th) + 47^(th) Batteries fired at suspected ANTI-TANK guns on ridge S.W. of NIERGNIES with good results.	
	6-		Again fired at suspected guns - would harass fire. Received orders for attack on NIERGNIES and FORENVILLE tomorrow, but this was eventually postponed 24 hours. MAJOR DYSON W. 47^(th) Battery went on leave to England.	
	7^(th)		Details of attack made out. Battery Commanders meeting at 17.30. Return of 16^(th) Battery under Major G. MEISERVY to advance in close support. NOYELLES as Battery area. Heavy shells during night. Sergeant PARSONAGE (H.Q.) and FORN TORIANCE (9^(th) FBS) awarded M.M.	
RUMILLY.	8^(th)		Barrage opened at 04.30. 2^(nd) Div. (9^(th) Brigade) attacking FORENVILLE with 62^(nd) Div. on their left attacking NIERGNIES. At Zero + 30 4^(th) Brigade moved forward to valley in front of RUMILLY, with 16^(th) section about 1500 yards N.E. Progress fried un railway behind NIERGNIES - FORENVILLE to cover final line. Counter attack by Tanks supported by enemy infantry forced on look from FORENVILLE, but the TANKS	

WAR DIARY
or
INTELLIGENCE SUMMARY.
(Erase heading not required.)

Army Form C. 2118.

6th 3. 41st Bde JC KER

Place	Date	Hour	Summary of Events and Information	Remarks and references to Appendices
RUMILLY	8th Cont'd		was heavily shelled with Trio Bomps & Whiz Bangs. FORENVILLE at 15.00 and again at 18.00. Wagon lines very heavily shelled all day with gas and 8" Hows. Lt/Benton[?]&Shone wounded at 10.45 and command passed to Major Quiller-Couch. The senior officer at the Guns. Major G. MESSERY M.C. 16th Battery was killed riding to Bdy Hd Qrs. from the section during the morning. Capt Greig M.C. 47th Batty 2/Lt Milley wounded but at duty, also 2/Lt GIBBS (17th5) 41st Bde had 8 killed, 32 wounded, 1 missing.* Attack was successful and many prisoners taken - NIERGNIES - FORENVILLE SERANVILLERS being captured and CAMBRAI invaded by the evening.	
"	9th		Shelling very heavy until 02.30 when the hostile artillery became very quiet evidently retiring. Big fire truck at CAMBRAI and damage from attack by GUARDS DIVISION at 05.20 men filed in quite a good light. GUARDS Attack went straight through without opposition. 41st Bde remained at positions and did not advance. On reassuming MESSINES and Tank Battery reported on 5th one found it & a damaged by on fire — & one gun turned — the ammunition in many cases had blown up. Major MESSERY M.C. buried in NOYELLES church-yard. Brigade returned at 09.00 to wagon lines at NOYELLES.	*On 8th/9th Major Monk PRICE, RE, left the Brigade after being attached
NOYELLES	10th			

D. D. & L., London, E.C.
(A10261) Wt.W. 5300/P713 750,000 4/17 Sch. 52 Forms/C2118/16

Army Form C. 2118.

WAR DIARY
or
INTELLIGENCE SUMMARY.

(Erase heading not required.)

6th the 4th Brigade R.F.A.

Instructions regarding War Diaries and Intelligence Summaries are contained in F. S. Regs., Part II. and the Staff Manual respectively. Title pages will be prepared in manuscript.

Place	Date	Hour	Summary of Events and Information	Remarks and references to Appendices
NOYELLES	11th		Rested at NOYELLES. Colonel P. RAITON D.S.O. returned from his hospital and resumed command of Brigade.	
"	12th		Rested at NOYELLES	
"	13th		" " " Church Parade. 2nd Division Infantry moved up to SERANVILLERS area.	
"	14th		Rested at NOYELLES. 2/Lieut C.A. FISHER (R) attached to 17th Battery.	G.S.
"	15th		" " " Informed that German Government have accepted unconditional terms on which Franco-British Peace. Belgian & troops took ROULERS with several thousand prisoners & guns. French took LAON with 12000 inhabitants. British attacking also at Roye well.	
"			Rested at Noyelles - Divn. Concert party visited and gave 2 performances	
"	16			
"	17		Moved towards Divn. Party.	
	18		4th Brigade marched via CAMBRAI to ST. VAAST coming under Guards Division - Billets for night in ST. MIHARD - H.Q. at ST. VAAST. 16th Battery lost 2 teams going up to their position. 2 men killed & 2 wounded. Position taken up about a mile N.E. of ST. VAAST.	

Army Form C. 2118.

WAR DIARY
or
INTELLIGENCE SUMMARY.
(Erase heading not required.)

Instructions regarding War Diaries and Intelligence Summaries are contained in F.S. Regs., Part II. and the Staff Manual respectively. Title pages will be prepared in manuscript.

Place	Date	Hour	Summary of Events and Information	Remarks and references to Appendices
ST VAAST	19th		Batteries took up position between ST VAAST and ST PYTHON. Misty day – Enemy guns normal. On Railway line – STTHIBRE and ST VAAST seen at intervals. R.O. meeting 18.00. Lieut. Col. P. BARTON DSO (4th Bty RFA) commanding to attack. Left Group RFA – comprising 36th, 41st & 76th Bties. Enemy Trees Lhone around SAUZOIR.	
	20th	Zero Hour 02.00.	Slight rain but fairly bright. Attack took place on 3 Corps front. XVII on left, VIth in centre, IVth Corps on right. VIth Corps advancing with GUARDS DIV. on Rt. 62nd DN. on Right. Artillery Barrage Hvy good. HAUSSY – ST PYTHON – SOLESMES was taken and W. edge of VERTAIN. By night we held N. bank of RHA HARPIES. 75th Brigade moved forward to LECATEAU VALENCIENNES railway. S. of HAUSSY at 10.00. Casualties very slight. A large amount of prisoners several field guns, many M. Gns and TMs captured. Left Group supported 3rd Guards Brigade. While 4 BELGIAN Battn. spotted experiences. Whole front advanced. No casualties amongst the Batteries.	
HAUSSY	21st		41st Brigade RFA advanced to Junction S.E. of HAUSSY at 10.30 AM. HAUSSY and ST PYTHON during day. H.V. gun active. Prominence – E aeroplanes active. Lieut Capt. A.E.J. WRIGHT promoted MAJOR while commanding 16th Battery RFA.	
	22nd		Quiet day – Group H.Q. moved to HAUSSY – 2nd Division relieves GUARDS DIVISION arrangement for attack on 23rd completed.	

Army Form C. 2118.

WAR DIARY
or
INTELLIGENCE SUMMARY.
(Erase heading not required.)

Instructions regarding War Diaries and Intelligence Summaries are contained in F. S. Regs., Part II. and the Staff Manual respectively. Title pages will be prepared in manuscript.

5th Brigade

Place	Date	Hour	Summary of Events and Information	Remarks and references to Appendices
HAUSSY	23rd		✱ VI Corps attacked in conjunction with IV Corps on Right and XVII Corps on left. The 2nd Division advancing through The Guards Division. 3 separate barrages were fired from times 0320 - 0840 and 1426 hours respectively. We took the villages of VERTAIN ESCARMAIN CAPELLE BEAUDIGNIES ST MARTIN BERMERAIN and SOMPIANG - The Germans held on stoutly at VENDEGIES below the railway point near Jenlair pouls early attack over the river ESCAILLON where they held the line LE QUESNOY RUESNES and VENDEGIES. Lieut JEPHSON 16th Battalion ✱✱ FOO for 45th Bde. Inf. being wounded when getting information at an outpost 15. 4th Brigade arrived at 10:30 ✱✱Positions at 4am; 9thH.Bde.Reach seven miles BERMAIN. Taking high ground and RUESNES. Guards push on Railway - 36 - 41 Brigades advance - 36th near PONT DE BUAT. being near ESCARMAIN 41 over river (NE) of CAPELLE. Very successful attack. 9000 prisoners and 150 guns taken by 3rd Army.
VERTAIN	24th		Tried Brange at 4 am; 9th H.Bde. Reach seven miles BERMAIN. Taking high ground and RUESNES. Guards push on Railway - 36 - 41 Brigades advance - 36th near PONT DE BUAT. being near ESCARMAIN 41 over river (NE) of CAPELLE. Very successful attack. 9000 prisoners and 150 guns taken by 3rd Army. H.Q. ECCAPELLE
CAPELLE	25th		Remained in position threatened by min ECAILLON putting main line of Resistance - front B RUESNES.
	26th		Position unchanged -
	27		

Army Form C. 2118.

WAR DIARY
or
INTELLIGENCE SUMMARY.
(Erase heading not required.)

Instructions regarding War Diaries and Intelligence Summaries are contained in F. S. Regs., Part II. and the Staff Manual respectively. Title pages will be prepared in manuscript.

Place	Date	Hour	Summary of Events and Information	Remarks and references to Appendices
CAPELLE	28th		Found Left Group enemy outpost line at 10.00 running between S2 D.19 – covering 76th Inf Bde. Enemy H.V. guns active on this covering N.E. of EECHE & area S of ESCARMAIN. Aeroplanes active on both sides	ON
	29th		**5th Allie on our front** Quiet day – 2nd Div Troops over line again at 78.30. M Arty mvmnts smaller H.V. guns active near Escarmain & CAPELLE areas. Observing balloon at ST MARTIN brought down by hostile plane. Bombing aeroplane photo visible active at TRIGNIES.	
	30th		Quiet day – Orders received for attack by XVII Corps on MARESCHES m15.4.11.8.6 (opening) in France, but postponed for 24 hours.	
			H.V. guns active in back areas. Shell wounded Deunn ETWE8 18/11.2.5.4 HQ and killed five horses in Buzzi Pk near the BUSHMAIN. Driv Shepard slightly wounded remaining at duty	
	31st		16th Artillery wagon lines moved up from VERDAIN to ESCARMAIN. Enemy high velocity guns active. 16th Battery lost 7 horses killed and 17 Battery 2 horses killed during night 31/10. News received that Turkey signs ARMISTICE. Captures in British Italian attack now exceed 33,000	

C Mantin
Warwick

Lieu.-Col. RFA
Regiment 74 & Reg. ARFA

2nd Divisional Artillery.

41st BRIGADE R.F.A. ::: NOVEMBER 1918.

Army Form C. 2118.

WO 49

WAR DIARY or INTELLIGENCE SUMMARY.
(Erase heading not required.)

41st Brigade RFA

November 1918

Place	Date	Hour	Summary of Events and Information	Remarks and references to Appendices
CAPELLE	1st	02.00	16th Battery took part in conjunction with barrage by Musgrave Group RFA in raid on LA FOLIE FARM, SOUTH of VILLERS-POL. Raid successful, 9 prisoners being captured including one officer. Own casualties 4 O.R. slightly wounded.	
		05.15	Barrage opened for attack on MARESCHES and high ground near ST. HUBERT by XVII Corps. 41st Brigade co-operating in barrage – successful.	
		10.23	O.P. report Evening counter-attack at ST. HUBERT accompanied by TANK. Batteries fired barrage from position N. of River EQAILLON near PONT DE BUAT.	
		19.30	Barrage arranged on high ground S.E. of ST. HUBERT and batteries fired up to limit of range. Also night harassing fire. Enemy H.V. gun active on back areas.	
	2nd		Attack resumed in early morning. 1st & 41st Brigade did not co-operate – XVII Corps successful – MARESCHES, PRESEAU, MARLY and VALENCIENNES being occupied. Attack arranged for 4th Divn on large front. Battery position reconnoitred N.E. of MORTRY FARM about 600x behind an outpost-line held by 2nd GUARDS BRIGADE. Usual harassing fire in both sides. GUARDS D.A. Ammunition taken up. Take over at 18.00 hours and 1st & 2nd GUARDS BRIGADES took over front from 2nd DIVISION – BARTON GROUP RFA becomes RIGHT GROUP. Comprising 36th & 41st Brigades R.F.A.	

Army Form C. 2118.

WAR DIARY
or
INTELLIGENCE SUMMARY.
(Erase heading not required.)

2.

Place	Date	Hour	Summary of Events and Information	Remarks and references to Appendices
CAPELLE	3rd		Batteries moved forward to new positions commencing 15.00 hours. Enemy reported to have action over LA ROUELLE river and to be shelling VILLERS-POL. Lieut. J. P. WILSON M.C. 92 Battery reported to be wounded by shell on way to O.P. Barrage eventually arranged to begin at 1st Artillery Barrage line (BLUE LINE) and advancing due East.	
VILLERS-POL	4th	Zero Hour 06.00	41st Brigade advanced at 10.00 with rear divisions at LE QUATRE VENTS Cross Road VILLERS-POL, followed by 36th Brigade. 74th and 75th Brigades R.F.A. going in in support of 1st and 2nd Guards Brigades. Flanks held up and the infantry did not pass the FRASNOY - WERGNIES-LE-GRAND Line. LE QUESNOY on right was taken after rather stiff fighting. Our casualties normal, many prisoners taken. 41st and 36th Brigades eventually billeted for the night at VILLERS-POL and remained in Reserve, with no horses actually to move.	! The last barrage fired by 2nd D.A. before dilution of ARMISTICE.
"	5th		Very wet day. 2nd Divisional Artillery still in reserve at Villers-Pol - Guards D.A. moved up to Sirver village and went on at Midday to PREUX-AU-SART. At dawn 3rd Monde Brigade moved up and through 1st and 2nd Brigades taking WARGNIES-LE-PETIT PREUX-AU-SART - FRASNOY - and at 10.00 were East of AMFROIPRES, taking BERMERIES before nightfall with left flank back at LE COURTIL FOI FORAM	

Army Form C. 2118.

WAR DIARY
or
INTELLIGENCE SUMMARY.
(Erase heading not required.)

Instructions regarding War Diaries and Intelligence Summaries are contained in F. S. Regs., Part II. and the Staff Manual respectively. Title pages will be prepared in manuscript.

Place	Date	Hour	Summary of Events and Information	Remarks and references to Appendices
VILLERS-POL	6th		Very wet day. 34th Brigade entrained advance and reported BRY GNIES spur 4th Brigade received orders to be prepared to move forward at 09.00 but eventually remained in reserve at Villers-Pol and did not move. The whole line advanced well. The day penetrating as far as BAVAI.	
PREUX-AU-SART	7th		Wet day - Brigade advanced to meet forward to PREUX-AU-SART. Brigade marched at 13.30. On arrival Col. P. Barton DSO returned to RA at Bt PYTHON to act as CRA while Brig General. 2/4 Sanders CMG DSO departed to England on leave.	
AUDIGNIES	8th		Brigade marched from PREUX-AU-SART To AUDIGNIES via FOREY-du-MORVAN - LE SAULE - B MECQUIGNIES. Very wet and tedious march owing to congestion of traffic on road B MECQUIGNIES. Major W.G. DYSON M.C. in command of Brigade. Guards Division entered MAUBERGE.	
"	9th		In reserve at AUDIGNIES. 36th Brigade RFA relieved up to MECQUIGNIES. Lt.Col. P. Barton DSO received Bar to D.S.O.	
"	10th		In reserve at AUDIGNIES. Major R.T.BAYER M.C. went on leave to England - Major B.B. QUILLER-COUCH M.C. went to leave to PARIS.	
"	11th		In reserve at AUDIGNIES ———— ARMISTICE ————
"	11th 6-17th		Rested at AUDIGNIES and prepared to move towards GERMANY on 18th inst. ARMISTICE at 11.00 - 11-11-18 All batteries reorganised with 4 gun Batteries - 34th Brigade rejoins 2nd Divisional Artillery after being an Army Brigade since January 1917.	

Army Form C. 2118.

WAR DIARY
or
INTELLIGENCE SUMMARY.
(Erase heading not required.)

Instructions regarding War Diaries and Intelligence Summaries are contained in F.S. Regs., Part II. and the Staff Manual respectively. Title pages will be prepared in manuscript.

Place	Date	Hour	Summary of Events and Information	Remarks and references to Appendices
AUDIGNIES	18-11-18		Rested at AUDIGNIES – March postponed until tomorrow.	
"	19-11-18		" " " "	
MEUBERGE	20-11-18		2nd Divl. Artillery marched to MEUBERGE area – 4th Brigade billeted at PONT ALLANT. Route via LE LONGUEVILLE.	
"	21 "		Remained in billets at PONT ALLANT. Capt. L.L. REEVES and Lt K.B. McINTYRE rejoined 4th Brigade from England, attached and posted to 16th Battery respectively.	
"	22 "		" " " "	
"	23 "		Papers for marching to ESTINNE-AU-MONT	
ESTINNE-AU-MONT	24 "		Marched to ESTINNE-AU-MONT via GIVRY. Very bad weather. Intolerable rest halts – Brigade crossed BELGIAN frontier between VILLERS-SIRET-NICOLE and GIVRY.	
FONTAINE L'ÉVÊQUE	25 "		Marched to FONTAINE-LÉVÊQUE via BINCHE and ANDERLUES. Roads very congested.	
"	26 "		Billeted at Fontaine L'Évêque. 4th Brigade collected 3556.50 francs from R.A. War Commemoration Fund –	BHQ 413 9th Bde 780 16th 743.50 17th 855 47th 965 TOTAL 3556.50
"	27 "		Billets at Fontaine L'Évêque. The KING of England & Belgium at CHARLEROI.	
"	28 "		" " " No mail for 15 days.	

Army Form C. 2118.

WAR DIARY
or
INTELLIGENCE SUMMARY.
(Erase heading not required.)

Place	Date	Hour	Summary of Events and Information	Remarks and references to Appendices
PRESLES	29/11/18		2ⁿᵈ Division Artillery marched to Presles via Charleroi and Chatelet.	
"	30/11/18		Billeted at Presles	

Capt & Adjt
ᶠᵒʳ O.C.
4 ᵗʰ Brigade RFA.

2nd Divisional Artillery.

41st BRIGADE R.F.A. ::: DECEMBER 1918.

Army Form C. 2118.

WE 50

DECEMBER 1918

WAR DIARY
or
INTELLIGENCE SUMMARY.
(Erase heading not required.)

41st Brigade R.F.A.

Instructions regarding War Diaries and Intelligence Summaries are contained in F. S. Regs., Part II. and the Staff Manual respectively. Title pages will be prepared in manuscript.

Place	Date	Hour	Summary of Events and Information	Remarks and references to Appendices
PRESLES	1-12-18		41st Brigade billetted at PRESLES.	
	2-12-18		"	
	3-12-18		"	
MALONNE	4-12-18		Marched to MALONNE via FOSSE	
NAMÊCHE	5-12-18		" " NAMÊCHE via NAMUR	
HUY	6-12-18		" " HUY	
WARZEE	7-12-18		" " WARZEE via BARSE STATION and STREE	
HARZE	8-12-18		" " HARZE via OUFFET and COMBLAIN-LA-TOUR	
	9-12-18		Remained at HARZE - Outbreak of Influenza in village	
CHENEUX / MOREAU	10-12-18		Marched to CHENEAUX and MOREAU	
MALMEDY (GERMANY)	11-12-18		" " MALMEDY crossing the GERMAN FRONTIER	
ELSENBORN	12-12-18		" " ELSENBORN LAGER	
MONTJOIE	13-12-18		" " MONTJOIE	
KESTERNICH	14-12-18		" " KESTERNICH	

Army Form C. 2118.

WAR DIARY
or
INTELLIGENCE SUMMARY.
(Erase heading not required.)

Instructions regarding War Diaries and Intelligence Summaries are contained in F. S. Regs., Part II. and the Staff Manual respectively. Title pages will be prepared in manuscript.

Place	Date	Hour	Summary of Events and Information	Remarks and references to Appendices
KESTERNICH	15-12-18		Billeted at KESTERNICH	
GEY	16		Marched to GEY via GERMETER — 9th and 16th Batteries at GEY — 17th 147th at GROSS HAU	
"	17 & 20		Billets at GEY and GROSS HAU	
LANGERWEHE	20-12-18		Marched to Final Destination near West of DUREN — via BIRGER and GURZENICH — Brigade HQ at FREZENBURG. 9th Battery - LANGERWEHE 16th at LUCHEM — 17th at SCHÖNTHAL — 47th at STOTGERLOCK	
"	21-12-18 to 31-12-18		Billetted in LANGERWEHE area	

Capt & Adjt
4th A.R.F.A.

Army Form C. 2118.

WAR DIARY
or
INTELLIGENCE SUMMARY.

41st Brigade R.F.A.

January 1919

Place	Date	Hour	Summary of Events and Information	Remarks and references to Appendices
LANGEMECK GERMANY	January 1st to 31st		Billeted at Langemark area	

Sgd.
Commanding
41st Brigade. R.F.A.

Army Form C. 2118.

WAR DIARY
or
INTELLIGENCE SUMMARY.
(Erase heading not required.)

41st Brigade R.F.A.

WO 95 2

Place	Date	Hour	Summary of Events and Information	Remarks and references to Appendices
LANGERWEHE	Feb. 1st to 22nd	22nd	Brigade billeted at LANGERWEHE.	
	6th		Major R.N. Quiller Couch MC RFA commdg 9" Battery RFA. died at 17th C.C.S. from Pneumonia	
	11th		Major RN Quiller Couch MC RFA. buried with Military Honours DÜREN CEMETERY.	
	14th		Captain L.L. Reeves RFA. 16th Battery RFA died from Pneumonia at 17th C.C.S. DÜREN	
	16th		Capt L L Reeves R.F.A. buried with military honours at DÜREN Cemetery	
	22nd		9th & 17th Batteries & Brigade H.Q. move up by train & join remainder of the Brigade Barracks CÖLN-KALK.	
	23rd		16th & 47th Batteries move up by train & join remainder of the Brigade	
	24th & 26th		Brigade billeted in KRONPRINZ Barracks CÖLN-KALK.	

J.V. Pratt Lt.
Adjutant
41st Brigade R.F.A.
28/2/19.

2ND DIVISION
44TH B E R.F.A.

B.H.Q.
44TH (HOW) BTY R.F.A.
56TH BATTERY R.F.A.
60TH BATTERY R.F.A.
2ND DIVL AMMN COLUMN.

AUG - DEC 1914.

2ND DIVISION
44TH BDE R.F.A.

2ND DIVL. AMMN COLUMN
AUG - DEC 1914

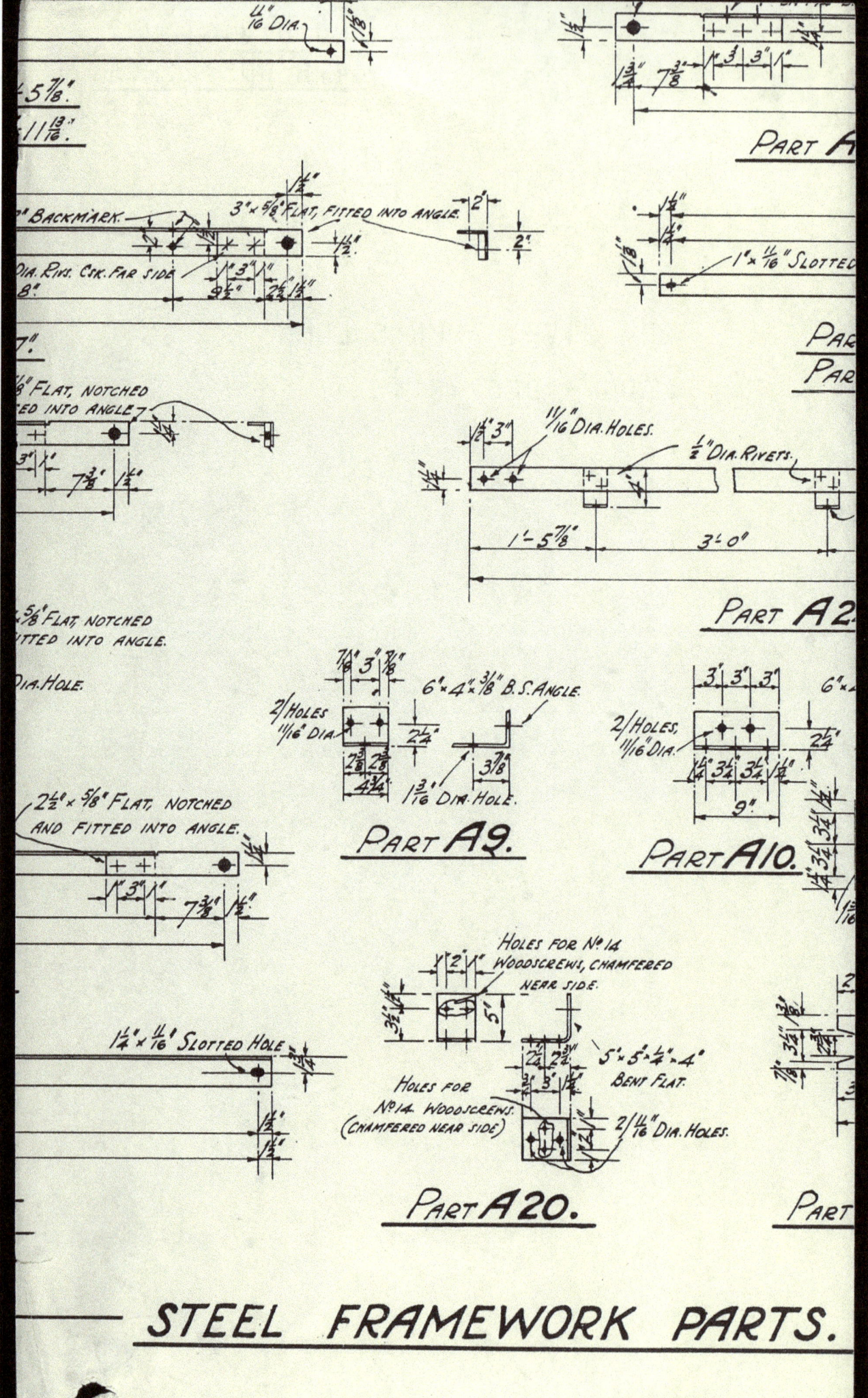

STEEL FRAMEWORK PARTS.

War Diary 121/357
2nd Divisional Ammunition Column
5 — 31-8-14.

Army Form C. 2118.

2nd Divison Ammunition Column

WAR DIARY
or
INTELLIGENCE SUMMARY.

(Erase heading not required.)

Instructions regarding War Diaries and Intelligence Summaries are contained in F. S. Regs., Part II. and the Staff Manual respectively. Title pages will be prepared in manuscript.

Hour, Date, Place	Summary of Events and Information	Remarks and references to Appendices
5th Aug 1914 Preston	(4) Orders 1905 Regular Reservists arrive about 70 Special Reservists — When 50 were up for issue of Equipment — Issued + were started off same night to the Aldershot Command. at WO/P.T Rawalden as O/C W Cornel and Capt Hick as Adjt. Eqpt. to Aldershot.	
6th Aug 9am Aldershot	(5) Commenced looking to personnel and Eqpt mes for H.Q and No 2 Sec. 2nd B.A.C. Found O.C. 3+4 B" 9.7.A. Strouden to his troopships and excellent arrangements Every assistance was made (weather showery)	
"	(6) Reserves put to Public and market. Vehicles painted Commenced arriving. & the horse /power 11pm Water proofs.	
8 "	(7) Receipt progress monthly. Both Fitters + preserves Weather showery and colder.	
9 "	(8) General progress — to Curenedo Checkered Weather showery & fine.	

2nd Division Ammunition Column

Army Form C. 2118.

WAR DIARY
or
INTELLIGENCE SUMMARY.
(Erase heading not required.)

Instructions regarding War Diaries and Intelligence Summaries are contained in F.S. Regs., Part II. and the Staff Manual respectively. Title pages will be prepared in manuscript.

Hour, Date, Place	Summary of Events and Information	Remarks and references to Appendices
Aug 10. Aldershot	(a) Instruction in Gun Drill. Spare kits always to be worn — Braces over tunic. Running hours pad 12 pm.	
11. "	(b) " kits "	
	(c) Horn Kout & Wain rides Troops Leading Draft	
12. "	(d) Teaming horses & fitting harness. Horse movement Breaking draft	
13. "	(b) Still raw - need Earth with horses. Horse shod Very hot day	
14. "	(b) Marching order - Teams went round billets. Bright sunny	
15. "	(b) Drill Order, morning and afternoon. Showing tent. Steady trifle all day	
16. "	(b) Drill Order - Inspection harness Buckingham Shorley tent. Weather dull & fine	
17. "	(b) All trans went out to Aldershot 8.30–9.30. Ammunition & Supp Ration issued to all Entrained Farnborough [?JWR?] 11 pm. Weather still very warm	

(9 29 6) W 5532-1107 100,000 10/13 H W V Forms/C. 2118/10.

Army Form C. 2118.

WAR DIARY
or
INTELLIGENCE SUMMARY.
(Erase heading not required.)

Instructions regarding War Diaries and Intelligence Summaries are contained in F.S. Regs., Part II. and the Staff Manual respectively. Title pages will be prepared in manuscript.

Hour, Date, Place	Summary of Events and Information	Remarks and references to Appendices
18. Aug Aldershot	(t) No 2 Sec entrained in 2/portion (Lt. S. Le Roy.) 3.30 am 0'4's are Entrained & Val, Northampton.	Horse picking iron very rattle
18 Do At 1 am Southampton	Hd Qrs & No 1 Section arrived Victoria 1 & 3 ads & unload wagons ade 7.30 am for Transport E 26 (U.S. Merchant) Embarkation completed 1 pm batten hiker & horses	much delay in entraining wagons caused by train only being att to lift 3 sever while wagons with ammunition weighed 4.6 cwt. ×
19. 6. am Havre	(t) Rupert Harrys – Entrain R. Seven 7 am.	
2 pm Rouen	Reached Rouen & began disembarkation completed 6 pm & marched 7 pm to Camp de Bon Pleur. Got Camp (Tents) before day pat.	
20. 6 pm to 8 pm Rouen	(t) No 2 & 3 + Heavy Jackson No 4 joined at Rest Camp – walker papier –	
21. 3 am & 3 50 am Rouen	(t) No 1 & 2 Sections entrained – at 3 am & 3 50 am Hors portion (No 4 Sec) arrived in Rest Camp 12 noon No 3 & 4 Section entrained 8 pm & 6.25 pm brother Shoving & Scatty. Parked Eulogie Sum.	

Army Form C. 2118.

WAR DIARY
or
INTELLIGENCE SUMMARY.
(Erase heading not required.)

Instructions regarding War Diaries and Intelligence Summaries are contained in F.S. Regs., Part II. and the Staff Manual respectively. Title pages will be prepared in manuscript.

Hour, Date, Place	Summary of Events and Information	Remarks and references to Appendices
22nd Aug — Rouen	(h) Bivouac in Rest Camp. Weather perfect. Left by train at 9 pm for Amiens	
23. Aug Various Sunday	(h) Entrained from ly TANGIER BUSIGNY. Arrived & detrained at Aut NOYE at 1.30 pm. Marched 2.30 pm to LE LONGUEVILLE and QUÉVY LE PETIT. Bivouac in a farm house. Gained touched with H and 2 Div at 9 pm. Fairly heavy and the infantry is to move. Weather warm & sultry	
24 Aug Various	(h) Moved to reconnaissance of K.O.M. NE of BEBOÉ — CHASLE ROYAL Road at 5.45 am. Withdrawn at 6 am via QUÉVY LE GRAND — QUÉVY LE PT & LA LONGUEVILLE. Another 4 wh to encounter at this place by 3pm at 4 pm withdrawn to bivouac S/und W of HARGNIES 12pm. Suffered 30. 000 rounds S.A.A. 18pm. Very warm day.	2 guns 70 battery RFA broken in to pieces. Repair kit & carried with totally lost. During the panic in infantry by XXXXX

(9 29 6) W 3852—1107 100,000 10/13 HWV Forms/C. 2118/10.

WAR DIARY
or
INTELLIGENCE SUMMARY.

Army Form C. 2118.

Hour, Date, Place	Summary of Events and Information	Remarks and references to Appendices
25th Aug. Various	(A) 21 lorries (1½ton vans refilled from Army Park at LAVAL during night & proceed in to PONT SUR SAMBRE. Others received at BISON KMPARK & ½ run to LANDRECIES via PONT SUR SAMBRE – LEVAL NOYELLE – Sadrot – bdlub – ST. REMY BRETON (2 K.Sy LANDRECIES) at the Rous & together with French Troops & our own First Row together with French Troops & our own First...	Horses suffering from heat & general exertion. Battation considerable jaded without whom had to transfer from to BASE.
Various 4 pm	Sudden orders to move at once to LE GRAND FAYT in company with 35 Coy 1 Heavy R.S.A. After bitter & lengthy (?) discussion & heavy thunderstorm came on at 8.30 pm. West – Heavy thunderstorm came on at 8.30 pm. Where 1st Brigade 1st Div and 1st Bde A.A. left us... LE GRAND FAYT. Arrive at LANDRECIES clearly heard all night. My got up in open...	
26 Aug. 145a	(A) Returned to march to ETREUX nr PRISCHES BARZY and BUE much together in Fatty crowd by French troops, motor lorries our vehicle... in all directions. Where 1st Army or ETREUX to the higher. Where 1st Army or ETREUX all day – hot kept.	

Army Form C. 2118.

WAR DIARY
or
INTELLIGENCE SUMMARY.
(Erase heading not required.)

Instructions regarding War Diaries and Intelligence Summaries are contained in F.S. Regs., Part II. and the Staff Manual respectively. Title pages will be prepared in manuscript.

Hour, Date, Place	Summary of Events and Information	Remarks and references to Appendices
27 Aug 6 am	(A) left at 6 am in motor & Train for GUISE via MONT D'ORIGNY — rested horses for all afternoon - marched to [?] from [?] very [?] all [?] to I hr [?] at Sudden [?] of march at once for ANDELAIN via LUCY, MAYOT and DAMIZY. [?] [?] Arr [?] [?]. (B) Horse [?] [?] Marched - [?] ANDELAIN at 7 am. [?] to an [?] through a DEUILLET and S' GIBAIN AMIGNY, [?] of S' GOBAIN and [?] BARISIS to [?] Pierre. Very warm in day & warm but cold at night.	Left 3rd [?]- Hospital & My [?] to [?] [?] MONT D'ORIGNY. Supplied 34 D, R+ F [?] with 15 [?] [?] came up [?].
28 Aug	[?] [?] at 7 am to move to new bit bivouac at 2.30 and then marched via BARISIS to PIERREMANDE. All 5 Div D+H left a Field Hospital and [?] [?] CR in [?] [?] return in [?]	

WAR DIARY
or
INTELLIGENCE SUMMARY.
(Erase heading not required.)

Army Form C. 2118.

Instructions regarding War Diaries and Intelligence Summaries are contained in F.S. Regs., Part II. and the Staff Manual respectively. Title pages will be prepared in manuscript.

Hour, Date, Place	Summary of Events and Information	Remarks and references to Appendices
30th Aug/14 3 am	(k) Ordered to march at once on POISEAUX but at SOISSONS rec'd counter orders — went to park at VAUX BUIN. Road fully congested with columns and fighting troops, very wearisome day.	Supplied 3 complete lines transport Brigt Am Col. — Efficiency of Supplies is everywhere —
31st Aug/14 4.15 am	(k) Marched to VILLERS COTTERET — arrived gave "today a rest". No 2 Ammunition Park at same place — met for first time. Up to date the following has been supplied to Artillery: 1772 Rounds 18pr 1.18 How. 52 Shrap } as 4.5" How. 4 Pos. Wheels G.S. Wag } 12 Rds } as 60 pr. 2 Poles Sq Stores } 374,350 r. J A A. 1 Wagons 18 Horses And in addition the following: 20 horses died or him...	Memorandum WPS Conf 2. F. TAP 31/8/14

WAR DIARY. 121/1063

Ammⁿ Column 2nd Division

Volume II. 1-30.9.14

2nd Division Ammunition Column

WAR DIARY
or
INTELLIGENCE SUMMARY
(Erase heading not required.)

Army Form C. 2118.

Hour, Date, Place	Summary of Events and Information	Remarks and references to Appendices
1st Sept 14. 3 a.m.	(1) Marched to MAREIL SUR ORACQ — halted 7 am till 2 pm & proceeded to NEUFCHELLES — MAY-EN-MULTIEN & the CANAL de L'ORACQ N.E. of MEAUX. Arrived 9 p.m. till 12 midnight. (2) Reorganization in Et. at Lilberaux ordered by GOC 1/9/14. Left — Each section retains 18 wagon (4 pr + 3 loaded) SAA + 2 pr Shrapnel + Shrapnel — N.4 section kept 6 wagon (4w) and 3 pr 60 pr ammunition — the remainder departed with full teams (one for 4 pounders) & the 2nd Brit'n to carry of packs and Infantry soldiers. Misty cloudy day — very hot afternoon.	
2nd Sept 14 midnight	(4) Moved on till 1st Brig. Am. Col. on MEAUX to left forward S. of ST GERMAIN. Very hot all day.	
3rd Sept 6.30 am	(4) Marched to VILLERS — CRECY — La HAUTE MAISON & PETITS LES HOUIS — at 8 pm again moved L. GREMENTER. Very hot all day.	3 wagons 18 pr. Limit K 41 — 18 pr. 9372

WAR DIARY
or
INTELLIGENCE SUMMARY.
(Erase heading not required.)

Army Form C. 2118.

Hour, Date, Place	Summary of Events and Information	Remarks and references to Appendices
4 Sept 14. 6.30 am	(H) Marched via MOUROUX and FAREMOUTIERS to PEZARCHES. Very hot all day	days known from 5th to 8th partially compiled with
5 Sept 14. 4.45 a.	(H) Marched for L'ETANG via ROZOY and COURTOMER. Cheered & bowers in all Villages there day – thirsty strand.	
6 Sept. Sunday	(H) Army moved forward to attack. Remained at L'ETANG till midday when met move to CHAUMES. Very hot even day.	
7 Sept. Tuesday	(H) Marched 3 am for PEZARCHES - forced 6. Ms. Arriv'd at 6 km ché at CHATEAU DE LA FORTELLE - halted there Very hot all day.	
8 Sept. Sunday	(H) Marched 1.30 am for REBAIS Cool day - heavy thunder storm 5 pm	

WAR DIARY
or
INTELLIGENCE SUMMARY.
(Erase heading not required.)

Army Form C. 2118.

Hour, Date, Place	Summary of Events and Information	Remarks and references to Appendices
9. Sept. Sunday	(4) 1.30 pm Marched fr CHARLY-SUR-MARNE but patrols were N.Y LA BELLE IDÉE & road was blocked for 5½ mls. Cavalry lost day.	Captured a Inf/Supply Co. Brigade in reserve
10. Sept. Sunday	(4) Marched ? am f. F Mon between DOMPTIN and COIPRU - arrived 10 am Received from 2 Army Ida 11 am	
11. Sept. "	(4) Marched from MARIGNY - BUSSIAIRES and MONNES & NEUILLY and billeted at LATILLY. very wet afternoon & night.	heavy baton opposition & communie Goneromn They see Am. Lt. f. & Div
12. Sept "	(4) Marched 9 am via WADON, BRENY and OULCHY LE CHATEAU & ARCY. Showing all day - very wet night.	
13. Sept "	(4) Marched via BRANGE and JOUAIGNES & QUINCY SOUS LE MONT - hard the Column billeted. Storms very bad there. Showing wet day.	
14. Sept "	(4) Marched via BRAINE thro' PONT D'ARCY but packed 2 mls N.g. BRAINE Cold windy day - lay wet night.	

Army Form C. 2118.

WAR DIARY
or
INTELLIGENCE SUMMARY.
(Erase heading not required.)

Instructions regarding War Diaries and Intelligence Summaries are contained in F. S. Regs., Part II. and the Staff Manual respectively. Title pages will be prepared in manuscript.

Hour, Date, Place	Summary of Events and Information	Remarks and references to Appendices
15 Sept Sunday	(h) Move bivouac 15rd coy to boat ecoul of bivouac	
16 Sept "	Heavy rain all afternoon & night	
	(b) Remained in bivouac	
17 "	Fine day	
	Remained in bivouac	
18 "	Very hot day, viually	
	(h) Shifted bivouac	
	Capt Jamieson + party went to Esil Kind for remounts	
19 "	Windy hot piece	
	Remained in bivouac	
	Very hot night — also windy day	
20 "	Remained in bivouac	
	Capt Jamieson returned with 2 g. O. R. no for 27 Sowars	
	Very hot other day	
21 "	Remained in bivouac	
	Remounts handed over to Squads	
	Very cold showery day	
22 "	(h) 2nd Dy Posten to 44th Rgts remounts whether are transferred to Brigade Hm Cols.	

WAR DIARY
or
INTELLIGENCE SUMMARY.

(Erase heading not required.)

Army Form C. 2118.

Hour, Date, Place	Summary of Events and Information	Remarks and references to Appendices
23rd Sept	(b) Moved into MONTHUSSARD FARM. Heavy expenditure Ammunition. Enemy very busy.	
	(4) N. & See receives signal to fill establishment by hand returned from 2" Div to have Ammunition preserved. received during morning.	
24 Sept	(4) Nothing to report. Enemy very busy.	
25.	(4) Quiet day.	
	(4) 18 wagons from 2nd Division Ammn Park to receive Mark.	
	(4) Quiet. Guns.	
26.	(5) Moved to VAUBERLIN. Enemy very busy.	(5) 18pr 266 rounds
	Abnormal expenditure of Ammunition.	4.5 1021 —
		tops 65 —
		S.A.A. 119,000
27.	(4) Nothing to note.	Expenditure to date
28.	(4) nil	18pr 11,075 rounds
29.	(4) nil	4.5 How 514 —
30.	(4) nil	tops 456
		18pr How 500 —
		4h 36,000
		S.A.A. 476,300
		Enemy guns 650

J Manrieu ADC
Comd 2 DAC

HQ ~~...~~ 2 Div

Herewith returned
copy of report + sketches
taken.

10.9.14 }
5.10 pm }

DH
44 R F A

OC GRESLINES.

Dates

30.9.14
2.35

44 Bde RFA

R.A. 2nd Division

Forwarded as
requested please return

E Seagrave Lt Col
G.S.O 2nd Div

30/9/14

2nd Division

I forward herewith a report on the German Trenches having RIFLE POINT as a RIFLE mound. These reports are the result of a Reconnaissance carried out by a patrol of the Rifle Brigade. The Brigadier General considers the report an excellent one and that the N.C.O. and men who carried it out have done Excellent work. When you have finished with it would you please forward

to the OC 47th Battery
as the sketch should assist
him in artillery co-operation.
I intend to ask him to fire
on — mound F and trench
C. I have an artillery officer
observing at RIFLE POINT

W D Bran Brig Gen
Comdg 17th Infy Bde

30 - 9 - 14.

Report on German Trenches
immediately in front of
8th Bn The Rifle Brigade
on RIFLE POINT & RIFLE MOUND

(vide rough sketch map attached)

1. **Trench A.**

    about 300" away from our position. About 150" long and protected by high wire entanglement close to the trench, and then low wire entanglement. A large deep strong trench. Flanked on W by mound F which scouts report holds 2 Machine Guns in a sort of redoubt. On E this trench A runs to the belt of trees B which runs along the edge of the hill.

2. **Belt of Trees B.**

    about 15–20 yards broad which runs along the side of the hill. Very thick undergrowth for about 150"–200" from own position ... after that it gets thinner and is almost clear opposite trench A.

3. Trench C.

A small trench being now under construction about 20ˣ long extends from bottom edge of belt and is connected by a communication trench to Trench D.

This trench C. holds a Machine Gun at the end where it touches the belt C. The parapet is still brown earth and unfinished except for 5 yards at E. End.

This trench apparently is only for occupation by night in opposition to our new trenches held by C. Coy.

4. Trench D ...

A well concealed trench running along a copse about 30ˣ from belt B. About 50ˣ long and protected by 2 bays of low wire entanglement. This trench

...eeps the small valley to its front.

Trench E. I have not been able to reconnoitre owing to excessive sniping.

For this information I am chiefly indebted to
    Sergt Hornby Scout Sergt
    Corpl Wheeler
    Rfn Lawler
    Rfn Appleton
who have shown much skill in reconnoitring along the belt B as far as trenches A & C, and who have brought back very good information and incidentally disposed of 4 Germans.

C Swan Lieut
3rd Bn The Rifle Brigade
29 - Sept 1914

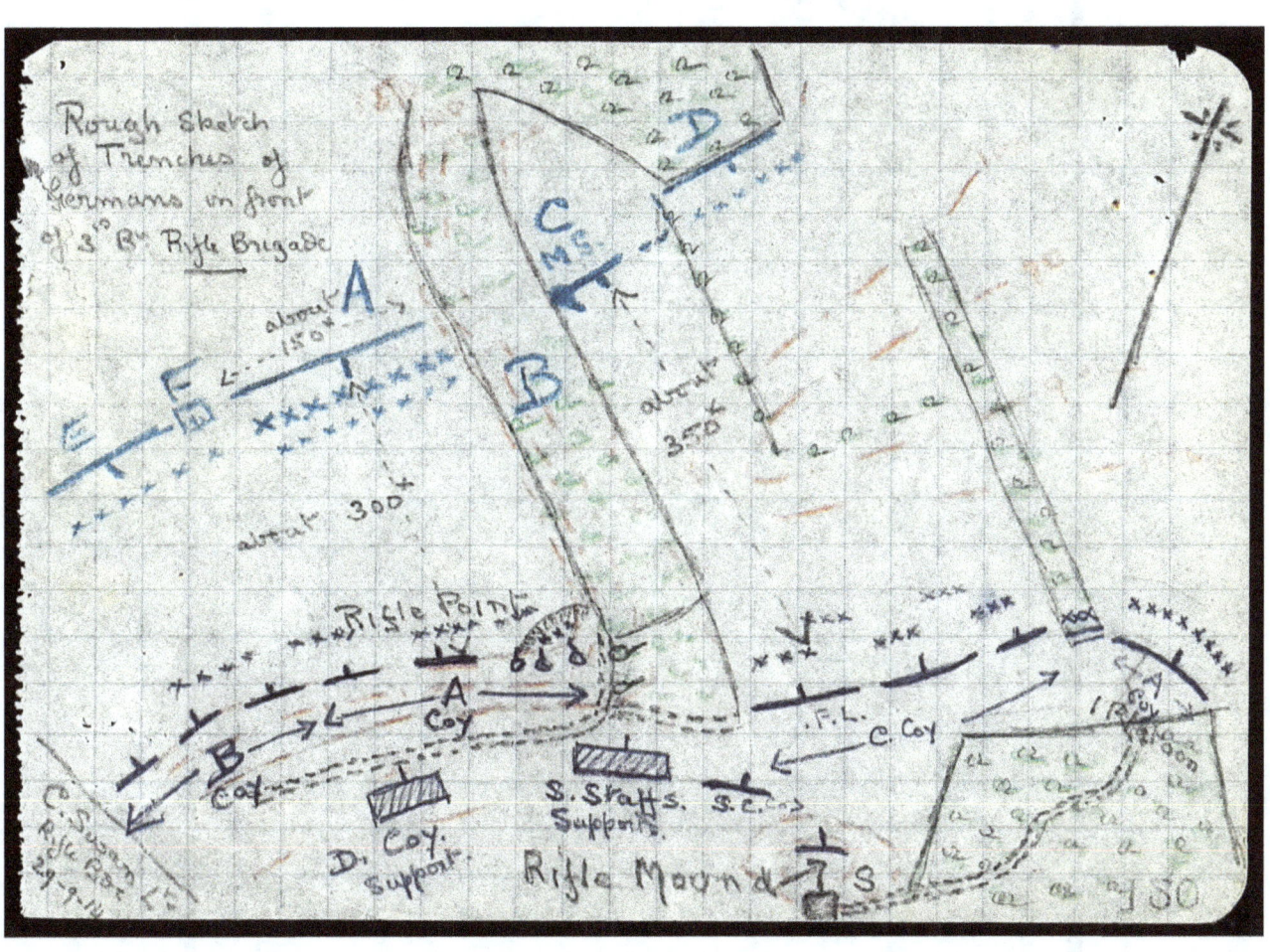

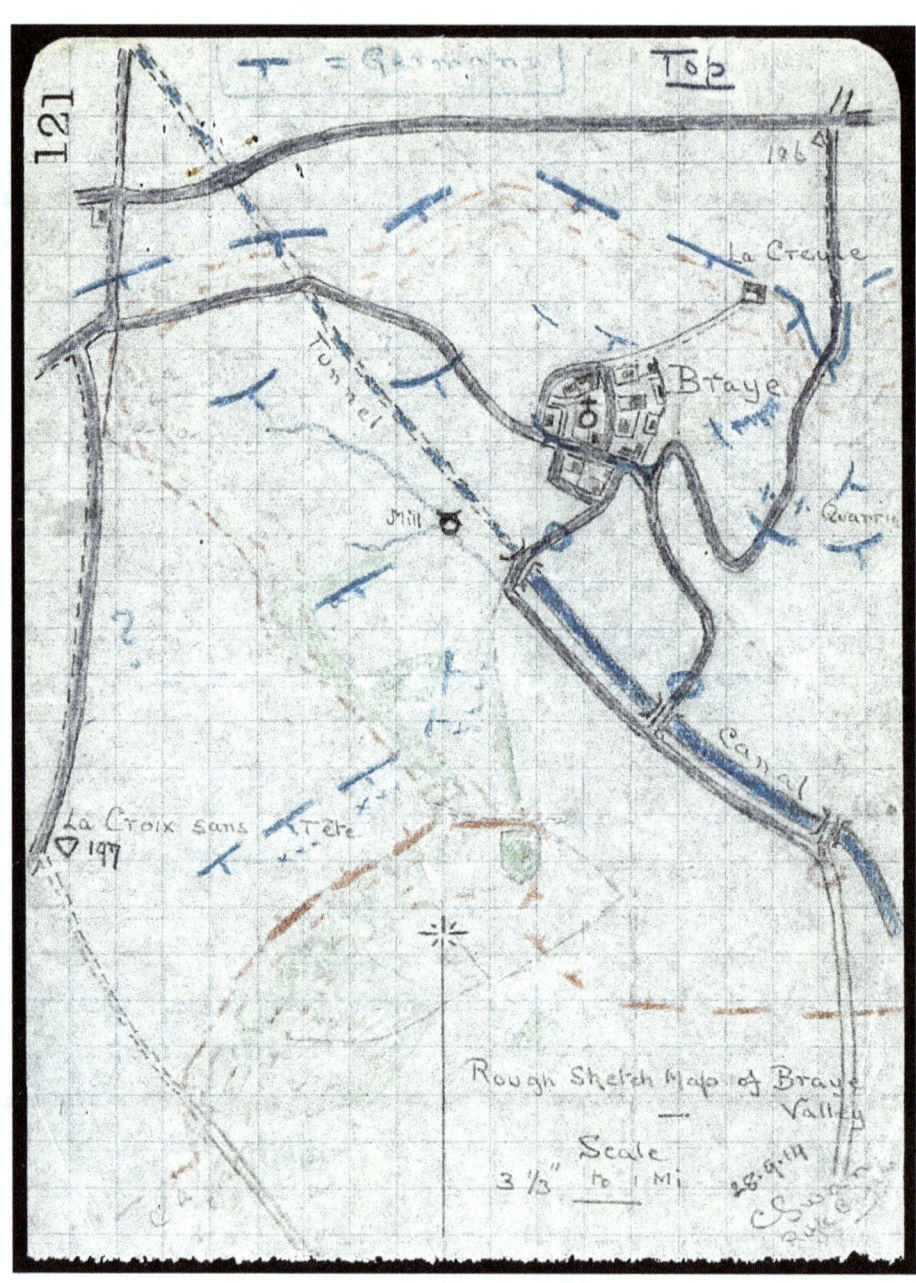

2nd Divisional Artillery.

2nd DIVISIONAL AMMUNITION COLUMN R.F.A.

OCTOBER 1914

Army Form C. 2118.

2n Australian Division

WAR DIARY
or
INTELLIGENCE SUMMARY.
(Erase heading not required.)

Hour, Date, Place	Summary of Events and Information	Remarks and references to Appendices
1 Oct 1914 ...	...	

WAR DIARY
or
INTELLIGENCE SUMMARY.
(Erase heading not required.)

Army Form C. 2118.

Hour, Date, Place	Summary of Events and Information	Remarks and references to Appendices
14 Oct. N. COURCELLES	(4) Orders given to move HdQrs. Bay to Stephen b/w 1st FISMES and N.3 Sec to FERE EN TARDENOIS & entrain for night. Showery all day with rain — the Empty Amm Park Lorries could not reach our camp owing to greasy roads. (4) HdQrs train left 6 am, N.1 9 am. M.2 12 noon & N.4 3pm N.3 1 am & travelled via OULCHY BRENY- FERTE LE — MILON — MAROEUIL SUR OURCQ — PARIS — CREIL — AMIENS ETAPLES — CALAIS & ST OMER.	
16 Oct. S' OMER	(4) arrived to an instant & entrained — Marched to billets at AROUES (M.O tey) & remainder to RENECURE still day	
17 Oct. RENESCURE	(4) kept letters relieving to work still day – no rain –	
18 Oct. HALLON CAPPEL	(4) marched 9 am. to HALLON CAPPE where worth between billettes. Major Cotton forced to commence R.T.a Col.	
19 Oct. do	(4) rain – do work proceed & replace Major COTTON Amperer avy	
20	(4) Marched via HAZEBROUCK and S'SYLVESTRE & EEKE Showery with all day.	

WAR DIARY
or
INTELLIGENCE SUMMARY.

(Erase heading not required.)

Army Form C. 2118.

Hour, Date, Place	Summary of Events and Information	Remarks and references to Appendices
21st OCT RENINGHELST	Bn marched at 11am to OUDEZEELE and BIESTHOEK was considered too bustling - Abnormal expenditure ammunition as per Remark 4C. Our chills any arrived to train arrived 1am too. Bn lent up to a Retain particular to not look showing all day.	18/- 27/30 ct /pt 162 m c
22	""	
23	Bn 7:30 am joined Brigade. Brigade expenditure ammunition as per Remark 4C. Rather fair day.	17/- 4 w m +5" 5:00 m 1/7 140.000 Bydecart 18/4 /w2nd extgn
24 VLAMERTINGE	Bn marched toward 11 am to VLAMERTINGE. Bn crossed with Recce Trench + Refuge. Showery series.	
25	Bn Batain to rest.	
26	Bn Trenchlips dug.	
27	Bn Trenches to nine. Rain serve in 8pm.	
28	Bn further to rest. Little rain day.	
	Bn still - rain day.	

WAR DIARY
or
INTELLIGENCE SUMMARY.
(Erase heading not required.)

Army Form C. 2118.

Hour, Date, Place	Summary of Events and Information	Remarks and references to Appendices
29 Oct VLAMERTINGE	(4) Holding to north Sharp four interval to men at 4pm. Rain had to him	
30. "	(4) Holding to report. her showing	
31. "	4pm REMEMBER (4) hrs heavy bombardment all over enquire on interior PoPPERINE & 9. Went 4pm to make way for Kips rev. of the main road. very cold night.	
	Ammunition expended near Oct.	
	18 pr Shrap. 31,191	
	" H.E. 1335	
	4.5" How Shrap 2643	
	" H.E. 3002	
	6 pr Shrap 5724	
	" H.E. 984	
	S.A.A. 1,874,150	
	Gun Am. 9631	
	Very Pistol Lights. 1750	

2nd Divisional Artillery.

2nd DIVISIONAL AMMUNITION CLUMN R.F.A.

NOVEMBER 1914.

Army Form C. 2118.

2nd Division Ammunition Column

WAR DIARY
or
INTELLIGENCE SUMMARY.
(Erase heading not required.)

Instructions regarding War Diaries and Intelligence Summaries are contained in F. S. Regs., Part II. and the Staff Manual respectively. Title pages will be prepared in manuscript.

Hour, Date, Place	Summary of Events and Information	Remarks and references to Appendices
1st Nov 1914 HQ REMINGHOLST POPERINGHE Rd	Remained in bivouac. Nothing to report. Cold but dry.	
2 "	Nothing to report. Received half bag man. Cold but sunny.	
3 "	" St Chiers joined from train — 30 Remounts joined	
4 "	Fine day	
5 "	2nd Syren joined W. & W. W. from Br. — Some from 6/R	
"	Nothing to note. Fine day — but cold	
6 "	Major E.W.M. Powell joined us W. & W. and proceeded to take command	
"	Major Seymour also joined & was promoted to Lieutenant Colonel	
"	2nd Lieut Argier joined	
"	Raw dull day	
7 "	Nothing to report. Still cloudy day	
8 "	2nd Lt Thurburn, Lieutenant & Sch. Pratt & Markham joined	
9 "	Dull cold day	
"	Nothing to note. Later saw heavy day	
10 "	Nothing to note. Demon louis met any face	
"	Aect was much attempt — Remainder	
11 "	Nothing to report. Sale flown all day — received from 5/—	

Army Form C. 2118.

WAR DIARY
or
INTELLIGENCE SUMMARY.
(Erase heading not required.)

Instructions regarding War Diaries and Intelligence Summaries are contained in F. S. Regs., Part II. and the Staff Manual respectively. Title pages will be prepared in manuscript.

Hour, Date, Place	Summary of Events and Information	Remarks and references to Appendices
12. Nov. RENING HELST.	(a) Battery to rest, preparation cut new dug.	
13. do	(a) Battery to rest — Reg int — fd all day.	
14. do	(a) Maj. Ewen Powis L.S.W transferred to 4th Bty. 2nd Lt. Denham to S.L. Hargreaves from L/c " Lt. Clivick " 3rd " " " " " Lt. Burden " 4th " " " " " Lt. Killogher " 44 " " " "	
15. Nov do	Reg duty days, (a) Battery to rest. Gales all day.	
16. do		
17. do	(a) Battery to rest — even but day. (b) Retain to rest — moving its day. 2nd Lt Compton Potter { buries from leave 2nd Lt O. Gann to At work	
18. do	(a) Retain Worth — Cold morning	

Army Form C. 2118

WAR DIARY
or
INTELLIGENCE SUMMARY.
(Erase heading not required.)

Instructions regarding War Diaries and Intelligence Summaries are contained in F. S. Regs., Part II. and the Staff Manual respectively. Title pages will be prepared in manuscript.

Hour, Date, Place	Summary of Events and Information	Remarks and references to Appendices
19 Nov Rouge Croix	By 2pm marched to Billets, which were warm. Road very bad - much enquired was to this. Hard of Division ordered that 9pm sharp every one off at 1.30 am while Division met us for the march at 2.0. Heavy firing from N.Y. all manoeuvre to suppl. 8. 5. M. R. Ex.	Bruno cut out from leg & kneels & parts to 4 & 5
20 " "	Nothing to note - hope there all day. Remained ready for distribution to trenches.	
21 " "	6. Batteries to note - hope hard all day.	
22 " "	6. Heavy firing from N.4 Avenue 4pm. Hard front all day.	
23 " "	6. Nothing to note. Very cold day - kept for miles.	
24 " "	Nothing to note. Trenches open. Waiting for higher water.	
25 " "	Nothing to note. Thawing all day - with 1/2 Major T.G. May C.M.S. joined from leave.	

Army Form C. 211

WAR DIARY
or
INTELLIGENCE SUMMARY.
(Erase heading not required.)

Instructions regarding War Diaries and Intelligence Summaries are contained in F.S. Regs., Part II. and the Staff Manual respectively. Title pages will be prepared in manuscript.

Hour, Date, Place	Summary of Events and Information	Remarks and references to Appendices
26 Nov ROUGE CROIX	Nothing to report. Misty day – thawing	Surg/Lt.N Fatherston Haugh (Temp'y Cmd) R.A.F. att'd 8. 9. 14. Lieut M.G. Carrie D.S.O. (Temp'y Cmd) DSO joined Oct 1914
27 Nov. Rouge Croix	Nothing to report. Took over 8 riding & 24 light draught Horses from Remount.	News 26.11.14
28 Nov ROUGE CROIX	Nothing to report. Still thawing	Major T.V. May C.M.S. posted to No 2 Am'n Park and left for route.
29th Nov ROUGE CROIX	Inspection by O.C. RA 2d Division who expressed himself pleased with the horses – very wet night Trucks established with No 6 Am'n Park.	
30 Nov. ROUGE CROIX	Day spent in refilling column with ammunition. Nothing special to note	L't G.E.H. Fatherston-Haugh joined 4th M Bde (attached) L't. M.G. Carrie joined 34 Bde (attached)

Marshall
Major 9th
Comd 2" DAC

Forms/C. 2118/10.

2nd Divisional Artillery

2nd DIVISIONAL AMMUNITION COLUMN R.F.A.

DECEMBER 1914.

Army Form C. 2118.

WAR DIARY
or
INTELLIGENCE SUMMARY.
(Erase heading not required.)

Instructions regarding War Diaries and Intelligence Summaries are contained in F. S. Regs., Part II. and the Staff Manual respectively. Title pages will be prepared in manuscript.

Hour, Date, Place	Summary of Events and Information	Remarks and references to Appendices
Dec 1st ROUGE CROIX	Nothing special to note – misty cold weather. Much correspondence all day	M.O. Lt Dunlop returned from leave to England.
Dec 2nd ROUGE CROIX	Nothing special to note – misty and cold. Still receive 15 PCM.E shell which were forwarded to B & A Cos. Shifted camp of H.Q. No. Sect. much correspondence.	Lt Cooke RAMC returned from leave to England.
Dec 3rd ROUGE CROIX	2nd BAC marched dismounted to METEREN on the occasion of the visit of his Majesty King George V. The route was lined between cross roads 1½ kils S.E. of METEREN and METEREN by the Artillery II nd Division. Weather raining hard and very muddy. at 9.30 AM	
Dec 4th ROUGE CROIX	Shifted camp of No 2 Section – weather brighter – high winds – nothing special to note.	

H Ernest
Major RFA
Comdg 2nd BAC

WAR DIARY
or
INTELLIGENCE SUMMARY.
(Erase heading not required.)

Army Form C. 2118.

Hour, Date, Place	Summary of Events and Information	Remarks and references to Appendices
5th. ROUGE CROIX	My hostein is now - hot all day	
6 -	" " Showery with strong wild wind	
7 -	" " Very hot ru day	
8 -	(K) dur Ers. ways received 31.8.14	
	tea completed suited 31.8.14	
	a Bulls NCE brews (see those)	
	Mice and strong	
9 -	(K) 30 strong suppler to breakfast house lies in	
	reserve (to from) transport to B. Ko	
	Strong. quite all day	
10 -	(K) Stone treyes cause to let us -	
	heir touch - steady rain all - 2 pm -	
11 -	Withinging (M.q sectin left 6.30 am 5 pm 3 SW MFRC	
	dust much rm	
12 -	(K) Lieut J. Lampson prices to duty from K.6 7th ml	
	No. In 6. took to air from to N. 4 F. Am	
	his day - the night	

WAR DIARY
or
INTELLIGENCE SUMMARY.
(Erase heading not required.)

Army Form C. 2118.

Hour, Date, Place	Summary of Events and Information	Remarks and references to Appendices
13th Xbr ROUSSEROIX	(4) Sgt. G. Matthews from Gun Halle Note [received in from Sgt]	
	B/A ammn	
	Coke unices key	
	(6) Been to mess & has notice received.	
14	Battery busy	
	Concertoning all day.	
15	(4) battery G note	
	Coke wet day	
16	(4) Capt Fitz. Simon. Snow. Kaufman. E. 34, 15 L. Am Col.	
	Caper M Farmer from 26 Bty R.S.a. L.G. Sider 2. Staff E	
	Lt. H.L. Long tendered to 41, 18, 19, R.S.a.	
17	(4) Battery G note	
	Lui Key Miller	
	(6) Gen. Percival in future known	
18	Cold and showery	
	(4) battery G note — long day.	
19	(4) Nothing to note	
20	Threatened rain	

WAR DIARY
or
INTELLIGENCE SUMMARY.

(Erase heading not required.)

Army Form C. 2118

Hour, Date, Place	Summary of Events and Information	Remarks and references to Appendices
21 Mar. ROUGE CROIX	(h) Relieving to note. Come through all day.	
22 —	(h) Hor: patrols N.Y. & left Hill 44 W.P., 4 OR, Hill 83's. br BETHUNE at 7 a.m. Heavy patrols N.Y. station shelled at 1 pm under St Yvon Res: crew over day.	
23 —	(h) Holding to note — still cold day.	
24 —	(h) Holding to note — cleared up little in the eng.	
25 —	(h) Holding to note. Frip rain all day.	
26 BOHEME	(h) Marched 7.30 a.m. via STRAZEELE - NEX BERQUIN and MERVILLE and took over from Indian (Meerut) Divn. Front white fuis ready — Relieved 9/11/12 & Reserve for 4/pm.	
27 —	(h) Holding to note. Etr. c.f. WRIGLEY/Dease from home area Tot. Frip Rain —	
28 —	(h) Holding to note. Very cut all day.	
29 —	(h) Holding to note. Violent Thunder Storm & gale during night — much rain — place inundated.	
30 —	(h) Holding to note. Frip rain — rain with afternoon	
31 — ROBECQ	(h) Marched 7.30 to ROBECQ — still raining heavily Le Sart rain.	J. Macintosh Ltt Col Comdg

WAR DIARY or INTELLIGENCE SUMMARY

Statistics of Ammunition Expenditure 19.8.14 to 19.11.14 ('90 days war')

Army Form C. 2118.

2nd Division. Ammunition Column.

Nature	Hour, Date, Place	Heaviest Expenditure	Date	Summary of Events and Information Continuous Expenditure	Date	Remarks and references to Appendices Average Expenditure in Action Days (or rpg)
18 pr Shrapnel	68,403	4068 3540 3424	30.10 31.10 11.11	2708, 1707, 2009, 4068 3508, 1672, 2432, 3540 1844, 2936, 2644, 1824 3424, 1160, 1344, 2144	21-24 Oct 28 Oct – 1 Nov 11-14 Nov	760
4.5" How Shrapnel (insufficient data)	12,090	882 682 736	20.9 1.11 26.9	534, 600, 145, 224, 882, 738 236, 200, 280, 504, 736, 432	16.4 29 Sept	124 6
ditto H.E.	10,975	514 446	29.10 5.11	Supply never up to demand – any figures would be misleading	aug	121 6
60 pr Shrapnel	1856	153 132	2.11 24.10	Daily issues always above the average – but seldom for any continuous period		20.5 5
ditto HE	2410	145 120 192	5.10 4.11 27.9			26 7
S.A.A.	4,448,765	350,m 224,m 251,m 216,m	4.9 25.10 31.10 1.11	100,m, 244,m, 132,m, 20,m 84,m 148,m, 224,m, 96,m, 10,m 146,50, 158,m, 157,m 182,m	20-23 Oct Sept 24 Oct 16 3 Nov	49,432 4

(Machine Guns are not allowed for in the average. They have been used throughout most of the amount shown)

Au 1914. Manchester 8th
cont. 2 stat.

A.A.G. Police

Herewith [illegible] Dec 14.

The accompanying figures of Ammunition Expenditure are submitted for information.

Any other statistics required will be supplied if possible.

Several points concerning the organization and working of a D.A.C. recommended for future guidance are held over until the end of the Campaign.

The nature and condition of roads, congestion of traffic &c. have necessitated a change in the system laid down for Rendezvous and Refilling Points — these I presume will be considered hereafter.

J. Mansell
Lt Col
Comdg 2 DAC

31/12/14

Index..........

SUBJECT.

Major Desmond G. Froulton's experiences in the early fighting of 1914.

No.	Contents.	Date.
	With 2ⁿᵈ Divnl. Ammn. Colm. August 1914	

Major Desmond G. Trouton's experiences in the early fighting of 1914.

(2nd Lieut. D.G. Trouton went out with No. 3 Section of the 2nd Divisional Amm'n Col. - Lt.-Col. F.T. Ravenhill).

I had very fortunately, as it turned out, joined the Special Reserve of the Royal Field Artillery a few weeks before war was declared in the beginning of August 1914.

I was first of all ordered to Woolwich and three days' later transferred to Aldershot where I took up the duties of an officer in charge of the Details left behind.

I was attached to a section of the Divisional Ammunition Column to assist them in the work of mobilisation.

Now an Ammunition Column is non existant prior to the mobilisation order and consequently the work attached to process of turning it out ready for the field is immensely greater than that in any other unit. The C.O. of this unit utilized me to carry on with the routine work leaving the others free for mobilisation work.

During that time we were all inoculated against Typhoid which was administered in a single dose as time was too short for the usual procedure. I was very bad the next day as the heat at that time was very severe for England and as we were all working against time and could not be spared my first experience of soldiering was in a rough school.

On Saturday morning I was sent for by the Adjutant who told me that I might be needed for one of the other sections as they were short of an officer and to get my things in readiness. I sallied out into the town and bought all the service kit available and wired home to town for the rest.

That evening I got the expected orders and after saying good-bye I drove over to Melbrech in a taxi where I spent the night and next morning Dorothy Donald left me at Borden.

I then met Capt. Dresser my new C.O., who told me

Quiller-Couch was the other Sub., so I felt I had at last dropped among friends. I heard at the same time that there was no time to be lost, in fact we sailed on the following Monday night.

I spent the morning making the acquaintance of the N.C.O's, procuring a batman, Gnr. Scott, and a charger, a little black mare.

That was one of the luckiest mornings' I ever had as both Scott and the mare became devoted friends later on; were absolutely paragons.

Time flew as there was so much to do and we were parading for our final march out into the unknown future before one could realize that the hour had come. There is only one incident worth mentioning and that was in mess on Sunday night, when we all drank the Gunner toast of "Fat targets and straight shooting" to the batteries of the 41st Brigade which marched out that night. This was the brigade that blew back the Prussian Guards from the muzzles of their guns on the memorable 11th November when our line was broken for a short time in the first battle of Ypres. If ever a wish came true that toast did.

Monday 17th.

Tuesday 18th.

Wed. 19th.

Of our march to the station and the trouble we had with the untrained horses I will say nothing, we got there and were very thankful. We also got on to the ship without serious trouble and very soon found ourselves sailing out into the channel. We reached Havre at daybreak next morning having crossed between continuous lines of destroyers who kept a broad belt across the channel free from any enemy vessel. When I came on deck I found that we were racing another transport for first place in the river. We ran side by side past the ever narrowing banks till you could nearly have jumped from one boat to another. The men on both ships were in the greatest spirits and we joined together in singing every popular song of the moment "Tipperary" included. We retired to breakfast after we had won the race and were very disappointed to

find the whole river covered in mist when we came on deck
again as we had been filled up with stories of the beauty
of the river by the genial skipper.

Later on it cleared a bit and we had our first taste
of French hospitality from the villagers who lined the banks
cheering and singing our National Anthem, when we tried to
sing the Marseillaise in return it was rather a failure at first.
Soon after lunch we got to Rouen and started to disembark as
soon as we were wharfed. It was rather slow as there were not
the same facilities for disembarking as in England.

We got away finally and spent the night in the huge
rest camp that had sprung up on the outskirts of the town.
Next day we met the other sections and the Colonel made a
speech to all the officers of the combined column.

Thursday 20th.

We all left next evening and found entraining wagons
on the French trucks very different from the end loading in
England. However the men worked like heroes and at last we
were all on and started on our journey towards the Germans and
Berlin as we then thought.

Friday 21st.

We had all night and next day in the train and finally
reached our detraining station Landrecies about 3 p.m., next
afternoon.

We got out pretty quickly and had orders to spend
the night there and move up after the army next day.

Saturday 22nd.

I was sent on ahead next day to find the rest of
the column and get orders. I found   deserted so had
to push on to Maubeuge where I found that 2nd Div. H.Q'rs
were just moving on to a place 10 miles north on the Mons road.
As I had already done about 16 miles I tried to get a wire
through for orders. While waiting I watered and fed the mare
and had lunch myself in the adjoining hotel. After lunch I
found most of the headquarters gone and not much hope of getting
an answer and until one of the clerks remembered an old message
relating to the D.A.C., I was in rather a quandary. He soon

found it in the waste paper basket and luckily it gave the position for the D.A.C. for that night.

As I had now got what I wanted I started back and found the Section about 6 miles short of Maubeuge. They were all talking about a "Zep" they had just seen brought down away to the south and I saw smoke rising from where it had fallen.

We were not far from the place mentioned and by striking northwards through bye-roads were soon there and in bivouac for the night.

I had been very interested during the day by the preparations the French were making for the defence of Maubeuge, chiefly barbed wire. Subsequent events showed that deep trenches and dug-outs would have been more to the purpose.

There was a lot of work being done all over the country by civilian labour gangs in putting up barbed wire and levelling trees to improve fields of fire and for making barricades.

As it happened all the work was wasted as we retired rapidly across this ground and helf the line through Landrecies.

Sunday 23rd.

Early next morning the rest of the Column came in from the north and we joined them in an orchard near our bivouacs where we all stood in readiness to move at a moment's notice.

Here we heard of the fight of the previous day and saw our first of the effect of shell fire; a gun hit in the fight being sent back to us on its way to the base. The only two survivors of the detachment filled us with stories of the fight but always kept coming back to poor Bill the layer and showed again and again the hole in the seat made by the case which had first passed through Bill. They seemed a bit dazed by it all and certainly that gun with the still fresh/blood marks of brought it home to us all for the first time.

Tuesday 25th Aug.

At about 9 a.m., we got the expected orders and moved to a place just north of Leval where we had lunch. Here we first came across the difficulties of watering 800 horses at one spot, one of the chief items of our daily life and thought for the future. Quiller-Couch was a master hand at this and we came off best that time but on other occasions we were not always so lucky. I was in charge of the Mess and after lunch I procured a hen from an old lady near by who also gave us some most excellent .

In the afternoon we were off again and moved through Leval to another field just south of Landrecies, where we got ready to spend the night.

Many of us got a wash in a stream near by and jolly glad we were after two such hot days and our first night in the open.

But the fates were not done with us yet and we were turned out again at about 6 to move to Le Grand Fayt about 4 miles due east.

When approaching this place we had our first excitement. A few shots were heard in rear and word was passed up for the gunners to fall back as a rear guard. No sooner had these gone, under Quiller, than a couple of shots passed over the wagon I was riding behind. I got hold of three men and got out on that flank on the only hedge coming near the road. On of my men said he saw a man at the hedge but at that moment a line of infantry came out from the village and advancing in open order covered our flank from any more trouble. By this time it was nearly dark and I found to my horror that the section with my horse were going on at the trot so I and the men had to sprint for the last wagon on which we jumped exhausted. I there learned a lesson I never forgot. Never dismount when you are with mounted troops without keeping your horse and a horseholder with you. And many a time has that saved me a two or three mile run.

We came into a field in the centre of the village passing through the cordon of infantry which was drawn round it. There was considerable confusion already and our hasty entry did not lessen it, one man evidently thought us to be

Uhlans as he stuck his bayonet through the leg of one of
Quiller's drivers. Soon the rear guard arrived very breathless
but triumphant and as most of them knew nothing about a rifle
being reservists they began investigating. We had to make
them unload as one shot went too near Quiller's head to be
comfortable. Things quickly quieted down then except for a
heavy battery in the next field which kept banging away into
the dark. A cold drizzle started then and we spent a
miserable night getting what shelter we could from the wagons
and warmth by crowding together.

Wed.
26th Aug.
We moved off at daybreak and struck the Landrecies Etreux road
about 5 miles south of Landrecies turning south then to Etreux
where we arrived about noon. The early part of this march
was exciting as we had our decks cleared for action metaphor-
ically speaking. I gathered that some Uhlans had been located
to the south of us, in fact one was pointed out to me about
a mile distant by a machine gun officer who was acting as a
flank guard to the column. But nothing came of it all and
we reached Etreux safely in bright sunlight which dried us
after the wet night.

We lunched here and spent a lazy afternoon getting
some sleep. Our bivouac was on the high ground to the South
of the town and in the evening we watched some heavy guns
coming into action on the ridge to the north of the town.
We heard about the fight of the Guards at Landrecies the night
before and all were wondering what the meaning of this
retiring was when on every occasion the men concerned said
that they beat the Germans. Rumours of all kinds flew about
with lightning speed; one of the most persistent ones was
that the Germans had pushed in between us and the 2nd Corps
at Le Cateau about 15 miles west of us. This one was so persistent that the Veterinary officer rode off in that direction
going out 4 or 5 miles but came back saying that there was
nothing there.

Thurs.
27th Aug.

We were off again at dawn the next morning and by eleven we were bivouaced again on the side of the road. Water was a difficulty here a marsh being the only available source. I remember it was down at the bottom of a six foot bank and our horse nearly mad with thirst from the dust on the roads came slithering down the bank and floundered into the mud. We had an awful job getting him out and in the end got about 40 men on to a rope and pulled him up by main force. Here again we had a slack afternoon but at about 5 we were just finishing a second water when we had to stand to and get orders to move soon after. Our section was to be left behind as the 41st Bde. Ammn. Col. was temporarily lost and the brigade were coming into action about ½ mile back along the road and wanted a reserve.

28th Aug

We moved to a sheltered spot more directly behind them and spent the night ready to stand to at a minute's notice. We were off before dawn and soon rejoined the rest of the Column as they were moving off from where they had spent the night.

We passed La Fere next day and the next break we had in the monotony of the march, of getting off at daylight with a stop at mid-day and then on again till dark, occurred at Villers-Cotterets. We came into the woods soon after passing La Fere and making our way south we finally approached Villers-Cotterets from the east coming into the wonderful cathedral of trees which seems to be art right into the centre of the Forest just as the rising sun shone down the centre, lighting up the trees with a soft pink effect. To me it seemed so strange to pass through this beautiful country just a day ahead of the Germans and all that their coming must mean. This leads me to speak of the refugees which I have left out so far, to make the thread of the narrative clearer.

From the moment we started the backward move the natives came with us. Even when passing through Leval, a few hours after we had started on our long retreat; we noticed an enormous difference to the appearance of the day before. Many houses were closed and shuttered and carts, prams and every other available vehicle were being hastily loaded with valuables. We left them and passed on but everywhere we came we saw the same thing, the streets being lined with people asking why. Why should England retire, what is the meaning, and next, what are we to do ? But one of the things that all of us noticed was the wonderful welcome we got everywhere and the simple faith these poor people had in the power of the British to protect them. Later on when I/was in France nearly two years later, I was sorry to see this had largely disappeared and very often the British troops were treated as an unavoidable nuisance. But to get back to the early days, everybody who could gave us something if only a drink of water which I am not sure was not the most acceptable gift of all as the weather was nearly tropical and the dust on the roads dried up the throat till one could hardly swallow. Nothing was too good for the men. Bread, eggs, wine, cider, fruit of all sorts, cigarettes, matches, milk and finally the cool water from the depths of some shady well were among the most frequent presents. I have seen a man well on in years rush into a tobacconists and come out with his hands full of cigarettes soon distributed among the passing men who laughed and thanked and said "Vive la France" and all were happy. And yet all the time these people were getting ready to fly, this greeting was nearly their last act before leaving, as many towns were deserted when the Batteries half a day after us passed through.

Another form of generosity that I think shows the spirit of France as much as anything was the way these small farmers when leaving their homes with what valuables and stock they could take with them, would willingly give chickens and anything they could to us and would often take no money saying "it is better you should have it than the Bosche".

How they hated the Bosche! To us it seemed rather ludicrous their earnestness. The old men as we passed would draw their hand across their throat and then make a stabbing movement, calling out some curse on the hated Hun.

The whole matter of the refugees was often comic in spite of the intense tragedy of it all. To see a huge farm cart drawn by a huge ~~a huge~~ Flemish stallion a milch cow and a dog no matter under what circumstances makes you smile and yet perhaps there were two or three families on top with the old grandmothers and hoards of children, the younger women leading the whole along, tramping sturdily beside, sometimes taking their turn for a lift. Many curious collections used to be piled on top of the carts, the Family bed was one of the favourite things in spite of its bulk.

Then on the other hand there were those who had no vehicle at all, these used to generally collect into bands of about 100 and trudge along the road together. It was pathetic to see the children dragging themselves along, but they were all very ~~thankful~~ thoughtful for the weak ones, and our men used also to take the children from the arms of the tired mother or elder sister and put them on to the wagons and often the mother too, although this meant that they themselves had to walk as we could not load up the horses any more than necessary. This was no slight thing as it meant a walk of thirty miles for the man himself.

But the saddest part of all was when the number of refugees on the road threatened to block the army and they had to be turned on to side roads. I was detailed to do this one afternoon of the later days and hated every minute of it. I had to turn the stream off the main road on to a side road which lead on to another parrallel road to us but made a good big round and I found the best way was to tell them this way was shorter, some used to plead tearfully and some with anger but I had a guard and they had to go; many saw how tired I was and just went on without any arguing.

Two girls I remember argued for over half an hour, they tried every means in their power to try and get past, so in the end I handed themm over to the Corporal who could not speak French but cleared them down the other road amid roars of laughter. These girls were typical of a large group who took it all as a great joke and were much less trouble to deal with than those who burst into floods of tears and asked you if the germans were close behind, what they had better do, and innumerable other questions which you could not answer. But on the whole they did what they were told without a murmur. I wonder would English refugees be as amenable and what would have happened if they had not obeyed as the guard had loaded rifles and I had orders to let no one pass on any account. I suppose a shot over their heads would have brought them to their senses.

While I am talking on this subject I must mention one woman who stood looking down the road along which we were coming with such a look of unutterable sadness that at the time I longed to be able to put that look on canvas as it seemed to me to contain all that the womanhood of France was passing through with their men in the unknown and their houses about to be destroyed. She xxxx stood unmoving looking into the far distance and her face seemed to me to contain all the sadness of the motherhood and wifehood of France in that one strained look.

But to get back to my story we reached Villers-Cotterets early in the morning and had great difficulty in getting water for the horses but in the end got the fire hydrant in a wood factory going and kept some tubs filled where we could water the horses satisfactorily. Towards evening we got orders that half the wagons were to be emptied at the station and sent back to carry the packs of the Infantry. Quiller-Couch was sent with the wagons of all the four sections and we did not see him for 5 days during which time he was roaming round on his own and had many interesting experiences.

The rest of the retreat was uneventful except for

the minor details of the march such as horses casting shoes or galling, and occasionally we had to shoot one thatwas too done to come any further with us.

Before I start on the term back across the Marne and the subsequent advance to the Aisne I will tell a little of our method of living.

We lived very differently from a mess as known in the subsequent stages of the war. We were travelling light, in fact we were down to our 35 pounds. A valise, a sleeping bag, a change of clothes and linen, our washing things and a burberry was roughly our kit. Our mess kit was very simple, a knife, fork and spoon, a mug and two plates each and plates for the food. We nearly always had stew when we had hot food and had plenty of vegetables as we just helped ourselves in passing. We bought bread, butter, eggs and chickens which we had when we had time to cook them. We generally only had one hot meal a day at about 4 p.m., and used to eat chocolate in the early morning when starting, have some cold bacon and bread or bully and bread at breakfast time and then a hot meal in the evening when we got in, and we used to sleep when we were doing nothing else.

Getting into camp became a matter of a few minutes and moving out quicker. We have all been asleep in an hour and half after turning into the field having watered and fed the horses, cooked our daily meal and washed. And later on we used to allow three quarters of an hour after reveille before marching out, all the harnessing and hooking in being done in the dark. In fact during those days we developed from a collection of novices into a fairly efficient body although we never got the smartness and discipline of regulars.

Sept 6th

Quiller-Couch rejoined us just before the turn came. That turn it sounds a little thing to march back along the road you came the day before but I can't say what it meant to us. We heard nothing only on marching out of the field we turned to the right instead of the left as we had expected and found ourselves going towards the germans. It took some time before the significance sunk in and then the joy; all were laughing, they could not help themselves and all tiredness was forgotten, we seemed to have become a new lot, everything was done with a will and nothing was too much.

Up to this time we as an Ammunition Column had not been used as we were such a huge and unwieldy thing on the road that we were bundled on out of the way as fast as possible so as not to block the road for others. We officers used often to talk about this and Captain Dresser said that if he never saw any more fighting than this he was going to pretend he was not out, and we were quite of the same opinion. We need not have worried as we all got our turn later but somehow those first men did the most wonderful thing of all. A rear guard action of 200 miles in ten days without ever losing touch with the enemy, always turning on him and hurling him back in confusion, seems to me the most wonderful feat of all times when we remember the difference in numbers.

At the time I heard it estimated that the germans had 100,000 casualties during the fighting to the Aisne and our total number was not more than that. We I believe lost 23,000.

Sept 9th

The first couple of days forward were very similar to the earlier days and I myself did not see any fighting till after the Marne was crossed when I was sent on with ammunition to replenish them after the battle. I got up with the army in the evening and got my wagons well caught in the block of traffic at the top of the long hill on the north side of the river. I rode on ahead to find the Bde. Ammn. Col. for which I was bound and met some gunner officers I knew. One of them told me a lot about the fight. How his battery had had to leave the guns owing to the amount of german shell coming over, and how Major, Sergeant Major and he had gone back later and got one gun into action at the retreating germans. What pleased him most was that he had pulled the trigger and wiped out so many himself. I only saw solid masses of Germans retreating over the hills in the distance accompanied by white puffs of shrapnel. I then went back to my wagons having heard my destination and after a long time got them up to the field where the whole brigade was bivouaced with the best part of the rest of the 2nd Division. It was dark when I got there and spent the night with the Ammn. Col. who gave us a share of their meal.

Sept 10th

Next day I had to wait behind to refil from the lorries and got orders from the Colonel where to rejoin as he passed on with the rest of the Column. I had to wait some time and when I finally got off it was afternoon. However I got along and got on to the road leading to this place. The whole road for miles forward and backwards was packed and I found that I was in the middle of the 5th Division. However I was on the right road and they were bound for the same place so I left my wagons in the line and pushed on ahead which turned out to be very lucky as when I got to the village I not only found no signs of the 2nd Div, Ammn. Column but heard that the 2nd Divn. was about 15 miles to the east. I also learned that this village was our outpost line; certainly no place for General Service Wagons. So I hurried back and was able to turn them off into a field about 2 miles back along the road. It was pitch dark by this time and the last wagon was badly driven in at the gate and got one wheel into a deep ditch. Do what we liked we could not get it out and had to unload it and reload after we had got it clear. By this time rain had come on and it was ~~bitterly~~ bitterly cold; we had no food as we had expected to be back with

the rest by then. So I gave the order for half the
emergency rations to be used and we had some hay ready
cut in the field for the horses. Soon we had all fed
and turned in for a few hours rest. We started off at
1 a.m., next morning so as to get clear of the 5th Division
before it started, and as soon as we were clear made our way
along a main road running due east. We stopped for breakfast in a village after we had done about 12 miles, and
there I had rather an amusing experience.

I was hunting round the village for bread when a
very excited native came up and told us of a german with
a gun, whose presence had got them into a state of
panic. We drew our revolvers and set out to capture him
with four men, expecting a desperate villain. Our guide
led us to a large house with a red cross flag and then
pointed us on ahead. We entered the courtyard with
caution, found it empty, the guide then followed us and
pointed to a french window "in there, in there" he kept
repeating. We quickly entered the room ready for anything
and found ourselves in a sick ward with about a dozen
cases, nothing else, so we hauled in the man and he pointed
to one of the cases. This man turned out to be a german
who had gone to bed. He had tied a huge bandage round a
cut in his arm and pretended to be badly wounded. I
think he had hit on this plan as the safest way to surrender,
anyway he had given this old man and his wife an awful
fright, the night before, when he had arrived and demanded
admittance. We soon had him out of bed and made him dress.
One of the men found his rifle under his matress so we
brought him along with us. I got the badge of his helmet
as a souvenir of such an amusing incident.

After breakfast we pushed on and found the rest
still in camp though about to start in an hour's time.
It turned out that they had had their marching orders
changed after they had left us and had left an orderly

to redirect us but he had got tired of waiting and had come on without us; hence our little pilgrimage.

The remainder of the advance to the Aisne was without special incident, and two days later we found ourselves on the plateau between Braisne and Bourg, where we were destined to remain for many a long day.

Up to this time we had never spent more than one night in any place so that here we entered into quite a different phase in the fighting. The first night we spent at the top of the long hill above Braisne, having got into our bivouac after dark. Early next morning we were up and moved along the road towards Bourg but only for a short distance, where we waited in a field beside the road. Here we saw shrapnel at close hand for the first time. A couple of batteries were in action about 500 to 800 yards north of us and the germans were trying to get on to them. They put most of the "stuff" over, some rounds coming fairly close to us, so we were moved along the road to a safer spot. We spent most of the day there without any incident. Quiller and I went across the road and over the fields till we could see down into the valley of the Aisne and there I saw a battle field for the first time. My first impression was acute disappointment. I had expected to see something exciting going on, instead everything seemed normal, but presently one began to pick out little things that a trained eye would have seen at once. Little puffs of white smoke which quickly dissolved in the breeze, gradually obtruded themselves on your notice and by using field glasses you could catch glimpses of the moving troops. Some wagons in the bottom of the valley carefully drawn up behind a line of trees, occasionally a little line of men would appear for a moment, advance and disappear again as suddenly as it appeared, but the whole impression was of a deserted countryside, except for the noise which had first drawn us there in expectation. This noise is a sound that once heard is never forgotten. The boom of the guns and the occasional shriek of a shell are the sounds that first obtrude themselves to the ear, but presently the continuous rumble or rather crackle of musketry seems to dominate all. This is one of the most fascinating sounds imaginable, in the distance it is like the sound of a bright log fire on a frosty night; suddenly quickening up and then dying away again to burst out once more in waves of sound. I have often lain awake during a night attack in the distance, listening to it gradually growing up then dying away, only to flare up more loudly, ever increasing in volume till the guns begin to speak, first one and then more and more as the fight thickens till the maximum intensity is reached with a roar of sound as the machine guns rattle out their stream of lead, and then suddenly silence; another attack has failed. One shot followed by two or three, then a little burst of fire and all is over for that time, quiet again reigns and back to the land of "nod".

However we could not stop watching for long and had to get back to the section where we then lunched but were unable to water the horses. Suddenly we had the stand to, and at the same moment a broken line of infantry straggled back over the spot we had been watching the fight from. We began moving out and back along the road with orders to put out a flank guard on our right. There was no need to bustle the tired men, the stories of the infantry who had joined us was sufficient, they jumped and we were quickly back in our former position. I remember a machine gun belonging to them was put into action on the rear wagon as the gun detachment expected the germans over the ridge at any moment. It was the first real panic I had ever seen; this company had got caught by a large number of machine guns and had been very badly cut up and these men had come the whole way back thinking they were followed by the germans. They had lost all their officers and N.C.O's, whether knocked out or left behind I never heard, but the men were quickly collected and went back again under a P.M., who turned up. I always felt sorry for those fellows, they were done to the world with the last few weeks hard work and undoubtedly had been very roughly handled; very few could not show a hole in their clothing and a lot had minor cuts on some part of their bodies. They got very little sympathy and got a pretty good dressing down, but at that time local panics like that might have serious results and were very quickly sat on. It was the only case I have ever come across and was of course due to there being nobody to take charge. I felt sicker than ever at being in an Ammunition Column after that, where like a hare you have to run at the first sign of danger, as it would be impossible to do anything with a line of wagons over a mile long with about eighty untrained riflemen to defend it.

So when we had been there for about a week you can imagine our joy when we heard that all the subalterns were going to be sent up to the Brigade Ammunition Columns to replace the officers there who had been drafted into the batteries to fill up casualties. So that my time with the Divisional Ammunition Columns practically coincided with the moving fighting and I spent the best part of this first spell of trench fighting in the Brigade Amm'n Column.

I think I better break the narrative at this time to explain the composition of the Artillery and Ammunition supply of a division. In a division, this does not hold now as things have been altered to fit new conditions, there were four brigades of artillery each containing three 6 gun batteries. Three brigades consisted of 18 pdr Field guns and the fourth of 4.5" Howitzers. In addition there was one battery of Heavys, composed of four 60 pdr guns. In each battery there were two limbered ammunition wagons for each gun as well as the ammunition carried in the gun limbers. Thus each brigade had an ammunition column of its own which had one limbered ammunition wagon for each gun of the brigade, making 18 wagons. It also had 7 small-arm carts and two G.S. wagons (General Service) for supplying the infantry. Each infantry brigade is attached to an artillery brigade for ammunition supply and are worked together as much as possible for this reason. Thus we have the four Brigade ammunition columns who in turn are supplied by the Divisional column which is composed of four sections, three carrying 18 pdr ammunition and small-arm, while the fourth supplies the howitzers and heavies. Each section contains 28 G.S. wagons which are drawn by six horse teams, so that the whole column is much bigger than an entire brigade of artillery including its own column. The Divisional Column is supplied by motor lorries from the Ammunition Park at rail head.

Well I had now joined the 41st Brigade and was in part of a combatant unit and although we did no fighting it was no rare thing for us to get under fire. I joined the unit when it was camped just beside the canal on the east side of Bourg. By this time we had given up trying to push the Germans any further and were ourselves again on the defensive and I remember on my first afternoon watching the 'Jack Johnsons' bursting round a french battery on a spur to the north-east of us. We had never imagined anything so big then and watched the sight of cottages going skywards with a kind of incredulous fascination. I must now describe

the unit I had joined. Capt. Thornton was O.C.; he was
an ideal soldier to work under for a beginner like me.
He demanded the best of everybody and got it, saying very
little the whole time. He did most things by fixed rules
which everyone knew and there was never any doubt about
what to do in consequence. I dont think he was very
pleased when he first got me, he had just lost two regular
subalterns, and I was a very poor substitute with all my
inexperience. However I soon settled down and he left me
most of the routine work when once he had explained all
his methods. He was one of the finest of horse masters
and never left anything undone that might help the beasts,
with the result that he had the finest lot of horses in
the division as certified by both the C.R.A., and the
A.D.V.S., when they came round on their inspections.
There was a great difference in the discipline of the
whole unit to that in the one I had left. For all the
N.C.O's were regulars and also nearly half the men, the rest
being old soldiers of the reserve, and this had given
them much more chance of settling down to a proper state
of things that we had had when our Sergeant Major had
been a reserve corporal and the rest had been picked from
the ranks.

When I joined the unit I found that a neighbouring
straw stack had been raided and all the horses were standing in a foot of bedding thus getting very much better
rest at night. Even then after that short rest all but
a few looked in the pink of condition and this was explained
to me by the superior march discipline Thornton had organ-
ized. He had it as a standing rule that at every stop all
the horses were to be watered without any orders if there was
water within 100 yards, and consequently the horses got
many drinks during the day and could be given plenty of
time for feeding during the mid-day halt, when most people

had to start by watering and then had to move on before the horses were half finished with their oats. He was also extremely particular about the grooming which was as thorough as in barracks, and he used to spend an hour himself every morning vetting all the sick horses and looking out for any thin ones who needed extra food or rest.

The 41st Brigade was in reserve if its position can be called reserve, as the guns were in action and constantly used, but they were on the hills to the south of the Aisne while the rest of the Divisional Artillery was on the northern bank of the river. Now all the Brigade ammunition columns were collected in the flat stretch of land on the south of the canal so that we had to go back to supply the batteries. It seemed a silly state of affairs but it enabled us to give the horses a little draught exercise thus keeping them used to the work. The first trouble we had came very soon; one day while going along the road to Pont D'Arcy on the way to the batteries, a sudden screech and bang; a shell burst right above the head of the column scattering its bullets well over. I was behind but soon had them trotting out round the corner into the woods and safety, but they got in a second round at us just before the rear was away, one shell bursting on each side of us. One of the horses shied and the driver who was equally frightened left go, so I and the sergeant stopped to catch it for him to have the pleasure of another salvo on each side of us. But we all got away without a scratch and for ever after avoided that corner which later on became locally known as "dead man's "corner". That road then being shut we had to find other ways. For the next few days we came up and down a parrallel valley to the east but the germans got on to the road just above the village where there was an open bit and that became unhealthy.

So later I got a way where by starting up the eastern
valley and then cutting round the shoulder of the hill
into the other valley through the woods we were only
visible for a few yards. This worked alright for a
couple of days but coming back just before lunch one day
we no sooner brought the first wagon down a bank into the
open bit than "bang, bang" they dropped a couple of rounds
about 200 yards short. I did not wait for the next round
but trotted out till we were well clear and then halted
for a bit to throw them out with their timing. We had
the pleasure of watching them shell the spot where we
joined the main road at the time they thought us due and
when they had finished we went home.

Next afternoon was exciting, we had made our trip
without any excitement and were resting when we saw some
horses being shelled at dead man's corner. The horses
bolted and the bulk made for our camp which was best part
of a mile off so we had plenty of time to get the men to
our horses heads. We caught the horses, they were glad
of any protection, and were looking at their wounds, most
were dripping with blood when I noticed that the german
shells were following them into our camp. I gave the order
to file out of camp and the men were just filing out when
a six gun salvo burst right over the spot where I had the
N.C.O's collected for instructions. I had a very narrow
shave the fuse of one shell landing just beside my foot
and the man on either side being hit. I saw the Sergeant
Major go flat on his face but found him later perfectly
fit and looking after the two wounded who were the only
casualties besides Sergeant Smith who was killed on the spot.
We were very lucky to get off as well as we did as the whole
lot of us were in the danger zone which I afterwards
examined and found that there were bullet marks in every
yard of the area. I quickly got the men and horses clear
of the camp and away to the woods and sent a messenger for

stretchers for the wounded men who were under cover of the wagons, and then I had to see to the horses. One was down and nearly dead and another had lost a foot so I had to shoot them as well as another who was badly hit about the head and was perceptibly dying. They put over a few more rounds but we were able to shelter behind the wagons and had no more trouble. I then went over to the rest and got them back from the front edge of the wood just in time as the Germans began searching it almost as soon as we were clear. After dark we came back to camp and next day moved to a place on the hills behind very near where I had been with the Divisional Ammn. Col. This was the first time I had ever had a near shave and made a great impression on me although I have since been in worse corners. We were very lucky to get off so lightly with men although we had 18 horses hit, thirteen of which subsequently died. I put this down to the fact that the men were leading their horses out and were sheltered between the two animals.

This makes it sound as if we were having a bad time but we were there for a fortnight altogether and that was all the trouble we had. I had great times on the whole and used to be out riding on my own a lot. We had the small arm carts with the H.Q. of the Guards Brigade whom we supplied and I used to often visit them on the days when the Captain did not. I got to know all the country round very well and enjoyed my time there more than any other I can remember.

-x-x-x-x-

2ND DIVISION
44TH BDE R.F.A.

56TH BATTERY R.F.A.

AUG - DEC 1914

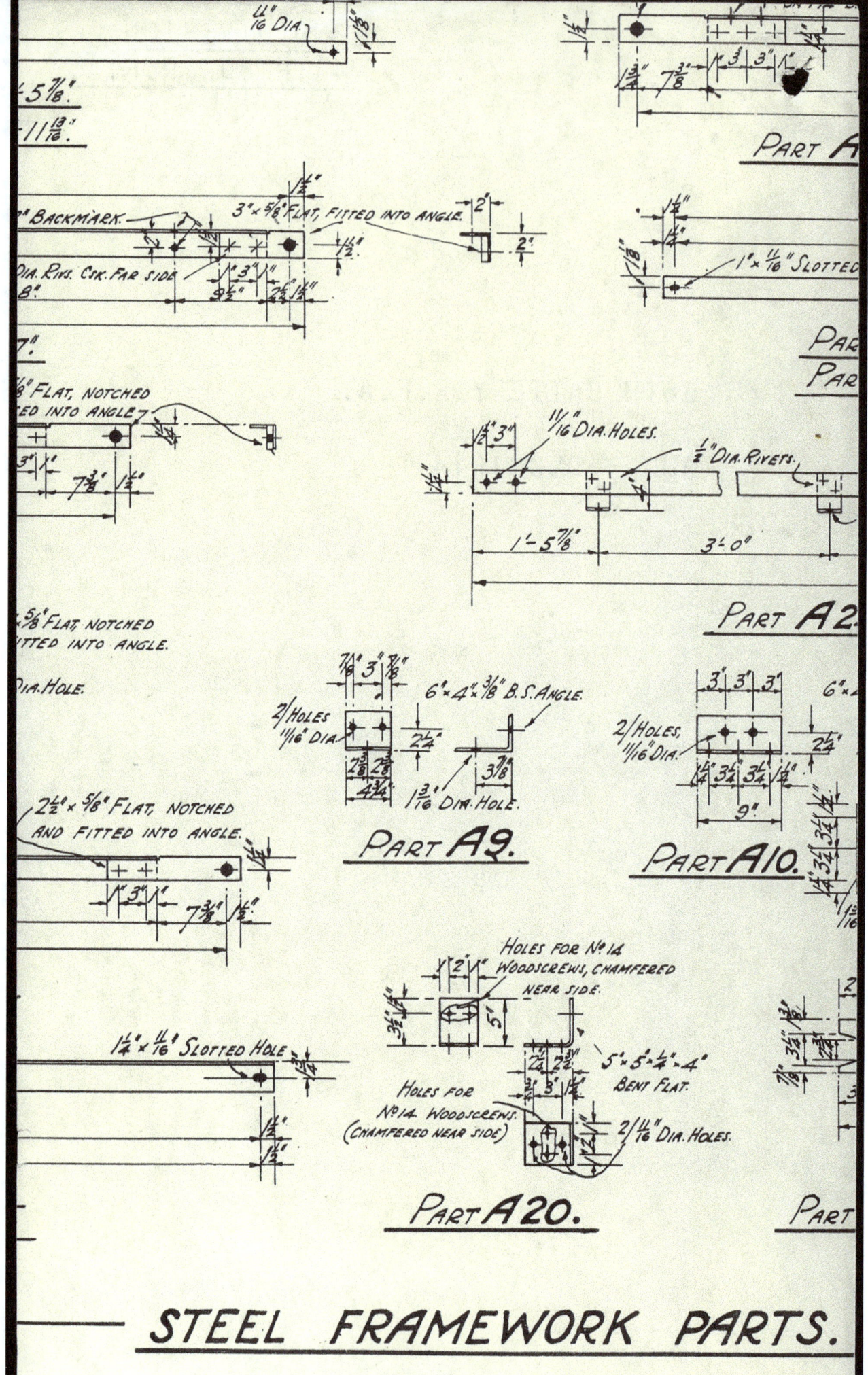

2nd Division

WAR DIARY

56th BATTERY R. F. A.

August

1914

War Diary of 56 Battery R.F.A.
From 18-8-14 to 23-11-14.

18-8-14 The Battery mobilized at BRIGHTON and left there for SOUTHAMPTON port of embarkation.

19-8-14 Arrived BOULOGNE in S.S. ARMENIAN and disembarked.

20-8-14 Rest Camp outside BOULOGNE leaving by rail to NORTH FRANCE in the evening.

21-8-14 Arrived by train WASSIGNY and went into bivouac.

22-8-14. Marched to LEVAL.

23-8-14. March continued to HARVENG. came into touch with enemy. LT. HARVEY'S section brought into action but did not open fire.

24-8-14. Retired to LA LONGUEVILLE and bivouacked.

25-8-14. Retirement continued reached LANDRECIES. Enemy tried night attack on LANDRECIES. Kept back by Guards Brigade and one section of 60 BTY RFA.

26-8-14. Moved before daybreak to ETREUX. Battery brought into action Gun pits prepared, did not open fire.

27-8-14. March continued and went into bivouac at ORIGNY.

28-8-14. SERVAIS.

29-8-14. SERVAIS.

31-8-14. CRECY-AU-MONT.

31-8-14. LAVERSINE.

2nd Division

WAR DIARY

56th BATTERY R.F.A.

September

1914

1-9-14. BARGNY.

2-9-14. MEAUX.

3-9-14. GRAND-BILBARTERU.

4-9-14. MOUROUX.

5-9-14. CHATEAU-LE-VIVIER.

6-9-14. CHATEAU. DE-LA-FORTELLE.

7-9-14. ST SIMEON.

8-9-14. BOITROM. Right Section under LT. TIDMARSH in action at LA PRETOIRE.

9-9-14. DOMPTON.

10-9-14. BUSSIARES. CHEVILLON south of MONNES.

11-9-14. OULCHY LE CHATEAU.

12-9-14. COURCELLES.

13-9-14. DHEUZEL. Bivouaced at DHEUZEL after being in action on the ridge south of the AISNE supporting the 4th Guards Brigade in their advance on CHAVONNE.

14-9-14. Crossed river AISNE and came into action at VERNEUIL. Battery under heavy fire and had several casualties. CAPT. G.W. BLATHWAYT and six men being killed. LT G.D. TIDMARSH and six men being wounded.

15-9-14. Same position. Bombr HOSKINS killed and three men wounded.

16-9-14. VERNEUIL. Continuation of battle of the AISNE

The battery remained in this position until 6.10.14

17-9-14. VERNEUIL.
18-9-14. VERNEUIL.
19-9-14. VERNEUIL.
20-9-14. VERNEUIL.
21-9-14. VERNEUIL.
22-9-14. VERNEUIL.
23-9-14. VERNEUIL.
24-9-14. VERNEUIL.
25-9-14. VERNEUIL.
26-9-14. VERNEUIL.
27-9-14. VERNEUIL.
28-9-14. VERNEUIL.

during which time it engaged targets in the vicinity of BRAY, CROIX-SANS-TETE and the country North West and West of TILEUL
On 19.9.14 the battery, with the 47th RFA, assisted in repelling an attack on the 4th Guards Bde.

29-9-14 VERNEUIL
30-9-14   do.

2nd Div

WAR DIARY

36th BATTERY R.F.A.

October

1914

29-9-14. VERNEUIL.	
30-9-14. VERNEUIL.	
1-10-14. VERNEUIL.	Continuation of battle of the AISNE.
2-10-14. VERNEUIL.	
3-10-14. VERNEUIL.	
4-10-14. VERNEUIL.	
5-10-14. VERNEUIL.	

6-10-14. About one mile NE of CHASSEMY. The battery was ordered to take up a position at this place, previously occupied by 43 BDE. RFA. Moved out of position at VERNEUIL during the night and the transfer was carried out without casualties.

7-10-14. About one mile NE of CHASSEMY. From 7-10-14 to 11-10-14 The battery was in action engaging targets to the North of VAILLY and in the vicinity of ROUGE-MAISON

11-10-14. About one mile NE of CHASSEMY. The line held by the BRITISH troops along the river AISNE was relieved by FRENCH troops. This was partly carried out during the night of the 11th. The battery was relieved and proceeded to MONTHUSSART FARM where they spent the night.

12-10-14. MONTHUSSART FARM the battery rested and proceeded to NEUILLY ST FONT to entrain for CASSEL (N.E. FRANCE) and bivouacked en route at ARCY on the night of 13th.

13-10-14. ARCY.

14-10-14. Entrained at NEUILLY ST FONT and left at 12.51pm proceeding via outskirts of PARIS, BOULOGNE and CALAIS.

15-10-14. Arrived CASSEL at 2 pm and
detrained. Then proceeded to
BLARINGHEN to billet.

16-10-14. BLARINGHEN.
Joined up with the remainder
of the 44 Bde R.F.A. from whom the
Battery had been separated since
6-10-14.

17-10-14. EECKE.

18-10-14. EECKE.

19-10-14. EECKE.

20-10-14. YPRES.

21-10-14. ST JULIEN.

22-10-14. FREZENBERG. The battery remained in action about ½ mile South of FREZENBERG until 23.10.14, engaging targets in the vicinity of ZONNEBEKE

23-10-14. FREZENBERG. Right Section detached from Battery and proceeded to HOLLEBEKE for duty with the cavalry who were entrenched in the vicinity.

9-10-14 FREZEN. BERG.

25-10-14 GHELUVELT. lent to 7th DIVN. Came into action here. Right Section rejoined. The battery assisted in repelling attacks from the east.

26-10-14 GHELUVELT.

27-10-14 HOOGE. } Rejoined 2nd Division & came under orders of O.C. 41st Bde R.F.A. Took up a position about 1500ˣ east of HOOGE where the battery remained till 3.11.14. engaging targets in the neighbourhood of REUTEL, BECALEARE, VELDHOCK, GHELUVELT

28-10-14 HOOGE.

29-10-14 HOOGE.

30-10-14 HOOGE.

31-10-14 HOOGE.

Battery under heavy fire during the afternoon. LT. H. Le F.E. HARVEY and two men being wounded.

2nd Division

WAR DIARY

56th BATTERY R.F.A.

November

1914

1-11-14. HOOGE. GR HANLON killed and one man wounded.

2-11-14. HOOGE. Battery under heavy fire. SERGT. EMERY and three men wounded.

3-11-14. Battery under heavy fire all day. SERGT. GRIFFITHS and two men killed. LT. MONTANARO and Fourteen men wounded. Three guns out of action temporarily. Battery withdrawn under cover of darkness.

4-11-14. ESTERNEST. Came into action but did not fire. Marched to POTIZJE that night & bivouaced under orders of OC 35" Bde RFA

5-11-14. Marched to DICKEBUSCHE. 2nd LT. W.G. DYSON joined.

6-11-14. Marched to HAZEBROUCKE.

7-11-14. HAZEBROUCKE.

8-11-14. HAZEBROUCKE.

9-11-14. HAZEBROUCKE.

10-11-14. HAZEBROUCKE.

11-11-14. HAZEBROUCKE.

12-11-14. HAZEBROUCKE.

13-11-14. HAZEBROUCKE.

14-11-14. HAZEBROUCKE.

15-11-14. HAZEBROUCKE.

16-11-14. HAZEBROUCKE.

17-11-14. HAZEBROUCKE. Marched to FLETRE.

18-11-14. FLETRE. CAPT. W.C.G. LYON joined the battery.

19-11-14. FLETRE.

20-11-14. FLETRE.

21-11-14. FLETRE.

22-11-14. FLETRE.

23-11-14. FLETRE.

24-11-14. FLETRE.

25-11-14. FLETRE.

26-11-14. FLETRE. Marched to LES HARISOM's near HINGES and came under orders of C.R.A. MEERUT DIVISION INDIAN ARMY. Went into billets.

27-11-14. LES HARISOM'S

29-11-14. LES HARISOM's.
of 44 BDE. A.C. joined the battery. No One section

30-11-14. LES HARISOM's

30/11/14.

J M Sawler
Lt Col R.F.A.
Cmdg 56 Bty R.F.A.

2nd Divisonal Artillery.

56th BATTERY R. F. A.

DECEMBER 1914.

Army Form C. 2118.

55th By RFA

WAR DIARY
of
INTELLIGENCE SUMMARY.
(Erase heading not required.)

Instructions regarding War Diaries and Intelligence Summaries are contained in F. S. Regs., Part II. and the Staff Manual respectively. Title pages will be prepared in manuscript.

Hour, Date, Place	Summary of Events and Information	Remarks and references to Appendices
1-12-14 LES HARISONS	Routine work in billets	
2-12-14 LES HARISONS	Routine work in billets.	
3-12-14 LES HARISONS	Marched to LE TOURET and came into action, relieving the 37th By RFA. A draft of 2 sergts, 3 bombrs, 13 gnrs, & 12 drs joined the battery from the Base at 4 p.m. The Right Section was detached under Capt. LYON at BURBURE.	
4-12-14 LE TOURET (4 guns) BURBURE (2 guns)	2nd Lieut. W.H BROOKES joined the battery from the 41st Bde Ammn Col.	
5-12-14 LE TOURET (4 guns) BURBURE (2 guns)	Detached Section shelled enemy's snipers' haunts - Effect good. N.W. of GIVENCHY	
6-12-14 LE TOURET (4 guns) BURBURE (2 guns)	fired on various trenches etc }	

Army Form C. 2118.

56 U 84 RFA

WAR DIARY
or
INTELLIGENCE SUMMARY.
(*Erase heading not required.*)

Instructions regarding War Diaries and Intelligence Summaries are contained in F.S. Regs., Part II. and the Staff Manual respectively. Title pages will be prepared in manuscript.

Hour, Date, Place		Summary of Events and Information	Remarks and references to Appendices
7-12-14	LE TOURET (4 guns) BURBURE (2 guns)	Detached Sect. shelled enemy's main trench W. of GIVENCHY by request of 58th Sikhs and silenced bomb throwers	
8-12-14	LE TOURET (4 guns) BURBURE (2 guns)	fired on enemy trenches etc	
9-12-14	LE TOURET (4 guns) BURBURE (2 guns)		
10-12-14	LE TOURET (4 guns) BURBURE (2 guns)	Detached section near Cte DU RAUX fired 30 rounds LYD. on enemy's cupolas near the PICKET HOUSE, causing considerable damage.	
11-12-14	LE TOURET (4 guns) BURBURE (2 guns)	Right section rejoined battery from BURBURE at 8 p.m.	
12-12-14	LE TOURET	enemy Couls	
13-12-14	LE TOURET		

Army Form C. 2118.

5/6 W 735 NFA

WAR DIARY
INTELLIGENCE SUMMARY.
(Erase heading not required.)

Instructions regarding War Diaries and Intelligence Summaries are contained in F. S. Regs., Part II. and the Staff Manual respectively. Title pages will be prepared in manuscript.

Hour, Date, Place	Summary of Events and Information	Remarks and references to Appendices
14—12—14 LE TOURET		
15—12—14 LE TOURET	Engaged enemy's support trenches without success.	
16—12—14 LE TOURET	} various targets	
17—12—14 LE TOURET		
18—12—14 LE TOURET		
19—12—14 LE TOURET	Took part in demonstration made by MEERUT Div? commencing firing at 4 a.m.	
20—12—14 LE TOURET	Major B.B. CROZIER joined the battery from 47TH BY. on promotion. Shelled MINENWERFER which caused firing and shifted its position. Fire kept up continuously throughout the night.	
21—12—14 LE TOURET	Opened fire at 5 p.m. in support of counter attack which however was delayed and finally did not take place	

(9 29 6) W 4141—463 100,000 9/14 H W V Forms/C. 2118/10

56 BG RFA

WAR DIARY
or
INTELLIGENCE SUMMARY.
(Erase heading not required.)

Army Form C. 2118.

Instructions regarding War Diaries and Intelligence Summaries are contained in F. S. Regs., Part II. and the Staff Manual respectively. Title pages will be prepared in manuscript.

Hour, Date, Place		Summary of Events and Information	Remarks and references to Appendices
22-12-14	LE TOURET	Lieut Col F.E.L. BARKER left Battery to join Home Establishment. Engaged houses in orchard on LA QUINQUE RUE with considerable effect. Intermittent fire was maintained throughout the night.	
23-12-14	LE TOURET	Effective fire again opened on the houses in the orchard.	
24-12-14	LE TOURET		
25-12-14	LE TOURET	At the request of 39th Garwhal Rifles opened fire on and put out of action a party which was flooding their trenches.	
26-12-14	LE TOURET	Battery was relieved at 2 p.m. by the 47th By. and marched to LESPESSES going into billets to rest and refit.	

50th Bty. R.F.A.

WAR DIARY
INTELLIGENCE SUMMARY.
(Erase heading not required.)

Army Form C. 2118.

Instructions regarding War Diaries and Intelligence Summaries are contained in F.S. Regs., Part II. and the Staff Manual respectively. Title pages will be prepared in manuscript.

Hour, Date, Place	Summary of Events and Information	Remarks and references to Appendices
27-12-14 LESPESSES	Routine work in billets	
28-12-14 LESPESSES	Routine work in billets	
29-12-14 LESPESSES	Routine work in billets	
30-12-14 LESPESSES	Routine work in billets	
31-12-14 LESPESSES	Routine work in billets	

2ND DIVISION
44TH BDE R.F.A.

B.H.Q.

AUG - DEC 1914

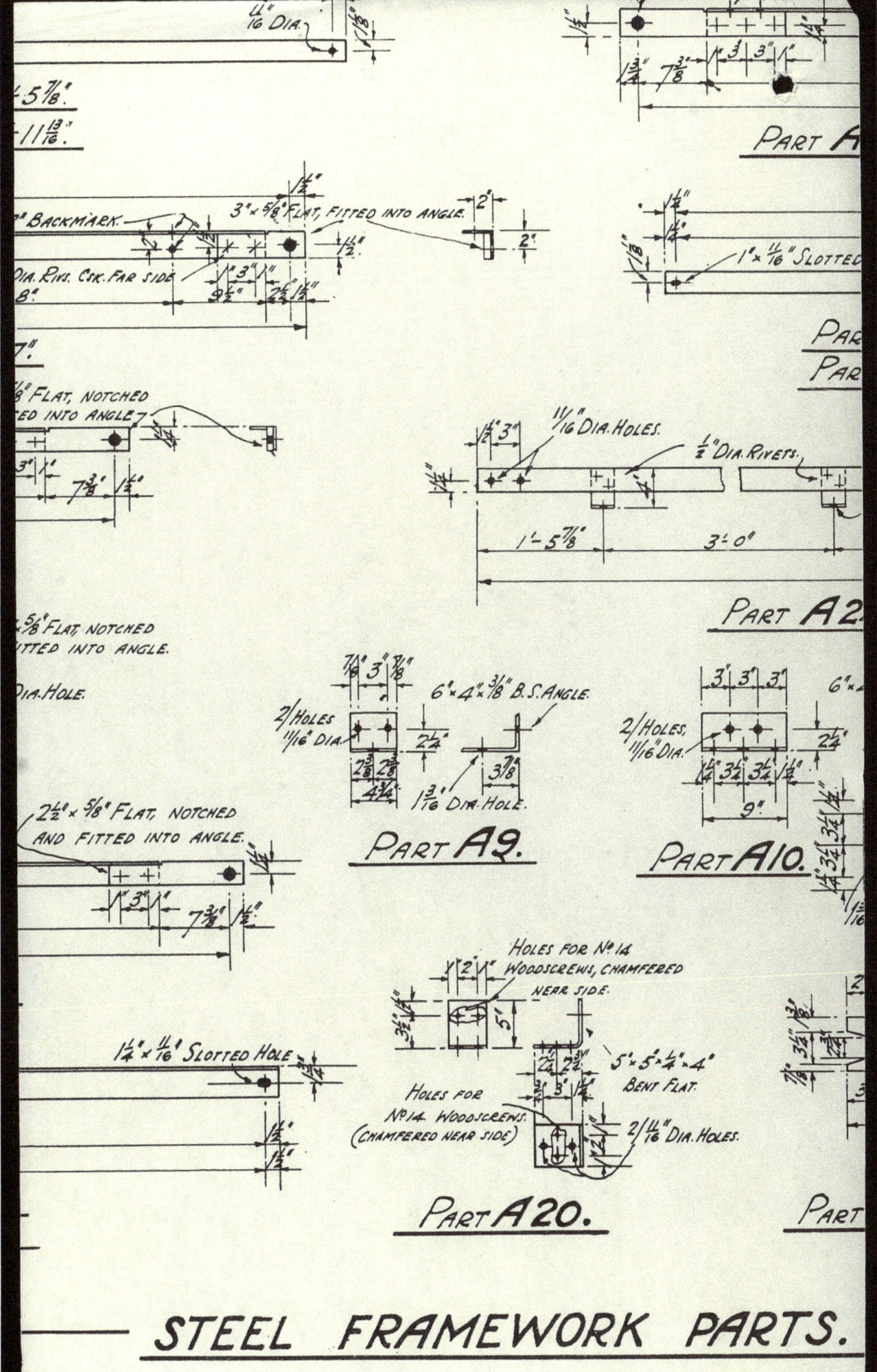

2nd Division

WAR DIARY

XLIV BRIGADE R. F. A.

AUGUST 1914

War Diary 44th Bde RHA.

4th.8.14. Orders to mobilize received at Brighton.

5.8.14. 1st day of mobilization

6.8.14 2nd day of mobilization. Lieut Knyvett & 2/L. Huggins posted.

7.8.14 3rd day of mobilization, reservists joined.

8.8.14 4th day of mobilization

9.8.14 5th day of mobilization

10.8.14 6th day of mobilization. Sergt Wing 47th Battery killed by horse.

11.8.14 7th day of mobilization

12.8.14 8th day of mobilization

13.8.14 Mobilization completed. Major Edwards 47th Batt dislocated his shoulder on parade.

14.8.14 Major Newcombe posted to 47th Batt in place of Major Edwards.

15.8.14

2

16.8.14.

17.8.14.) The Brigade started to entrain at Brighton
for Southampton at 11.40 p.m.

18.8.14 Arrived at Southampton, & embarked for
BOULOGNE.

19.8.14 Disembarked at BOULOGNE & went into a
rest camp about three miles from the
town. A list of officers is given below who
left Brighton with the brigade
Bde Staff. Lt Col. D Arbuthnot.   Am Col.
    Capt. G.C. Neville   Capt R.C. Miller
    Lt 7&V Mills   Lieut C L Montanaro
    Capt L L Dixon A.V.D
    Capt T.W.D Seaton R.A.M.C

  47th Batt.   56th Batt.   60th Batt
Maj H W Newcombe. Maj F Barker. Maj H J Mackey.
Capt. B Crozier Capt G W Blathwayt Capt H E Furse
Lieut C L Knyvett Lieut H. Harry Lieut A F Willcocks
Lieut K Caldwell Lieut G D Tidmarsh Lieut J P Knight
Lieut H W Huggins Lieut H E Barkworth Lieut R C Stillman

20.8.14 Brigade entrained at BOULOGNE, starting first
train at 11 p.m. & arrived

21.8.14 at VAUX & went into bivouac near the town

3

22.8.14 The Brigade marched to LEVAL & went into billets.

23.8.14 Moved at 3am & crossed the BELGIAN frontier near MALPLAQUET, we were then ordered to billet, ~~at~~ ~~~~, but moved on again at 2.30 p.m. The 47th Battery was attached to 6th Inf Bde & came into action in the evening near GIVRY.
The 56th & 60th moved to HARVENG where the 60th Battery & the 56th Battery came into action. These two batteries retired that evening with the Amn. Col. to
          where they slept for the night on the side of the road without unhooking.

24.8.14 Continued the retirement to LA LONGUEVILLE & bivouaced for the night. The 47th Batt rejoined the brigade.

25.8.14 Continued the retirement & bivouaced in LANDRECHES where we were shelled, two casualties in 47th Batt.

26.8.14 Retired to ETREUX where the brigade was brought into action & dug in, the men slept by their guns, a very wet evening.

4

27.8.14 Retired to RIREMONT where we again dug in, but were not attacked.

28.8.14 Retired to SERVAIS & bivouaced where we
29.8.14 remained for two nights to rest.

30.8.14 Retired towards TERNY & bivouaced at LE BANC DE PIERRE

31.8.14 Retired & bivouaced for the night at POMMIERS

2nd Division

WAR DIARY

XLIV BRIGADE R.F.A.

September

1914

1.9.14 Retired & came into action W of the village of CUVERGNON where the brigade dug in & remained in action for the night.

2.9.14 At 2.30 am continued the retirement & bivouaced close to the town of MEAUX

3.9.14 Retired to two miles S of PIERRE LEVEE & bivouaced.

4.9.14 Retired to MOUROUX & bivouaced.

5.9.14 Retired to CHAUMES & bivouaced

6.9.14 about 7.a.m we commenced advancing the 60th Battery came into action in the afternoon near PEZACHES The brigade bivouaced at Ch de la FORTELLE

7.9.14 At 7a.m continued the advance & bivouaced at St SIMEON

8.9.14 Advanced & came into action near LA TRETOIRE against the German rear guard, eventually crossed the PETIT MORIN river & again came into action near (S of) BOITRON. The 47th Battery took eleven German prisoners. We bivouaced for the night near BOITRON.

9.9.14 At 5am continued to advance & bivouaced for the night at VILLIERS-sur-MARNE.

10.9.14 Advanced to near MONNES where the brigade stayed the night.

11.9.14 Advanced again to OULCY-LE-CHATEAU & bivouaced.

12.9.14 Advanced to LA POTERIE (COURCELLES) & bivouaced

13.9.14 Advanced to DHUIZEL & bivouaced. 47th & 56th Batt came into action at ·175.

14.9.14 Moved via BOURG where we came under fire, came into action 3/4 mile S

of VERNEUIL. Eventually moved forward to position NW of VERNEUIL just S of point 158 TILLEUL.
Here the batteries having dug themselves well in, remained. Under a heavy shell fire Captain Blathwayt was killed & Lt. Tidmarsh was wounded.

15.9.14 Heavily shelled. Capt Fane wounded. Very wet.

16.9.14 Capt Fane died. Both he & Captain Blathwayt were buried in the CHATEAU grounds, the Brigade heavily shelled. A combined shelling of the enemy's position from 5 p.m till 5.30 p.m.

17.9.14 Very wet.

18.9.14 A good many horses killed in the horse lines. The 60th Battery were moved to a position N of SOUPIR

19.9.14 Wagon line of 47th moved.

20.9.14 Horses of 47th & 56th Batteries moved to BOURG.

21.9.14
22.9.14
23.9.14
24.9.14
25.9.14
26.9.14
27.9.14
28.9.14
29.9.14
30.9.14

During this period nothing of particular interest occurred. The Batteries remained in action in the same positions.

Lieut C H Montanaro was posted to 56th Battery & Lt Tidmarsh wounded. Lieut C L Ziegler to the 60th Batt in place of Lieut Willcocks killed

2nd Division

WAR   DIARY

XLIV BRIGADE   R. F. A.

October

1914

1.10.14
2.10.14
3.10.14 } Batteries remained in the same positions.
4.10.14
5.10.14

6.10.14 The 56th battery moved at night to a position nr BRAINE & were attached to the 34th brigade R.F.A.

7.10.14
8.10.14 } The 47th Batt remained in action at VERNEUIL & the 60th near SOUPIR
9.10.14

10.10.14 nothing of interest, a quiet day, heavy firing on our right flank at about 9 p.m.

11.10.14. Below are the number of remounts which have joined the brigade since coming to VERNEUIL

Date	No.	where posted	Bd staff	47th	56th	60th
	59	—	—	20	20	19
	30	—	6	0	16	8
3rd Oct.	25	—	2	13	10	—
11th	10	—	2	2	—	6

11.10.14 (continued) Still at VERNEUIL nothing of importance happened.

12.10.14 at VERNEUIL a quiet night & morning nothing to note. Twenty eight remounts joined & issued 10 to 47th Batt.
9 to 56th Batt.
9 to 60th Batt.

13.10.14 Nothing to note during the day. The 47th Batt & the Bde Staff left VERNEUIL at 8.30 p.m. marched via BOURG & BUIHZEL to LIMES. The Am. Col. joined us at BOURG, we billeted men & horses in a large farm for the night. The 56th & 60th Batteries marched independently.

14.10.14 Left LIMES at 9 a.m. & marched to NEUILLY station about 21 miles via JOUAIGNES – BRANGES – ARCY – OULCHY-la-VILLE arriving 4.15 p.m.
56th Batt entrained at noon
60th Batt — " — 2.30 p.m.
47th Batt — " — 4.30 p.m.
Hd Qrs & A.C. — " — 6.0 p.m.

15.10.14 Spent in the train route. AMIENS – BOULOGNE – CALAIS – CASSEL. The 56th Batt arriving by 1st train marched to BLARINGHAM arriving at 11.30 p.m., the 47th & 60th bivouaced for the night at CASSEL near the station

16.10.14. The Am Col & Bde Staff arrived at CASSEL at 2 a.m. detrained & marched straight to BLARINGHEM arriving 8 a.m. followed by 47th & 60th Batteries, horses were bivouaced & men billeted, requisitioned hay

17.10.14. The Brigade marched at 7.30 am to EECKE via HAZEBROUCK — ST SYLVESTRE arriving about 1.30 p.m., horses bivouaced men billeted. Com ration short.

18.10.14. Remained at EECKE

19.10.14 Draft of 35 gunners & 18 drivers arriving posted as follows:
	grs.	drs.
47th	18	7/11
56th	14	4
60th	3	7

later information the above have been hung up on the line.

20.10.14 Left EECKE at 5.30 am & marched to YPRES via GODEWARSVELDE — BOESCHEPE — RENINGHELST arriving 12.15 p.m., bivouaced just north of town & billeted the men

21.10.14 Left YPRES at 5.30am marched through ST JEAN - WIELTJE, 47ᵗʰ Battery attached to 5ᵗʰ Inf Bde. 60ᵗʰ Battery came into action near PT 37 NW of ZONNEBEKE, & then moved slightly forward & came into action again in support of 4ᵗʰ Guards Bde. One section of the 56ᵗʰ then came into action where the 60ᵗʰ Batt had first been in action. Bde Hd Qrs, 56ᵗʰ & 60ᵗʰ Batts returned to ST JEAN & billeted for the night.

22.10.14 Left ST JEAN at 7am (i.e. 56ᵗʰ & 60ᵗʰ Batts) & came into action just S of the Z in FREZENBERG facing ZONNEBEKE. The 56ᵗʰ Batt at 10 am was ordered to a point near St JULIEN to come under the orders of Col LUSHINGTON, only one section under Lt BARKWORTH remained there, this section rejoined at 11 p.m. The remaining four guns rejoined the 60ᵗʰ Battery which had moved forward to a position just S of the H in HALTE & both batteries came into action in support of the 22nd Bde 7ᵗʰ Div. remaining in action all day & at 7 pm returned to ST JEAN & billeted.
Serg S. KELLAGHER promoted 2ⁿᵈ Lieut.
Lt Col Arbuthnot, Major Mackey, Lieuts Knight & Huggins were mentioned in despatches

23.10.14 The 56 & 60th Batts were ordered back by 6 am to the same positions which they had vacated the previous evening. The 1st reinforcement referred to on 19.10.14 arrived. At 3.30 p.m. the 60th Batt was ordered back to the same position which it had occupied on 21.10.14 to better support an attack which was being delivered to the French along the line ST JEAN - WIELTJE on PASSCHENDAEL. The 60th Batt returned to ST JEAN at 9 p.m. for the night. The 56th Batt remained in action near the HALTE.

24.10.14 The 60th Batt starting at 5 am returned to the position vacated by them the previous evening, but later in the day join up with the 56th Batt near the HALTE. The 47th Batt also rejoined & came into action near the R of EKSTERNEST. About 7 p.m. the 56th Batt was sent to support the 7th Division near GHELUVELT. The 47th & 56th remained in action for the night. Bde Hd Qrs staying in a house near the HALTE.

25.10.14 In the evening about 4 p.m. both 47th & 60th Batts moved forward to a point about about half a mile NE of the 2nd T of ENSTERNEST & dug in. Bde Hd Qrs moved to farm S of the R of ENSTERNEST. The detached section of the 56th rejoined its battery

26.10.14. The 47th & 60th remained in action in the same place, forward observation stations were pushed forward, to just behind "the Kings" firing line. The 47th Batt knocked out two machine guns & Major Duncombe was hit by a bullet in the leg slightly. Reinforcements arrived & were posted as follows

  to Bde Staff.   1 Br   2 Dr.
  to 47th Batt   1 Cpl.   8 Dr   10 Grs
  to 56th Batt   2 Dr   6 Grs.

27.10.14. The 47th & 60th Batts remainded in action in the same position. Lt Huggins was sent out to a house in advance of the Guards trenches with a telephone wire, where he knocked out a machine gun near REUTEL. The 56th Batt moved to a position just N of Pt 64, N of 5 m. stone on the YPRES - MENIN road. The Bde Hd Qrs moved to a farm just N of the 2nd T of EKSTERNEST

28.10.14 The Batteries remained in the same positions. The 60th Battery tried to run out 2 miles of wire to the forward trenches of the S. Staffs, but could not get proper communication so returned to its old observation station about 700x in front of the battery. Capt Crozier did good work from a forward observation station on the enemy's trenches in front of "the Kings". The supply of lyddite running short, Div. A.C. have been ordered only to supply lyddite in proportion of one lyddite to two shrapnel in future, whatever the expenditure of lyddite. Bde provided with a 1/40,000 map of the country to our front.

29.10.14. The Division attacked all along the line at 5 a.m. Nothing of further interest, the two batteries were firing at many targets during the day. Still in same position

30.10.14 A lot of firing, the enemy made three attacks on our immediate front, without success. Still in same position

31.10.14 A quiet night, neither of the batteries firing during the night. Heavy firing all day Still in same position

2nd Division

WAR DIARY

XLIV BRIGADE R.F.A.

November

1914

16

1.11.14. Batteries (47" & 60") still in same position. The French attacked through our lines general direction ZONNEBEKE — BELELAERE attack commenced 6.30 a.m. A good deal of firing during the day. Sergt Kremer killed.

2.11.14. In the same positions, nothing of note. Capt Miller joined 60" Batt & Capt Hope the Bde. A.C.

3.11.14. Lieut Knight sent out with a telephone line to the trenches in large wood 800x E of B5 on ZONNEBEKE — BECELAERE road, batteries remain in same positions. Lt Hanrey wounded.

4.11.14. Sixty four remounts arrive distributed as follows:

	L.D.	H.D.
Bde Staff	4	—
47" Batt.	35	2
60" Batt	23	—

56" Batt badly shelled during the afternoon evacuated the position at night & retired to bivouac near ST JEAN. Lt Montanaro wounded.

5.11.14. Lt W.G Dyson attached temporarily to 44" Bde & attached for duty to 56" Batt. The 56" Battery moved back to ST OMER In the same positions.

6.11.14. In the same position, nothing of incident.

17

7.11.14. In same position. Major Barker, Capt Crozier, Capt Miller, Lieuts Knyvett & Maubarano promoted on gazette of the 3rd instant. The French attack on our left at MESSINES & gained a mile of ground.

8.11.14. Same position nothing of note, several small attacks by the enemy during the day & the night.

9.11.14. Capt C L Knyvett posted as Captain to 56th Battery, no change in position

10.11.14. Capt C L Knyvett's posting cancelled. German attacked on 5th Inf Bde right. About 20 men arrived as reinforcements for the Brigade.

11.11.14. Heavy attack by the enemy along REUTELBECK on VERBECK farm. Our brigade firing all day, very high wind

12.11.14 Enemy attacked ZONNEBEKE, again we fired a lot of ammunition at various targets.

13.11.14. In same position. Capt Lyon posted to 56" Battery from England. Enemy attacked on our left near ZONNEBEKE. 60th Battery had 30 horses in wagon line wounded.

14/11/14. In same position a quiet day.

15/11/14. In same position. ~~Arranged with French for "handing over" position.~~ 47th Battery left at 4 pm. and reached BRIELEN at 12 mn. Difficult march owing to bad roads and traffic. 60th Battery remained.

16/11/14. 47th Battery marched from BRIELEN (9.0 am.) to LOCRE (3.30pm) bad road. Bde Head Quarters left at 11 am. arrived FLAMERTINGE 6.0 p.m. Arranged "handing over" position with French. 60th Battery remained.

17/11/14. 60th Battery in same position. 47th Battery rested at LOCRE. Bde Head Quarters marched from FLAMERTINGE (9 am) to LOCRE (12 noon).

18/11/14. Bde H.Q. and 47th Battery left LOCRE at 5.30 am. reached FLETRE at 8 am. Proceeding into billets in 4 farms about 1 mile S.E. of FLETRE. Joined by 56th Battery from HAZEBRUCK. 60th Battery marched from near ZONNEBEKE at 3.30 am. arrived in billets near FLETRE at 5 pm.
 The move was carried out without any casualties.

19

19th In same billets. Brigade resting.
The following officers left at 6.30 pm.
on leave to ENGLAND.
  Maj. Mackey.
  Maj. Crozier.
  Capt. Nevile
  Capt. ~~Knyvett~~ Knyvett.
  Capt. Dixon. A.V.C. (attached)
  Lt. Caldwell.
  Lt. Knight.

20th In same billets. Brigade resting.

21st In same billets. Received 39 remounts
allotted as under.
  56th Battery:— 20 L.D. 2 H.D.
  60th „ :— 15 L.D. 2 H.D.

22nd In same billets.

23rd In same billets. 19 horses sent to
Mobile Section of Vet. Corps.

24th In same billets. Lt Mills & Huggins left
1/4 on leave for England.
25th In same billets. Lt Col Arbuthnot, Maj. Miller
Newcombe, Lts Barkworth, Ziegler, Stillman left for England on leave
26th 56th Battery marched to LOLON & ordered

to report to MEERUT division. 4 & 47th Batteries in same billets

27.11.14 No change

28.11.14 No change

29.11.14 No change. B.S.M. WALBY 47th Battery awarded a D.C.M.

30.11.14 No change

2nd Division

WAR DIARY

XLIV BRIGADE R.F.A.

December

1914

Army Form C. 2118.

WAR DIARY
or
INTELLIGENCE SUMMARY

(Erase heading not required.)

Instructions regarding War Diaries and Intelligence Summaries are contained in F. S. Regs., Part II. and the Staff Manual respectively. Title pages will be prepared in manuscript.

Place	Hour, Date, Place	Summary of Events and Information	Remarks and references to Appendices
FLETRE	1.12.14.	The 47th and 60th Batteries still billeted in farms near FLETRE the 56th Batt attached to the MEERUT division near LOCON	
"	2.12.14	The following decorations were awarded the brigade. (60th) Lieut J.P. Knight and (A) Lieut- H.W. Huggins D.S.O's. (60th) B.S.M Dryden D.C.M (47th) B.S.M Walby D.C.M. (47th) Sergeant Hours D.C.M. (60th) Gdr Ding D.C.M (47th) Cpl Adie D.C.M and (47th) B° Light - D.C.M.	
"	3.12.14	Visit of his majesty the King. The brigade was formed up with the rest of the Divisional Artillery S of METEREN at 11.15 a.m.	
"	4.12.14 to 6.12.14	No change	
"	7.12.14	Captain T.W.O Seaton R.A.M.C posted to 61st Field Ambulance & Lieut O. Wilson R.A.M.C. posted in his place.	
"	17.12.14	No change. Captain C.T. Confroe joined 60th Battery vice Major R.G. Sutton ordered to proceed to England. Captain Dixon A.V.D posted to England.	
"	19.12.14	Maj R.G. Sutton left for England & Lieut J.P. Knight D.S.O posted to "F" Battery R.H.A	
"	21.12.14	Lieut J.P Knight D.S.O left the brigade. At 10 p.m orders received to move at 7 a.m. 22nd Brigade and battery commanders to leave MERRIS by motor trips at 7am for BETHUNE	

1247 W 3299 200,000 (E) 8/14 J.B.C. & A. Forms/C. 2118/11.

Army Form C. 2118.

WAR DIARY
or
INTELLIGENCE SUMMARY

(Erase heading not required.)

Instructions regarding War Diaries and Intelligence Summaries are contained in F.S. Regs., Part II. and the Staff Manual respectively. Title pages will be prepared in manuscript.

Hour, Date, Place		Summary of Events and Information	Remarks and references to Appendices
VENDIN	22.12.14	The brigade and ammunition Column marched via BETHUNE to VENDIN were billetted in farms & remained there until 26th Dec	
"	23.12.14	The Brigade Comdr & O.C. Batteries met G.O.C. Perceval at LOCON & rode round battery positions. It was decided that the 47th Batt should take over the position held by the 56th Batt & the 60th Batt that held by the 19th Batt. Cold day, snow in the morning.	
"	25.12.14	Xmas carols received from H.M the King & Queen, 9/5 from Princess Mary.	
"	26.12.14	Lieut. J.E.M. Fetherstonhaugh attached to the 60th Batt. The brigade marched to LE TOURET & took over selected positions	
LE TOURET	27.12.14	Quiet day, batteries found their range is to reverse forests.	
"	28.12.14	ditto	
"	29.12.14	Very wild night, all very quiet.	
"	30.12.14	All quiet very little firing	
"	31.12.14	ditto	

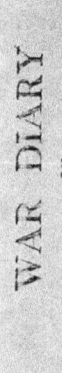

2ND DIVISION
44TH BDE R.F.A.

44TH (HOW) BATTERY R.F.A.

AUG - NOV 1914

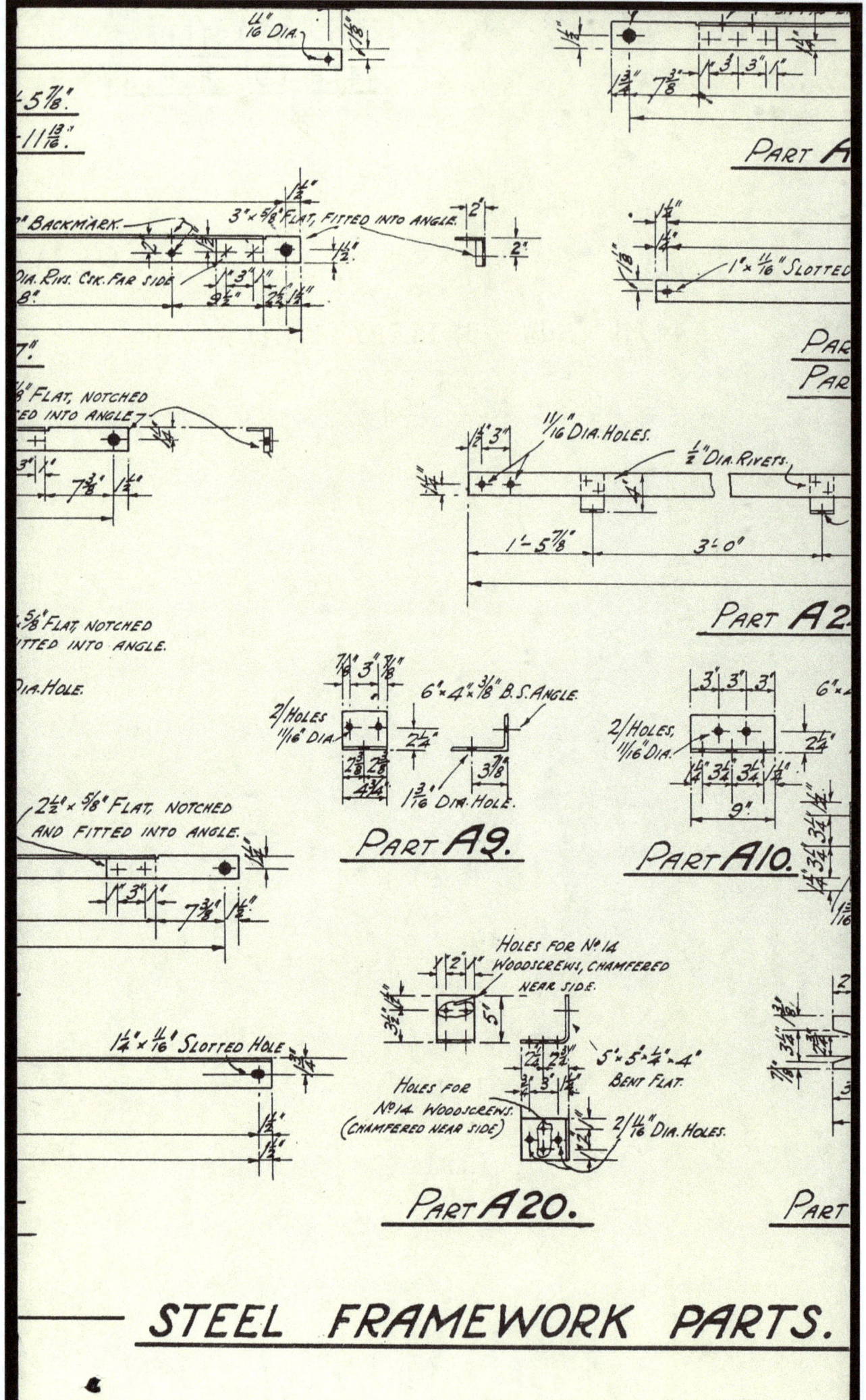

2nd Division
44th Bde. R.F.A.

WAR DIARY

44th (How.) BATTERY R. F. A.

August

1 9 1 4.

47th Battery. R.F.A.

WAR DIARY

1914

17th Augt. — Battery left BRIGHTON in two trains, 11.40 p.m.

18th Augt. — Arrived SOUTHAMPTON, 3 a.m., embarked on board S.S. ARMENIAN. Sailed 8 p.m.

19th Augt. — Arrived BOULOGNE 8 a.m., disembarked and marched out to Rest Camp, PONT FEUILLET.

20th Augt. — Entrained at BOULOGNE 11 p.m.

21st Augt. — Left at 3 a.m. Arrived at VAUX ANDIGNY at 2 p.m. Detrained and marched 3 miles to bivouack, at WASSIGNY.

22nd Augt. — Marched at 8 a.m, and arrived LAVAL 2 p.m. Bivouacked there.

23rd Augt. — Marched at 3 a.m. through MALPLAQUET, crossed frontier into BELGIUM, and halted for dinners at QUÈVY LE PETIT 2 p.m. Joined the rest of 2nd Division on the march, and the whole Division moved out at 4 p.m. to the attack. Remained in reserve at HARVENG till 6 p.m., and then received orders to join 5th Brigade at GIVRY. Entrenched a position N. of GIVRY

1914   on left of 34th Brigade R.F.A.

24th Augt   Finished entrenching at 2.a.m. Occupied observing station 3.30.a.m. and engaged German Batteries, 3500 yds. to the North. At 8.30.a.m. received orders to cover withdrawal of 34th Brigade R.F.A., which we did, and then withdrew at 9.30.a.m. to HAVAY. Joined remainder of 44th Brigade R.F.A. at 1.30.p.m., and the whole Brigade entrenched a position 1½ mile S. of QUEVY LE PETIT to cover the withdrawal of 2nd Division. Did not open fire, but retired at 2.p.m. and marched to HARGNIES, where we bivouacked at 8.p.m. Gr. Hartley injured + went to hospital.

25th Augt   Marched at 5.a.m. Arrived LANDRÉCIES 1.p.m. and parked in a field till 6.p.m. Then went into bivouack. Germans attacked heavily during the night and we took up a position for close defence. Bivouack shelled by German artillery. Sr. Farrell wounded severely and died next morning. Gr. Secker wounded and sent to hospital.

26th Augt   Marched at 3.a.m. Came into action on high ground S. of LANDRÉCIES, but did not open fire. Continued retirement 4.30.a.m. and marched to ÉTRUIE, where we again entrenched at 12 noon. No Germans appeared. Gr. Dobson to hospital.

1914

27th Augt. Marched 6.a.m. Arrived MONT d'ORIGNY 3.p.m. At 4.p.m attack threatened from ST. QUENTIN, so came into action, and eventually entrenched in the firing line with the King's. Lt. KNYVETT and one section to guard ST QUENTIN road with Guards' Brigade.

28th Augt. Marched 4.a.m. Arrived SERVAIS 3.p.m. Gt. Bird to hospital.

29th Augt. Remained at SERVAIS.

30th Augt. Marched 5.15.a.m. Passed COURCY-LE-CHATEAU and bivouacked 5.p.m. at BETHANCOURT.

31st Augt. Marched 5.30.a.m. Bivouacked 3.30 p.m. between LAVERSINE and COUTRY. Marched through SOISSONS.

WAR DIARY.

47th Battery. R.F.A.

Major H. W. Newcome.
Capt. B. B. Crozier
Lt. C. L. Kempsett.
Lt. K. F. T. Caldwell
Lt. H. W. Huggins.

2nd Division
44th Bde. R.F.A.

W A R   D I A R Y

44th (How.) BATTERY R. F. A.

September

1 9 1 4.

1st Sept.   Marched 4.a.m. Through VILLARS-COTTERETS
            to CUVERGNON. Came into action facing W.
            and then entrenched a position S. of the
            village, facing N. at 6.p.m.

2nd Sept.   Marched 2.15 a.m. Arrived MEAUX and
            went into bivouack S. of MEAUX 2.p.m.

3rd Sept.   Marched 5.30.a.m., crossed R. MARNE 10.a.m.
            Bivouacked in chateau 2 miles S.W. of
            PIERRE - LEVÉE at 2.30.p.m.

4th Sept.   Marched at 3.30.p.m. Arrived MOUROUX
            8.p.m. Went into bivouack.

5th Sept.   Marched at 2.a.m. Arrived CHAUME 3.p.m.
            and went into bivouack.

6th Sept.   Marched at 6.30.a.m. and began the advance
            to R. MARNE. Bivouacked in a chateau near
            RIGNY at 7.15 p.m.

7th Sept.   Marched at 6.30.a.m. Bivouacked at 7.30 p.m.
            at ST SIMEON. Gr Miles to hospital.

8th Sept.   Marched at 7.a.m. Halted near VOLIGNY.
            Trotted through REBAIS and came into
            action at LE TRETOIRE at 11.a.m. Shelled
            woods near the River and German maxims.
            Moved across the R. PETIT MORIN at 2.p.m.
            and came into action at BOITRON at 4.p.m.
            Engaged hostile infantry and artillery to
            the W. at 4000 yds., when hostile infantry
            opened on the Battery from a wood 300 yds. to
            our front. Turned one section on to them and
            also the Gunners with rifles. Captured nine
            prisoners. Went into bivouack at BOITRON 7.30 p.m.

1914

9- Sept.   Marched at 5.30 a.m. Came into action
           overlooking CHARLY-SUR-MARNE at 7 a.m.
           Crossed R. MARNE 12 noon. Moved into
           bivouack between VILLIERS and DOMPTIN
           at 6.30 p.m.

10th Sept. Marched at 7 a.m. to HAUTVENNES. Advanced
           at noon to MONNES. Went into bivouack
           there at 6.30 p.m.

11th Sept. Marched at 5.30 a.m. through BRENY, NEUILLES,
           VICHEL. Bivouacked at OULCHY-LE-CHATEAU
           at 2 p.m.

12th Sept. Marched at 5.45 a.m. Through JOUAIGNES
           to QUINCEY. Bridge at LIMÉ across River
           VESLE was blown up, so marched through
           BRAINE to COURCELLES. Bivouacked there
           at 8 p.m.

13th Sept. Marched at 5.45 a.m. to high ground S. of
           DHUIZEL. Waited there till 2 p.m., and then
           came into action near VIEIL ARCY at 3 p.m.
           Fired on the heights N. of R. AISNE till
           dusk. Then marched back through pt. 175
           to DHUIZEL and bivouacked there.

(6)

1914.

14th Sept. Marched at 6.30 a.m. Crossed R. AISNE and two canals at BOURG and came into action 1 mile W. of BOURG at 9 a.m. Advanced through VERNEUIL at 2 p.m. and came into action between VERNEUIL and MOUSSY, with observing station on TILLEUL. Fired at BRAYE-EN-LANNOIS and the CHEMIN DES DAMES. The enemy searched recure slope with High Explosive. Sergt Kenny wounded. GI Richards to hospital. Bivouacked in action.

~~15th Sept.~~

15th Sept. Heavy firing on both sides all day. Gr Middleton missing. Corpl Houston, Br Morris, Br Pickering, wounded. Bivouacked in action.

16th Sept. Heavy firing on both sides all day. No casualties. Bivouacked in action.

17th Sept. Heavy firing all day. ~~Dr James & Gr Nicholson killed. Br Saunders & Gr Woods wounded.~~ Bivouacked in action.

18th Sept. Heavy firing all day. Dr James & Gr Nicholson killed. Br Saunders & Gr Woods wounded. Bivouacked in action.

19th Sept. Heavy firing all day. Horse-lines moved to COURTONNE. B.Q.M.S. Tudge and Gr Bursey wounded. Bivouacked in action. Heavy attack by Germans on 4th Guards Brigade brought to a standstill by fire from 47th & 56th Batteries.

20th Sept. Heavy firing all day. Observing station moved to King's trenches, but returned to TILLEUL in the afternoon. Germans attacked TILLEUL but eventually retired. Great difficulty all these days to keep telephone working, as wire constantly cut by hostile shell. B.S.M. Walby, Cpl. Hines, Sgt. Thompson, Br. Adie, Br. Neale constantly went out to repair it under heavy shell fire. Gr. Wilkinson wounded. Bivouacked in action.

21st Sept. Battery ranged on by German aeroplane. Heavily shelled, but little damage done. Far Q.m.S. Gurling wounded. Bivouacked in action.

22nd Sept. Shelled LA CREUTE spur and MALVAL FARM. German aeroplane again ranged on Battery and many H.E. shell dropped near. Gr. Garbutt wounded. Bivouacked in action.

23rd Sept. Moved Battery to new position, about 200x more right. Firing all day. The telephone wire constantly cut, but repaired by telephonists under heavy fire, especially B.S.M. Walby and Cpl. Hines. Br. Traynor killed. Bivouacked in action.

1914

24 Sept. Usual fire on enemy's position. Drew heavy fire on Battery and Observing station. Bivouacked in action.

25th Sept. Usual fire on enemy's positions. Major NEWCOME slightly wounded in left hand by shrapnel bullet, and Capt. CROZIER took over Observing station. Lt. HUGGINS went up to our trenches opposite CHIVY and knocked out a German gun, communicating orders by chain of orderlies. German aeroplane over again, and we received much attention from "Black Maria". Bivouacked in action.

26th Sept. Capt. CROZIER still in command. Fired on usual targets. A lot of H.E. and shrapnel into the Battery. Lt. HUGGINS up to Camerons' trenches to engage hostile guns again, this time with telephone wire out. Gr. Bate, killed. Gr. Archibald, Gr. Diehl, Gr. Rouse, wounded.

27th Sept. Major NEWCOME back to duty. Tried a new Observing station on hill N. of BOURG. Fired at TILLEUL DE COURTECON. Decided to return to old Observing station on TILLEUL. Gr. Coleman wounded. Bivouacked in action. Not so much shell fire, but heavy rifle fire at 8 p.m. Turned out the gunners with rifles, but nothing happened.

1914.

28th Sept. Lt. CALDWELL and Lt. HUGGINS went out to trenches of 60th Rifles to locate hostile guns and trenches, and fired on them. Rest of Battery on usual targets. Laid out lines for night firing. Bivouacked in action.

29th Sept. Usual fire on enemy's position. Lt. CALDWELL out to 60th trenches, and Lt. MILLS to Rifle Point. Got on to hostile Battery S.W. of BRAYE. Both succeeded in stopping fire of enemy's batteries. Bivouacked in action.

30th Sept. Same as usual. Lt. CALDWELL and Lt. MILLS out to same observing stations. Located hostile observing station on LA CREUTE spur. Bivouacked in action.

2nd Division
44th Bde. R.F.A.

W A R   D I A R Y

44th (How.) BATTERY R.F.A.

October

1914.

1st Oct. Same as usual. Enemy quiet till 2.30 p.m. when he began shelling us. Lt. HUGGINS to observing station on our right, Lt KNYVETT to Rifle Point. He blew up one of enemy's guns on LA CREUTE Spur. Dr Bennett, Dr Holt, Dr Grant, wounded. 10 horses killed, 9 wounded. Bivouacked in action.

2nd Oct. Same as usual. Battery and Observing station heavily shelled. Bivouacked in action. Moved horse-lines to COURTONNE.

3rd Oct. Same as usual. Lt. HUGGINS Observing from Queen's trenches, Lt KNYVETT from Rifle Point. Bivouacked in action.

4th Oct. Rather quieter than usual. Combined bombardment of hostile position at 4.30 p.m. and 5.15 p.m. Bivouacked in action.

5th Oct. Engaged LA CREUTE battery under direction of an Officer and private of the King's, who had located it when on patrol. Battery was heavily shelled about 6 p.m. Bivouacked in action.

6th Oct. Heavy shelling from 2 p.m. till 4 p.m. Gr Westhead, Tpt. Long, wounded. Dr Martin to hospital. Bivouacked in action.

7th Oct. Usual shelling 6 a.m. to 7 a.m. and 11 a.m. Usual targets. Bivouacked in action.

8th Oct. Lt. HUGGINS to Rifle Point. Quiet day. Bivouacked in action.

9th Oct. Usual targets. At request of Queen's, shelled LES PARADIS at 5.30 p.m. and turned Germans out of the wood. Bivouacked in action.

10th Oct. Same as usual. Bivouacked in action.

1914   11

11th Oct.   Same as usual. Lt CALDWELL to observing
            station at Rifle Point. Quiet day. Bivouacked in action.
            Dr Gorman to hospital.

12th Oct.

12th Oct.   Quiet day. Lt HUGGINS to Rifle Point. Sgt Pidgeon
            posted from 56th Battery. Bivouacked in action.

13th Oct.   Fairly quiet day. Relieved at dusk by battery
            from 1st Division. Ran guns back to VERNEUIL
            by hand, limbered up in the village, and left
            at 8 p.m., having been 30 days in action between
            VERNEUIL and MOUSSY without a relief.
            Marched to BOURG, DHUIZEL, COURCELLES
            and billeted at LIME, 11.30 p.m.

14th Oct.   Marched at 9 a.m. to QUINCY, JOUAIGNES,
            BRANGES, BEUGNEUX, OULCHY-LA-VILLE,
            ROZET, NEUILLY. Entrained there and left
            at 6.50 p.m.

15th Oct.   Train route via AMIENS, ÉTAPLES, BOULOGNE
            CALAIS, ST OMER, HAARZEBRUCK to CASSEL.
            10.30 p.m. Detrained there and billeted.

16th Oct.   Marched at 9 a.m. EBLINGHEM, LYNDE,
            BLARINGHEM. 11.30 a.m. Billeted there. Dr George Joshua
                                                    Dr Marsham Joshua

17th Oct.   Marched at 7.30 a.m. HAARZEBRUCK, EECKE.
            Billeted at EECKE. Lt Whitehouse left on getting
                                                    commission.

(12)

18th Oct. Remained at EECKE. O. Woodward to hospital.

19th Oct. Remained at EECKE. G. Gardner, O. Cochrane, D. Faulk to hospital

20th Oct. Marched 5.30. a.m. via BOESCHEPPE - RENINGHELS, VLAMERTINGE to YPRES. Billeted at ST JEAN at 6 p.m. Cpl. Couchman to 60th Battery.

21st Oct. Marched 5.30 a.m. Attached to 5th Inf. Bde. Came into action ½ mile N. of ST JULIEN at 9.15 a.m. Observing station in a windmill. Enemy attacked from POELCAPELLE. We checked all the attacks with gun fire and enemy never got within rifle fire. D. Duffy and Cpl Pearson killed, G. Nicholson missing. Bivouacked in action.

22nd Oct. Engaged German Battery near POELCAPPELLE. Windmill and 2 cottages burnt. Observed from another cottage. Heavy attacks by Germans from POELCAPPELLE, but checked by gun fire. Located German Battery E. of POELCAPPELLE and stopped it firing. G. Jackson, D. Auchwity, wounded. Bivouacked in action.

23rd Oct. Located German howitzers S of POELCAPPELLE and stopped them firing. Heavy infantry attack from direction of PASSCHENDAEL. We turned on to it with lyddite and 15th Battery with shrapnel.

(13)

1914. Marked down a German field gun and wagon behind a farm and put 3 rounds of Lyddite there. One wagon with one horse in team seen going back. Gun not seen again. Sergt. Pittaway wounded. Bivouacked in action.

24th Oct. Rifle fire on Battery all the morning. Corpl. Patterson killed. 2nd Division moved S. during the night, but we remained to support the French. Moved at 2.30 p.m. to FREZENBERG and came into action 1 mile S.W. of ZONNEBEKE at 4 p.m. Fired by Compass at REUTEL at 6 p.m. Bivouacked in action.

25th Oct. Established observing station ½ mile S.W. of ZONNEBEKE. Fired at BECELAERE. Lt. HUGGINS went up to Bde. firing line and located a German battery, which we shelled. It then withdrew. Advanced at 5 p.m. into position on N. edge of POLYGON wood, ½ mile S. of ZONNEBEKE. Bivouacked in action.

26th Oct. Established observing station in a cottage just W. of PASSCHENDAEL – BECELAERE road. Major NEWCOME slightly wounded, Capt. CROZIER took over observing station. Engaged enemy's trenches, and knocked out 2 machine-guns. Bmr. Neale wounded while repairing telephone wire. Bivouacked in action. Gr. Furzman to hospital.

1914.

27th Oct. Capt. CROZIER to front observing station and engaged enemy's trenches in front of 6th Inf. Bde. Lt. HUGGINS went to 4th Guards Bde. trenches and then on to a cottage between their trenches and the Germans, taking telephone with him. He knocked out a machine gun and put a lot of lyddite into their trenches. Br Curry wounded. Bivouacked in action.

28th Oct. Capt CROZIER to observing station with 6th Inf. Bde. Lt. HUGGINS to observing station in the cottage in front of 4th Guards Brigade. Shelled enemy's trenches. Bivouacked in action.

29th Oct. Same as before. ~~[struck out]~~ Bivouacked in action. G. Curry to R.A. 2nd Divn. Lt. Williams from R.A. 2nd Divn.

30th Oct. Several attacks made on 6th Inf. Bde. and on 4th Guards Bde., which we helped to repel.

31st Oct. Heavy shelling all day on both sides. We shot a good deal by map and compass. CROZIER promoted to Major, KNYVETT to Capt., both to date 1st Oct., but to remain for duty with the Battery. Shelled trenches in front of 6th Inf. Bde. and 4th Guards Bde. Bivouacked in action. Farr-Sergt Steele to hospital.

2nd Division
44th Bde. R.F.A.

W A R   D I A R Y

44th (How.) BATTERY / R.F.A.

November

1914.

15

1914

1st Novr.   Shelled trenches in front of 6th Inf. Bde. and 4th Guards Bde. Fired at hostile batteries by map and compass. "Black Maria" into our wagon line. Saddr. Sergt. Cremer, Dr. Pittiers, Sr. Rudge, Dr. Woodey, killed. Cpl. Jeffs, Dr. Calder, Dr. Crossley, Dr. Kaye, Br. Diehl, wounded. 5 horses killed, 4 wounded. Bivouacked in action.

2nd Novr.   Heavy firing all day. Supported an attack by the French to S. of us. Fired at trenches in front of 4th Guards Bde. at 11 p.m. Bivouacked in action. Dr. Davies to hospital.

3rd Novr.   Fairly quiet day. Major NEWCOME back to duty. Bivouacked in action.

4th Novr.   Shooting by map and compass at hostile batteries. Dr. Bowyer wounded. Gr. Howell to hospital. Bivouacked in action.

5th Novr.   Capt. Knyvett established another observing station in the King's trenches to support 5th Inf. Bde. in direction of GHELUVELT. We now have 3 guns supporting 6th Inf. Bde. on PASSCHENDAEL — BECELAERE road, with observing station on the ridge S. of ZONNEBEKE; one gun supporting 4th Guards Bde. with observing stn. in their trenches — one gun supporting 5th Inf. Bde. with observing stn. in their trenches. Bivouacked in action.

/14

6th Novr: Shooting at various targets all day, sometimes in front of our infantry, and also at guns by map and compass. Lieut. KNYVETT located hostile battery opposite the King's trenches. Bivouacked in action.

7th Novr: Same as usual. Assisted in repelling a sharp attack on the Connaught Rangers about 4.30 p.m. Bivouacked in action.

8th Novr: Heavy attack on our right opposite 5th Inf. Bde. and 1st Division from 12 noon till 8 p.m. Lt. KNYVETT directed fire on German attack from observing station in the King's trenches. Bivouacked in action.

9th Novr: Fired on hostile batteries by map. Also on trenches in front of 4th Guards Bde. and 5th Inf. Bde. Also at 6 p.m. and 8 p.m. and in front of H.L.I. at 11 p.m. Bivouacked in action.

10th Novr: Heavy firing all day and night on our right and left, not much in front. Capt. LYON arrived, attached to 47th Battery. Gr. Toh, killed. Gr. Williams, wounded. Fired on batteries and trenches. Bivouacked in action.

(17)

1914

11th Novr. Heavy attacks all day on our right in direction of WELDHOEK. Assisted in repelling these attacks on 1st Division by fire directed by Lt. KNYVETT from the King's trenches. Went on till 6 p.m. when things quieted down. Bivouacked in action. Quiet night. Reinforcements arrived for us, 1 Br., 1 Wt., 1 shoeing-smith.

12th Novr. Turned out at 4 a.m. to support counter-attack by 1st Brigade, but nothing happened. French driven in on our left, so fired E. of ZONNEBEKE. Considerable excitement all day. Bivouacked in action. Gr. Popham, wounded. Supported French counter-attack.

13th Novr. Fired in direction of WESTHOEK. Went with Capt. Nevill to reconnoitre positions further back. Firing all the afternoon in front of trenches of King's and South Staffords to drive back German attacks. Bivouacked in action. Quiet night.

14th Novr. Quiet day on the whole, but some firing at night. Fired on trenches in front of Berks. Bivouacked in action.

15th Novr. Quiet day. Relieved by the French and left position at 4.30 p.m., marched through YPRES and billeted 4 miles W. of YPRES at 12 m.n.

1914

16th Novr: Marched at 9 a.m. Arrived at LOCRE at 4 p.m. and went into billets.

17th Novr: Remained at LOCRE.

18th Novr: Marched at 5 a.m. through BAILEUL and METEREN. Arrived FLÈTRE 8. a.m. and went into billets.

19th to 30th Novr:
Rested at FLÈTRE and re-fitted.
Started laying and signalling classes to replace casualties.
Officers in turn on leave to ENGLAND.
B.S.M. Walby and Q.M.S. Thompson also in turn to ENGLAND.

FLÈTRE
30th Novr 1914.

H W Newcome
Major R.F.A.
Commdg 47th Battery. R.F.A.

2ND DIVISION
44TH BDE R.F.A.

60TH BATTERY R.F.A.

AUG - NOV 1914

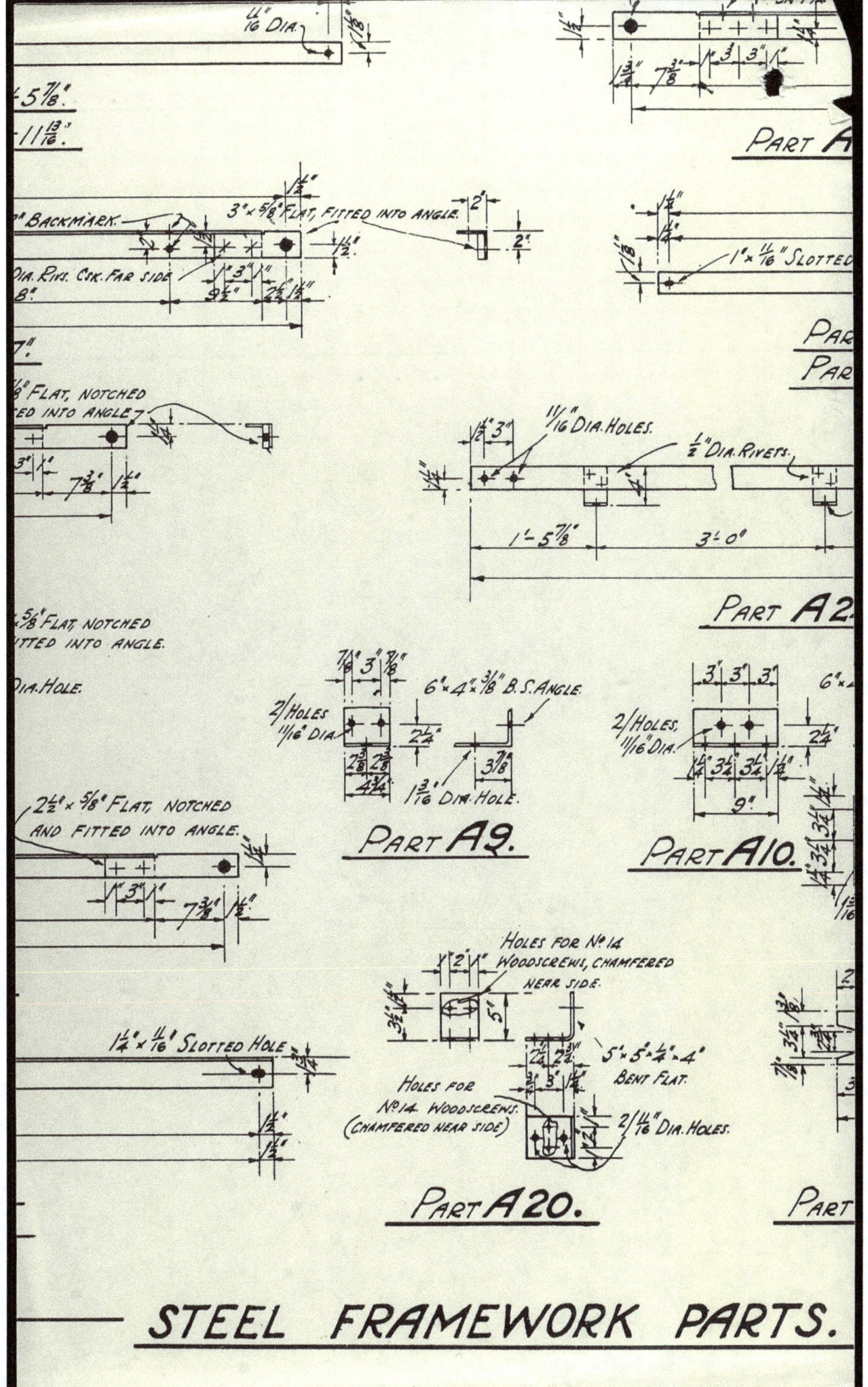

STEEL FRAMEWORK PARTS.

2nd Division

WAR DIARY

60th BATTERY R.F.A.

August

1914

60th Battery R.F.A.
War Diary.

August 1914

4th. Orders received to mobilise at Brighton

13th. Mobilisation completed.

18th. Left Brighton at 7am. for Southampton and embarked on S.S. Welchman for BOULOGNE. Sailed at 10 pm.

19th. Disembarked at BOULOGNE and went into rest camp about 3 miles out.

20th. Entrained at night at BOULOGNE

21st. Arrived at BUSIGNY and marched to WASSIGNY. Went in to bivouac.

22nd. Brigade concentrated and marched to LEVAL. Went into bivouac.

23rd. Moved at 3am. Crossed the BELGIAN frontier near MALPLAQUET and went into bivouac at BLARIGNY. 2.30pm ordered to move, went on to HARVENG and came into action, remaining in action without firing a shot until 9pm when orders to retire were received. Marched until about 1am. and then bivouacked without unhooking by side of road.

24th 3 a.m. reconnoitred for position and came into action. Fired a few rounds of lyddite at ridge above HARVENG. Retirement continued during day - came into action again thrice. Went into bivouac at LA LONGUEVILLE.

25th Retired to LANDRECIES and went into bivouac. Germans made a hot attack on 2nd Coldstream Guards and Lt. Willcocks was sent with his section to assist. The section was very hotly engaged, and destroyed a German gun which was doing great damage. There were no casualties in the section. The bivouac came under shell fire but there were no casualties in the battery.

26th Moved off at 2 a.m. came into action on heights above LANDRECIES but retired again to ETREUX where brigade came into action. 60th Battery on right with observing station on stack of wheat, guns dug in. Slept by guns that night - very wet.

27th Retired to RIREMONT - dug in again but were not attacked.

28th Retired to SERVAIS and went in to bivouac.

29th Battery ordered out about midday attached to 34th Bde to cover retirement of cavalry; guns dug in in very good position but no signs of enemy were seen and at nightfall battery rejoined brigade to find division was to move very early.

30th Retired towards TERNY and bivouacked at LE BANC DE PIERRE.

31st retired and bivouacked at POMMIERS.

2nd Division

WAR DIARY

36th BATTERY R. F. A.

September

1914

SEPTEMBER 1914.

1/ Retired and came into action W. of the village of CUVERGNON - dug in and remained in action for the night.

2/ 2.30am continued the retirement and bivouacked close to MEAUX by the canal.

3/ retired to 2 mile S. of PIERRE LEVEE - just getting into bivouac when ordered to take up a position covering the road from ST QUENTIN. Dug in in infantry outpost lines with Kings Regt. 2nd Coldstream Guards on our right. Night passed without incident.

4/ moved at daybreak retired to MOUROUX and bivouacked.

5/ retired to CHAIMES and bivouacked.

6/ About 7am. commenced to advance. Came into action behind 4th Guards Brigade near PEZACHES, battery dug in just outside wall of Ch. de la FORTELLE. Battery came under shrapnel fire when coming into action, but only casualty was one horse wounded. Fired a few rounds searching for german battery, and fired lyddite into village. Bivouacked for night in grounds of chateau.

7/ At 7am. continued to advance, came in to action near CILLY(?). Very steep pull up - had to use double teams. Did not fire much, but saw a good deal of fighting on left where a lot of prisoners were captured. Bivouacked near ST SIMEON.

8/ Advanced & came into action near LA TRETOIRE against the german rearguard. Had a perfect cavalry target here - cavalry retiring along a road just ranged on. Subsequently searched woods with lyddite whilst a

September, (cont⁰).

section of 18 pr. fired shrapnel. Eventually crossed PETIT MORIN and came into action just S of BOITRON, where there was some sharp fighting with the rearguard. Bivouacked close to position in action.

9ᵗʰ/ 5 am continued to advance & bivouacked for night at VILLIERS-sur-MARNE.

10ᵗʰ/ Advanced to near MONNES where we bivouacked.

11ᵗʰ/ Advanced to OULCHY-le-CHATEAU and bivouacked.

12ᵗʰ/ Advanced to COURCELLES & bivouacked.

13ᵗʰ/ Advanced to DHUIZEL & bivouacked.

14ᵗʰ/ Advanced via BOURG. Came under fire when column was just across canal. Came into action 3/4 mile S of VERNEUIL and later in day moved forward through village of VERNEUIL to position N.W. of village. Battery all day in at bottom of hill and observing station established near pt. 158 TILLEUL. Under very heavy shell fire that afternoon. Right section under Lt. Knight detached and placed direct under orders of B. Gen. Percaval. The section went into action almost in the infantry firing line, the guns remaining there during the whole battle of Aisne - personnel being relieved at intervals.

15ᵗʰ/ Very wet. Continued digging in both battery and observing station. Under very heavy shell fire which continued at intervals all day. Captain Furse wounded.

16ᵗʰ/ Capt. Furse died. He was buried in the grounds of the Chateau at VERNEUIL. Again heavily shelled. A combined shelling of enemy's position from 5 to 5.30 pm

September (continued)

17/ Very wet - shelled as usual.

18/ Shelled as usual all day. Moved at dusk to SOUPIR & placed under orders of O.C. 36th Bde. R.F.A. Bivouacked alongside road without unharnessing. Very heavy rain in night.

19/ At daybreak took up position just above CHAVONNE with observation station in Guards trenches. Enemy attacked in afternoon and offered a poor target. With-drawn at dusk to SOUPIR and again bivouacked by side of road without unharnessing.

20/ At daybreak back to former position, but observed from machine gun pit of 2nd Coldstream Guards. Withdrawn during afternoon and occupied new position close to SOUPIR.

21st/ A new observing station established, & battery told off to work with the infantry brigade holding line from the canal by MOUSSY to RIFLE POINT.

The battery remained in this position until end of month, the only alteration being that a fresh observing station further forward was established and telephone communication was established with RIFLE POINT, which increased the area over which fire could be brought to bear.

6

Casualties during September.

Killed   Captain G. A. Furse.   (died of wounds).
          No. 68287 Driver F. Butcher.
          No. 70659 Gunner H. Gascoigne
          60326   "   W. Hope   (died of wounds).

Wounded   No. 27253 Corpl. S. H. Garbutt.
          46296 Driver C. Fry.
          70113 Bmbr. S. Stuart
          27606 St. Corpl. B. Hemmings.

Sick   Mr. Lillcocks.

2nd Division

WAR DIARY

60th BATTERY R.F.A.

October

1914

October 1914.

1st to 12th. Battery remained in same position. The principal targets engaged being the BEAULNE ridge, FERME de METZ, FERME de BRAYE, guns & trenches in BRAYE spur, and trenches along the COURTECON ridge.

13th. French artillery officers arrived to take over position. The battery was withdrawn and marched at 6.45 pm to QUINCY - arriving there at 11 pm. Bivouacked - wet night.

14th. Marched at 7 am for NEUILLY, where we entrained. Leaving about 3.30 pm - via AMIENS - BOULOGNE - CALAIS

15th. Arrived CASSEL about 6 pm & received orders to march to BLARINGHAM. Subsequently these orders were cancelled & we billeted in CASSEL - finding good accommodation for both officers and men.

16th. Marched to BLARINGHAM. Billetted men in a school and all officers of brigade in large private house. Got plenty of hay for the horses.

17th. Marched via HAZEBROUCK & ST SYLVESTRE to EECKE. Arrived about 1.00 pm. Men in a school, officers in an empty cottage.

18th-19th At EECKE, had complete overhaul of equipment.

October 1914 (cont'd)

20th/ Left EECKE at 5:30am and marched to YPRES via GODESWAERSVELDE - BOESCHEPE - RENINGHELST. Long delay getting billets, but men finally billeted in large granary. Officers in empty private house.

21st/ Left YPRES at 5:30am and marched through ST JEAN - WIELTJE. Battery placed under orders of O.C. XIVth Bde R.F.A. in support of 4th Guards Brigade. Came into action on South side of road just East of the HAANEBEECK. Centre section under Lt. Stillman was detached and sent to ST JULIEN. Observed from haystack by point 27 N.W. of ZONNEBEKE. Targets enemy's infantry on the slopes NE of the HAANEBEECK. Shelled and set on fire two farms occupied by them, but observation very difficult & battery was shortly moved forward about ½ mile & came into action on N side of road. Observing station first at a farm & finally in the trenches of the Coldstream Guards along the N edge of the LANGEMARCK - ZON-NEBEKE road. Principal targets searching the valley of the HAANEBEECK and shelling some houses N of ZONNEBEKE in support of the QUEENS. Enemy retiring from these & subsequently massing for a counter-attack offered a good target. At 7.20pm battery was withdrawn and returned to ST JEAN & billeted.

22nd. In morning advanced to FREZENBERG, coming into action behind high ground W of mainroad with observing

October (cont.)

station behind haystack on top of hill. After a short time moved across railway and came into action about 500 yards S. of the level crossing, close to a farm. Observing station in a house. Acted in support of 22nd Bn. 7th Divn. Principal targets:- Guns behind Xroads on PASSCHENDAELE-BECELAERE road, and infantry in trenches & houses along this road. At 7pm returned to same billets at ST JEAN.

23rd/ Returned to same position leaving billets at 4 am. and remained in action there until 3.30 pm. when battery was ordered to return to position it occupied on 21st to support a French attack on PASSCHENDAELE. Observing station in trenches as before. Returned at night to billets at ST JEAN.

24th/ Started at 5am returned to position occupied previous afternoon, but later in day returned to the FREZEN-BERG railway position. Billeted that night in the farm, with detachments in their gun pits, drivers & spare gunners sleeping in barns.

25th/ In same position but about midday advanced to a position close to 6th Infantry Brigade HQrs. Did not fire from this position but about 4pm moved forward to a point about ¼ mile N.E. of 2nd T in EKSTERNEST 6 clay in. The position selected was in a grass field alongside a track with a fir wood some 50ª in front. Guns were concealed by cutting down firs and planting them so as to form a strip of wood along the track.

October (cont'd).

25th/ Wagon line in a wood about 300ᵡ in rear. Officers billeted in a semi-ruined house quite close to guns. All men in pits & detachments at their guns. The night was very stormy & wet but passed without incident.

26th/ In same position. Established a forward observing station in a house just behind KING'S firing line. 47th Battery also used this house and accordingly the two batteries did some combined shooting on German trenches, 47th firing Lyddite and 60th Shrapnel as the Germans showed out of trenches. Fire appeared to be effective. Later in day 47th moved to another house whence a better view of front & left was obtained. 60th then took over a zone further towards REUTEL. Gun position improved & all pits deepened during day.

27th/ In same position.

28th/ In same position. Ran't out with telephone to S. STAFFORDS trenches but this entailed 2 miles of wire and communication was hopeless, so returned to former observing station. Large scale map received this day, and shooting by map & compass began.

29th/ In same position. Enemy attacked all along the line at 5 am.

30th & 31st/ Still in same position. Wagon line shifted and horses scattered as far as possible so as to minimise casualties.

General remarks on this position.

During the whole time that the battery occupied the position it was never accurately located by the enemy's artillery. It was subjected to a good deal of searching fire, was enfiladed from the right and taken almost in reverse from the left & by a gun firing armour piercing shell. On two occasions wagon bodies were knocked over. The wagon line suffered badly on one occasion — R.S.M. S. and eight men being wounded and 30 horses either killed outright or so badly wounded that they had to be destroyed. The detachments stood to their guns most nights and night firing took place frequently. Targets were engaged over an arc of 180°. After the first few days No 1 gun was turned at right angles to the line of fire of battery and subsequently No 2 gun was run out into a new pit also to fire in same direction. Night attacks were frequent especially at first, and when attacks were made on our immediate front or on either flank the battery came under heavy rifle fire. There were several casualties amongst the men from rifle bullets & the horses suffered considerably. After first few days most of the firing was done by map assisted in some cases by forward observing officers, but the targets were spread over such a wide area and country was so close that much of the fire was of necessity unobserved.

October 1914.

Lieut. H. F. Willascher awarded the Croix de Chevalier
Major A. J. A. Mackay M.Kay
Lieut. J. P. Knight } mentioned in dispatches.

Captain G. R. Miller & Lieut. C. A. Ziegler joined the battery.

1 Cpl. 5 gunners and 8 drivers joined.
42 remounts received.

Casualties
Killed   No 56062   Bm. N. Hurle
          58130   gr. P. Hamilton

Wounded
          No 26186   gr. Tarling
          29921   Sgt. F. Pidcock
          26021   gr. H. Byfield

Sergts. G. Whitlam & F. Thomas commissioned.

2nd Division

WAR DIARY

60th BATTERY R.F.A.

November

1914

November 1914.

1st & 2nd. In same position – nothing of note.

3rd Lt Knight succeeded in establishing a forward observing station in firing line of the STAFFORDS, and did useful work knocking down houses occupied by enemy, firing on trenches etc. until the battalion finally withdrew from their forward position.

4th to 10th In same position – no special incidents.

11th Heavy attack by the enemy along REUTELBECK on left of 1st Division. Battery heavily engaged all day fired 366 rounds of which 182 were fired by No 1 gun. At one time each gun was engaging a different target – distributed over an arc of 175° – longest range 2400 shortest 1050.

12th Another heavy attack on our left in direction of [struck through] battery again heavily engaged all day. BSM Dryden wounded.

13th Lieut Knight withdrawn from forward observing station as battalion had retired from forward position during night. Wagon line heavily shelled.

14th-17th No special notes. The general remarks made in October apply to whole period from 1st to 17th.

18th Battery withdrew at 3.30 am and marched via YPRES VLAMERTINGHE – POPERINGHE to FLETRE. great difficulty in getting out of the position at all owing

November 1914

to mud, and roads were very bad all the way. Arrived at billets about 4 pm. Very crowded.

19th/ Billets improved by taking over more houses and billeting very comfortable. Started overhaul. Major Mackey and Lt. Knight left in evening proceeding to England on leave.

20th-25th In same billets continue overhaul of all equipment and inspecting class. Major Mackey & Lt. Knight return from leave on morning of 25th. Major Miller, Lts. Ziegler & Stillman leave that evening. 17 horses received & 3 destroyed & 11 to Mobile Section. Capt. Kettle received commission dated 17th.

26th In same billets.

27th " " "   20 horses received.

28th In same billets. one horse destroyed.

29th " " " one horse destroyed (broken leg) 2 horses received to complete establishment. Church parade service held by Rev. H. Henming Co.

30th In same billets. 3 horses evacuated.

November 1914.

Sergt. Kiteley given commission

The following joined the battery:-
    Remounts 23
    1 Bombardier, 1 Fitter and 2 Drivers

Casualties

Killed   No 2597. Gr Holden

Wounded   No 640 B.S.M. C. Dryden
          20324   Sr Hancock W.
          21790   Bam S Corbell H.
          58417   Gr Rankin J.
          56488   Gr Steele E.
          76975   Gr Wollerton W.
          54157   Gr Shorey J.
          62742   Dr Goldsmith A.
          24835   Dr Seager J.
          61079   Dr Moran J.

Sick   3 men.

2ND DIVISION
ROYAL ARTILLERY

H.Q. 44TH BRIGADE R.F.A.
56TH BATTY R.F.A.

1915 JAN — 1915 DEC

2nd Divisional Artillery.
44th Brigade R.F.A.

56th BATTERY R.F.A.

FEBRUARY 1915

War diary of 56th (How) Battery R.F.A.

Hour date & place	Summary of events and information	Remarks references & appendices
1-2-15 Croix Barbee	No firing	
2-2-15 Croix Barbee	Shelled hostile trenches E & S.E. of Northern end of Rue-de-Bois.	
3-2-15 Croix Barbee	No firing.	
4-2-15 Croix Barbee	No firing.	
5-2-15 Croix Barbee	Shelled house used as an observing post W. of Bois-Du-Biez.	
6-2-15 Richebourg St Vast	Battery marched at 1 pm & occupied position 1200 yards S. by W. of Richebourg-St-Vast joining the Meerut Division.	M

War diary of 56th (How) Battery R.F.A. Contd:

Hour date place	Summary of events & information	Remarks & Reference to appendices
7-2-15 Richebourg St Vast	Established & corrected line of fire. Registered trenches.	
8-2-15 Richebourg-St Vast	Shelled house used for artillery observation. Registration continued.	
9-2-15	Shelled his horses reported as Hanoverian stations for artillery. Maj. E. Eton 8th Hunter (Hr) Roe R.F.A. joined for a fortnight - attached under instruction. B.N.C.O's left the Battery & posting to 3rd C Reserve Brigade Christchurch.	
10-2-15 Richebourg St Vast	Registration continued.	

67

War Diary of 58th (How) Battery R.F.A. (continued)

Date Place hour	Summary of events + information	Remarks
11-2-15. Richebourg St Vast	Shelled observing Station at Distillery + also Redoubt in trenches	
12-2-15. Richebourg St Vast	Shelled Hearing Station Battery stopped firing	
13-2-15. Richebourg St Vast	Very quiet, no movement observed.	
14-2-15. Richebourg St Vast	Shelled Distillery when movement observed. Whistle Battery opening fire. Repulsed trenches round Cathedral N'and 17 Rue-du-Bois. Lahore Div: took over line from Meerut Division	

War Diary of 5th Battn. Batter P.P.C.L.I.

Summary of events + information

Date Place hour	
15-2-15 Richebourg St Vast	Registered trenches about the Rd. ORCHARD (LA-QUINQUE-RUE.)
16-2-15 RICHEBOURG ST VAST	Shelled hutting station at dusk enemies infantry observed working on entanglements in front of his trenches.
17-2-15 RICHEBOURG ST VAST	During morning enemy continued work on his entanglements. No firing
18-2-15 RICHEBOURG ST VAST	No firing Received preliminary orders to regain 1st Corps on relief 9am 19R inst by 4th R Bty. 6th Bty. later attached is evening of 19R on relief by 30R Bty.

69.

19-2-15 LES-HARISOIRS	On relief by 30th Battery R.F.A. marched at 3 pm via LOCON to LES-HARISOIRS + went into billets. The Battery came under orders again of O.C. 44th Brigade and G.O.C. R.A. 2nd Divn.
20-2-15 to 26-2-15 LES-HARISOIRS	} Routine work in billets
27-2-15 CAMBRIN	Marched at 8-15 am via BETHUNE to CAMBRIN + relieved the 60th Battery in action 150 yards N.E. of Village. Fired 30 Rds Registering
28-2-15 CAMBRIN	Casualties during month Ordinary at mnm L/Hble - 1 Gr 4 Dr = 5.

Mann
Major R.F.A.
Commanding 56th Battery R.F.A.

44th Brigade R.F.A.
2nd Divisional Artillery.

56th BATTERY R. F. A.

APRIL 1915

War Diary of the 2nd Dn R.W.

Hour, Date & Place		Summary of Events & Information	Remarks & references to Appendices
1-4-15	CAMBRIN	No firing	
2-4-15	CAMBRIN	No firing	
3-4-15	CAMBRIN	Fired at enemy trenches in connection with explosion of mine viz 8.30 a.m. and from 8 – 10.15 p.m.	
4-4-15	CAMBRIN	No firing	
5-4-15	CAMBRIN	No firing	
6-4-15	CAMBRIN	No firing	
7-4-15	CAMBRIN	No firing	

War Diary of 1st 53rd Bty R.F.A.

Hour, date & Place	Summary of Events & Information	Remarks Reference to Appendices
8-4-15 CAMBRIN	Shelled enemy gun on CANAL BANK. 2.30pm	
9-4-15 CAMBRIN	No firing	
10-4-15 CAMBRIN	11.45a.m. Shelled enemy brickstacks and Each support. 6.p.m. Shelled enemy gun on canal bank.	
11-4-15 CAMBRIN	12.30.p.m Shelled enemy brickstacks and trenches.	
12-4-15 CAMBRIN	12.30a.m & 3p.m. Shelled enemy brickstacks and support trenches.	
13-4-15 CAMBRIN	No firing.	

182

War Diary of the 35th Bty R.F.A.

Hour, date & Place.	Summary of Events & Information.	Remarks & References to Appendices
14-4-15 CAMBRIN	No firing.	
15-4-15 CAMBRIN	No firing.	
16-4-15 CAMBRIN	No firing.	
17-4-15 CAMBRIN	Fired 8 rounds (at 10.45 a.m) at trench guns behind redoubt. Fired another 4 rounds (5 p.m.)	
18-4-15 CAMBRIN	Fired 11 rounds registering at 3.45 p.m.	
19-4-15 CAMBRIN	3 p.m. Fired 10 rounds on MINENWERFER which ceased firing. 3.45 p.m. Fired 6 rounds registering on Fort just N. of canal.	

War Diary of the 368th By. R.F.A.

Hour, date. & Place.	Summary of Events & information.	Remarks & References to appendices.
20-4-15 CAMBRIN 2 p.m.	Fired 3 registering rounds on trench N. of CANAL	
21-4-15 CAMBRIN	No firing.	
22-4-15 CAMBRIN 2.15 p.m.	Fired 10 lyddite at trench of enemy mine in front of trench in BRICKSTACKS 8.10 p.m. & 9.30 p.m. Fired again as above. 2 rounds each time. 8.10 p.m. Fired 2 rounds at MINENWERFER near LA BASSEE Road which ceased firing	
23-4-15 CAMBRIN 1.15 p.m.	Fired 8 Lyddite on MINENWERFER in enemy trench near LABASSEE ROAD. MINENWERFER ceased firing 8.35 p.m. Fired 3 rounds on same.	182

39

War Diary of the 58th Bde. R.F.A.

Date	Place	Summary of events & information	Remarks & References to Appendices
24-4-15	CAMBRIN	10.15 p.m. Fired 3 rounds on MINENWERFER	
25-4-15	CAMBRIN	10.46 p.m. Fired 4 rounds on MINENWERFER	
26-4-15	CAMBRIN	1 a.m. Fired 3 rounds on MINENWERFER. 12.20 p.m. Fired 2 rounds on same. 4.5 p.m. Fired 4 rounds on mine 4 or enemy work adjoining	
27-4-15	CAMBRIN	10.30 a.m. Fired on enemy cup by the forward brickstack (2 rounds). 6.31 p.m. Fired on mouth of mine and enemy communications trench in (13 rounds)	

Hrs & dt & Place	War Diary of Field 38th Bg. R.F.A. Summary of Events and Information	Remarks & References to Appendices
27-4-15 CAMBRIN (continued)	5.45 p.m. Fired on MINENWERFER (3 rounds) 9.47 p.m. Fired on MINENWERFER (2 rounds) 11.45 p.m. Fired on MINENWERFER (2 rounds)	
28-4-15 CAMBRIN	9.53 a.m. Fired on MINENWERFER (3 rounds) 12.15 p.m. Fired on MINENWERFER (2 rounds) 12.35 p.m. Fired on MINENWERFER behind brickstack C. (1 round) 6.55 p.m. Fired at enemy field battery located at SW corner of RAILWAY TRIANGLE (8 rounds)	

WAR DIARY of 56TH BATTERY, R.F.A.

HOUR DATE & PLACE.	SUMMARY OF EVENTS & INFORMATION	REMARKS & REFERENCES TO APPENDICES.
29·4·15 CAMBRIN.	10 A.M. Fired Salvo (3 rounds) on Field Battery firing from behind S. corner of RAILWAY TRIANGLE 1·45 P.M. Fired 4 rounds on MINENWERFER N. of LA BASSEE ROAD. 10·55 P.M. Fired 2 rounds on MINENWERFER.	
30·4·15. CAMBRIN.	4·45 A.M. Fired 2 rounds on same target. 10·18 A.M. Fired 4 rounds on same target. 11·30 A.M. Fired one round on same target. 1 P.M. Fired 8 rounds on Fork on N. CANAL BANK. 2·30 P.M. Fired 10 rounds on junction W.½ 16th Regt. on Crater of mine N. of LA BASSEE ROAD. 3·50 P.M. Fired 2 rounds on same target. 10·15 P.M. Fired 6 rounds on MINENWERFER	

War Diary of the 57th By. 11??

Hour, date & Place	Summary of Events & Information	Remarks & References to Appendices
29-4-15 CAMBRIN	10.a.m. Fired Salvo (shrapnel) on field battery firing from behind S corner of RAILWAY TRIANGLE 1.45pm. Fired 4 rounds on MINENWERFER N of LA BASSEE ROAD 10.55 pm Fired 2 rounds on MINENWERFER	
30.4.15. CAMBRIN	9.45 am Fired 2 rounds on MINENWERFER	

M. Power
Major 9th??
Comg 57th By R.F.A.

30.4.15

44th Brigade. R.F.A.
2nd Divisional Artillery

56th BATTERY R.F.A.

M A Y   1 9 1 5

56th

2

HOUR, DATE, & PLACE.	EVENTS.	REMARKS.
CAMBRIN 1.5.15. 6.15 AM.	Fired 2 rounds on Fort on N.Bank of CANAL.	
8.30 AM.	Fired one round on MINENWERFER N. of LA BASSÉE Rd	
2.5 pm	Fired 6 rounds on New clos round N.E. BRICKSTACK.	
11.35 pm	Fired 2 rounds on Eastern edge of mine crater N. of LA BASSEE Rd.	
CAMBRIN. 2.5.15. 12 noon.	Fired 2 rounds on MINENWERFER.	
12.20 pm	Fired 2 rounds on MINENWERFER near above.	
CAMBRIN. 3.5.15.	No firing.	
CAMBRIN. 4.5.15. 10.00 am	Fired 25 rounds at enemy's mineshaft W. BRICKFIELDS.	
2.40 pm	Fired 25 rounds on same target.	

2

HOUR, PLACE & DATE	EVENTS	REMARKS
CAMBRIN. 5.5.15.	No firing.	
CAMBRIN. 6.5.15.	No firing.	
CAMBRIN. 7.5.15. 2:30 p.m.	Fired some registering rounds (shrapnel) on North side of CANAL.	
CAMBRIN 8.5.15. 4:30 p.m.	Registered LA BASSÉE ROAD and approaches from AVANY.	
CAMBRIN 9.5.15 5.35 a.m.	Fired on FORT on N bank of CANAL and the REDOUBT on S. bank of CANAL: at same time	

3

HOUR. DATE	EVENTS	REMARKS
10.53 am	An attack by 1st Div. etc further north. Fired on CANTELEUX communication trenches on reported movement of enemy there from VIOLAINES.	
CAMBRIN 10.5.15	No firing.	
CAMBRIN 11.5.15 12 noon	Very slow rate of fire maintained on enemy trenches on CUINCHY front.	
2 p.m.	At request of French Sniped enemy battery	
2.15 p.m.	S. of RAILWAY TRIANGLE. Rennes fire on enemy trenches.	
3.15 p.m.		
CAMBRIN 12.5.15	Fired at irregular intervals on enemy trenches	

DATE & PLACE	EVENTS	REMARKS
	N and NW of RAILWAY TRIANGLE.	
CAMBRIN 13.5.15	Fired at irregular intervals on enemy trenches and trevering stations.	
CAMBRIN 14.5.15 1 a.m.	Fired on enemy trenches and communication lines at intervals during day.	
CAMBRIN 15.5.15	Fired on enemy trenches, observing station and a working party.	
CAMBRIN 16.5.15 10.20 a.m.	Fired intermittently on enemy trenches. Searched for hostile guns reported moving to	

HOUR, DATE & PLACE	EVENTS	REMARKS.
11.15 am	CANTELEUX Engaged enemy batteries on CANAL BANK. Think stopped firing. Fired by night on enemy communications.	
CAMBRIN 17.5.15	Fired intermittently on enemy trenches and on communications at night.	
CAMBRIN 18.5.15 4.15 p.m.	Fired at intervals on enemy trenches. Fired on enemy communications about CANTELEUX and on straining station at moon time. An attack by 2nd Div.	
CAMBRIN 19.5.15. 10.45 am	Fired on enemy trenches. Engaged enemy field batteries active W. of LA BASSÉE.	
11. am	Engaged enemy field bty. batty. NW of LA BASSÉE	

HOUR, DATE & PLACE	EVENTS	REMARKS
CAMBRIN 20·5·15	Fired on enemy targets of interest and after dark on his communications about CANTELEUX.	
CAMBRIN 21·5·15 6.30 – 8.30	Fired at intervals on enemy trenches from 6.30 to 8.30 took part in bombardment of enemy trenches under orders of 1st Corps.	
CAMBRIN 22·5·15	Fired at intervals on enemy trenches LEFT SECTION (2 HOWITZERS) reporting battery from attachment to 60th Bde (1st Division)	
CAMBRIN 23·5·15 1.40, 2.35, 10.9 11.50am and 7pm 3.20 pm	Fires on enemy trenches in retaliation for gunfire. Fired on hostile section acting just S. of LA BASSÉE ROAD.	

HOUR, DATE & PLACE	EVENTS	REMARKS
CAMBRIN 24.5.15 2:30 pm 4:30 pm 10 pm – 10:50 pm midnight 12.22 am	Fired on enemy trench in retaliation. Shelled firing machine S. of LA BASSÉE RD. Fired on enemy trench.	
CAMBRIN 25.5.15 2 pm	Took part in operation 947th (LONDON) DIVN at GIVENCHY. Shelled trench to N and NE during afternoon and returned during night.	
CAMBRIN 26.5.15	Firing continued at intervals in manner trenches.	

HOUR, DATE & PLACE	EVENTS	REMARKS
CAMBRIN 27.5.15. 6:45 pm	Fired on French northern near LA BASSÉE Rd at enemy [infantry].	
CAMBRIN 28.5.15. 10:55 am	Shelled enemy new draft 700 yards S. of LA BASSÉE road	
12:10 pm	Fired on enemy trench W. of RAILWAY TRIANGLE in retaliation	
7:25 pm	Fired on trench northern at request of S. WALES BORDERERS.	
CAMBRIN 29.5.15. 7:55 pm	Fired on enemy trenches W. of RAILWAY TRIANGLE in retaliation.	

H.R. Date & Place	EVENTS	REMARKS.
CAMBRIN 30.5.15 2.30 pm	Hostile mine shafts in craters in front of enemy line.	
4.45 pm	Fired on enemy trenches W. of RAILWAY TRIANGLE in retaliation for his shelling ours.	
5.14 pm	Fired again as above.	
CAMBRIN 31.5.15 6.5 pm	Fired on trenches W. of RAILWAY TRENCHES TRIANGLE in retaliation for enemy bombing.	
6.30 pm	Repeated above.	

Casualties.
8 of C.O's Pr admitted to Hospital
1 Gunner Wounded

Reinforcements
6 Gunners.

[signature] 1/6/15
Major R.A.
Comdg 6th nd Battery R.F.A.

44th Brigade. R.F.A.
2nd Divisional Artillery.

56th BATTERY R.F.A.

JUNE.1915

War Diary of the 56th Bty for the Month of June

Place & Date	Hour	Events	Remarks
CAMBRIN 1.6.15	10.58 am	Fired on trenches in front of CUINCHY in retaliation	
	2.40 pm	Repeated	
	3.5 pm	Repeated	
	6.45 pm	Fired on trenches 400 yds S. of LA BASSÉE RD. in retaliation for bombing. Maj G.R.S. GARDNER. R.F.A. 53rd Divn joined for attachment. 2nd Lieut H.J. Wheatly wounded. 2nd Lt RALLHUSEN to Trenches.	
CAMBRIN 2.6.15	8.15 am	Retaliated on enemy trenches about CANAL and W. of TRAMWAY	
	8.45 am		
	12.35 pm		
	3.45 pm		

Hospital Plan	Events	Remarks
CAMBRIN 3.6.15	No firing 2 drivers wounded.	
CAMBRIN 4.6.15	Nothing	
CAMBRIN 5.6.15 S/D	Fired on enemy trenches near LA BASSÉE ROAD in retaliation.	
CAMBRIN 6.6.15	No firing	
CAMBRIN 7.6.15	No firing. Capt T.N. FRENCH joined in for Fig	

Hours dated Place	Events	Remarks
CAMBRIN 8·6·15 9:10 a.m. CAMBRIN	Fired on Trench W. of TRIANGLE in retn	
9·6·15 1:10 p.m. CAMBRIN	Fired 50 rds wire cutting E. of ORCHARD at GIVENCHY.	
10·6·15 11:37 a.m. 1·0 p.m. CAMBRIN	Fired 40 rds wire cutting NE of ORCHARD at GIVENCHY Fired on enemy trench S. of CANAL in retn for shelling our trenches.	
11·6·15 1:35 p.m. CAMBRIN	Fired on REDOUBT in retn	
12·6·15 8:45 a.m. 9:30 a.m. 11·2 a.m.	Fired on REDOUBT in retn to 4·2 how's shelling our trenches. Repeated above Fired in retn	

From, date/Place	Events	Remarks
CAMBRIN 13.6.15.	Nothing.	
CAMBRIN 14.6.15 9.50am 4.10p 6.8p	Ritchie(?) on enemy trench S. of CANAL. Removed wire cutting. NE. of GIVENCHY. Ritchie(?) on trenches W. of RAILWAY TRIANGLE.	
CAMBRIN 15.6.15 4.0p	Ritchie(?) enemy trenches W. of RAILWAY TRIANGLE. Maj G.R.S. GARDNER 3rd (Welsh) Battn. left for ENGLAND in complete of frame.	
CAMBRIN 16.6.15 10.30am 11.45am 4.0p	Ritchie(?) enemy trenches at N.E. BRICKSTACK. Fire returned onto RAILWAY EMBANKMENT in retaliation. Caused rather enemy REDOUBT and works in CANAL EMBANKMENT Simultaneous with attack in GIVENCHY trench.	

Date and Place		Event	Remarks
CAMBRIN 17.6.15	4.30 pm	Shelled enemy trench and terminals in RAILWAY AREA 1.1	
CAMBRIN 18.6.15	3.30– 4.10 pm	Shelled front enemy trench in REDOUBT in CANAL BANK & line in FORT on N. CANAL BANK in retaliation to bombing	
CAMBRIN 19.6.15		No firing	
CAMBRIN BETHUNE 20.6.15		Received orders 7.30 pm. to withdraw to BETHUNE with 1st Div. Arrived at 9.30 pm.	
BETHUNE 21.6.15		Routine work.	

10

Hour	Date & Place	Events	Remarks
	22.6.15 BETHUNE	Routine work in billets	
	23.6.15 BETHUNE	— ditto —	
	24.6.15 BETHUNE	— ditto —	
	25.6.15 BETHUNE	— ditto —	
	26.6.15 BETHUNE	— ditto —	
	27.6.15 BETHUNE	— ditto —	
	28.6.15 BETHUNE	— ditto —	
	29.6.15 CAMBRIN	marched at 7.45pm and reoccupied trenches vacated 20.6.15	
	30.6.15 CAMBRIN	Nothing.	

T. Sneed J.A.
Capts. O-S.A.

44th Brigade R.F.A.
2nd Divisional Artillery.

56th BATTERY R. F. A.

JULY 1915

War Diary of the 56th Battery R.F.A
commanding of wounded Major Crozier

Hour, date 1915		Events
1.7.15 CAMBRIN	9.35 am	Retaliated on enemy trenches on the RAILWAY EMBANKMENT
	9.50 am	Registered points S.9. BETHUNE – LA BASSEE road – light very bad. No firing.
2.7.15 CAMBRIN		
3.7.15 CAMBRIN	1.5 pm	Continued registration.
4.7.15 CAMBRIN	7.30 am	New vicinity of battery position heavily shelled by 105 mm and 150 mm howitzers with aeroplane observation for 2 hours and at intervals later. Cause – Exposure to observation by details C & B 1/7th Kings Regt billets alongside. C Subre Gun (Rt No 69) knocked out. Maj BB CROZIER slightly wounded (at duty).

Commanding 56th Battery R.F.A.

6

"War Diary of the 50th Battery"

Hour, date & Place	Events
5.7.15. CAMBRIN. 10.25 am	Fired on trench in BRICKFIELDS in retaliation.
6.7.15. CAMBRIN. 7.20 pm	Fired on house in AUCHY from which movement observed.
7.7.15. CAMBRIN. 6.30 pm	Fired on RAILWAY EMBANKMENT W of TRIANGLE where is covered way from barge bridge. New gun (No 47) arrived in place of one destroyed on 4th by enemy's fire.
8.7.15.	No firing.
9.7.15. CAMBRIN. 2.58 pm	Fired on enemy trenches S of CANAL in retaliation.
6.25 pm	
6.40 pm	Fired on dressing station E of AUCHY to stop shelling of CAMBRIN.

1 AUG 1915

COMMANDING 50TH BATTERY R.F.A.

War Diary (contd)

Hour, date and Place		Events
10.7.15. CAMBRIN	3.40 am	Shelled a piper issuing from enemy trench in BRICKFIELDS.
	8.50 am	} Retaliated on enemy trenches.
	9.35 am	
	3.0 pm	
	3.18 pm	
11.7.15. CAMBRIN.	9.35 am	} Retaliated on enemy trenches
	12.0 noon	
	12.16 pm	
	2.15 pm	Fired on enemy working party N of CANAL.
	2.38 pm	
12.7.15 CAMBRIN	10.15 am	} Retaliated on trenches E of CUINCHY.
	1.25 pm	

BATTERY
S.H.
11 AUG. 1915

Commanding 50th Battery

War Diary (contd)
minus appendices

Hour, date & Place		Events
13.7.15. CAMBRIN.	9.15 am 9.50 am	Retaliated on enemy trenches.
14.7.15. CAMBRIN.	9.0 am 10.45 am 11.8 am 1.0 pm 3.45 pm 4.10 pm	Retaliated on enemy trenches.
15.7.15 CAMBRIN		Registered points between BETHUNE — LA BASSEE RD and GIVENCHY from alternative battery position NW of ANNEQUIN.
16.7.15. CAMBRIN.	10.30 am 11.18 am 11.30 am	Retaliated on REDOUBT on CANAL BANK. Fired on trench mortar N of LA BASSEE road. Retaliated on trenches W of RAILWAY TRIANGLE.

War Diary (contd)

Hour, date & Place		Events
16.7.15 CAMBRIN	2.9 pm	Fired again on french mortar
	5.30 pm	Retaliation on FORT on N bank of CANAL.
17.7.15. CAMBRIN.	11.5 am	Stopped working party N of CANAL.
	11.20 am	Fired at french mortar N of LA BASSEE road.
	3.30 pm	Fired on working party N of CANAL
	4.40 pm	
	6.10 pm	
	10.0 pm	Fired on same party in conjunction with 16a.
	11.30 pm	and 50th Bty and infantry N and S of CANAL.
18.7.15 CAMBRIN	2.13 pm	Fired on working party moving up communication french N of CANAL.
	6.0 pm	Retaliated on trenches W. of RAILWAY TRIANGLE.
	11.65 pm	Fired on communication french N of CANAL.

7 AUG 1915

KL
MAJOR, R.F.A.
COMMANDING 50TH BATTERY R.F.A.

8

War Diary (contd)

Date & Place		Events
19.7.15. CAMBRIN.	10.57 am 11.12 am	Fired on working parties N. of CANAL.
20.7.15. CAMBRIN	12.45 am 1.29 pm 10.10 pm 10.30 pm	Fired on working parties N of CANAL
21.7.15. CAMBRIN.	2.12 pm 4.40 pm	Fired on working parties N of CANAL Retaliated on enemy trenches S of CANAL.
22.7.15. CAMBRIN.	9.37 am 3.55 pm	Retaliated on enemy trenches W of RAILWAY TRIANGLE.

Major,
Commanding 15th Battery, R.F.A.

War Diary (cont.)

Hour, date / Place	Events
23.7.15. 8.40 am CAMBRIN. 11.57 am 12.55 pm	Retaliated on enemy trenches around BRICKSTACKS.
24.7.15 10.5 am CAMBRIN 1.5 pm 5.20 pm 5.40 pm 9.20 pm 9.45 pm	Retaliated on enemy trenches W of RAILWAY TRIANGLE. Retaliated on trenches behind BRICKSTACKS at request of infantry.
25.7.15 9.40 am CAMBRIN. 6.40 pm 7.40 pm 2.10 pm	Retaliated on trenches in BRICKFIELDS. Shelled new work put behind enemy front line N of CANAL.

War Diary (cont).

Hour, date & Place		Events	
26.7.15. CAMBRIN	10.0 am — 10.30 am 7.50 pm	Retaliated on various trenches W of RAILWAY TRIANGLE.	Aug. 1915 Personale
27.7.15. CAMBRIN	10.50 am — 12.20 pm 1.20 pm	Fired on working party N. of CANAL Fired on RAILWAY TRIANGLE in retaliation to shelling of CUINCHY.	work stopped
	4.40 pm	Shelled new work in enemy front line just N of CANAL.	
	5.37 pm	Retaliated on enemy BRICKSTACKS.	
28.7.15. CAMBRIN	11.25 am — 12.35 pm	Fired on working party N of CANAL	work stopped

10

4th Army (contd.)

Time, date & Place		Events
29.7.15. CAMBRIN.	7.55 am 9.15 am 10.30 am 11.40 am 11.50 am 12.44 pm 3.10 pm 4.0 pm 6.55 pm	Fired on various trenches in retaliation to persistent howitzer fire on our own.
30.7.15 CAMBRIN.	9.58 am 10.12 am 4.15 pm 6.50 pm	Fired on various enemy trenches in retaliation.
31.7.15 CAMBRIN.	12.40 pm 2.42 pm	Fired on working party A.16 a 23. Work stopped.

Moore

44th Brigade R.F.A.
2nd Divisional Artillery.

56th BATTERY R.F.A.

AUGUST 1 9 1 5

War Diary of the 56 Battery for the Month of August 1915

Hour, Date and Place	Events	Remarks
CAMBRIN 1·8·15 9.20 am	Fired on enemy brickstacks in retaliation for shelling CUINCHY trenches	
11·10 am	Fired on trenches N. of BRICKFIELD in retaliation	
5·40 pm	Fired on party of 20 Germans in the open N. of CANAL	
CAMBRIN 2·8·15 5·40 pm	Fired on enemy BRICKSTACKS in retaliation to shelling of ours.	
CAMBRIN 3·8·15	No firing.	
CAMBRIN 4·8·15 9.0 am	Fired on NE BRICKSTACK in retaliation to shelling of our brickstacks	
1·10 pm	Fired on CANAL REDOUBT in retaliation to shelling of CUINCHY trenches	

RFL
MAJOR, R.F.A.O.C.
COMMANDING 56TH BATTERY, R.F.A.

War Diary of the 56 Battery for the 10th of August 1915.

Hour, Date and Place	Events	Remarks
CAMBRIN		
5.8.15. 10.20am	Fired on trenches behind enemy BRICKSTACKS in retaliation to shelling of mine.	
10.45am	Fired on REDOUBT in retaliation to shelling of HOLLOW	
3.35 pm	Fired on working party near A.6.c.8.4.	
CAMBRIN		
6.8.15. 8.45am	Fired on trenches W. of RAILWAY TRIANGLE in retaliation to shelling by IDS in Hohenzoll-	
11.55am		
12.55 pm	Fired on working party in communication trench at A17.a.7.6	
2.8./—} 2.13 pm	Fired in REDOUBT on S. CANAL BANK in retaliation to shelling of HOLLOW.	
2.55 pm	Fired on working party at A16.a.3.6	
4.25 pm	Fired on trench mortar at A21.6.8.7	
5.40 pm	Fired again on working party at A16.a.3.6	
6.30 pm	Fired on CANAL REDOUBT in retaliation	

M——
MAJOR. R.F.A.
COMMANDING 56TH BATTERY, R.F.A.

War Diary of the 58 Battery for the month of August 1915

Hour Date and Place	Events	Remarks
CAMBRIN		
7.8.15 9.20am	Fired on trench mortar at A21.b.8.7	
11.35am	Fired on working party at A10.d.2.5	
2.40pm	Fired on working party at A17.a.7.5	
3.17pm		
CAMBRIN		
8.8.15 12.35pm	Fired on working party near Alba S.S.	
2.38pm	Fired on house E of RAILWAY TRIANGLE.	
5.7pm	Fired on working party at A10.d.5.6.	
11.30pm	Shelled trenches opposite 60th Rifles at their request.	
CAMBRIN		
9.8.15 12.45pm	Fired on working party near Alba S.S.	
1.58pm	Fired on working party at A10.d.5.6	
4.15pm		
5.14pm	Fired on machine gun near NE BRICKSTACK which was carrying on fire on our aeroplanes	
5.25pm	Fired on 2 Krauts mortars N. of LABASSEE RD at request of 60th Rifles.	
10.45pm		

M.
MAJOR. R.F.A.
COMMANDING 58TH BATTERY, R.F.A.

War Diary of the 58 Battery for the Month of August 1915

Hour Date and Place		Events	Remarks
GANABRIN 10·8·15	1·15 am	Fired on Southernmost fixed mortars at 60°	
	9·18 am	Rifle request	
	1·43 pm	Repeated above	
	3·55 pm	Fired on trench mortars under RAILWAY EMBANKMENT in retaliation to shelling of HOLLOW	
	4·10 pm		
	4·20 pm	Fired on working parties near Alba S.S.	
	4·65 pm		
		Ratchets on trenches S. of CANAL BANK	
GANABRIN 11·8·15	8·37 am	Fired on Trenches near CULVERT in retaliation to 115mm Hows shelling on BRICKSTACKS	
	10·3 am	Repeated above	
	11·16 am		
	11·55 am		
GANABRIN 12·8·15		No firing	

Major. R.F.A.
Commanding 58th Battery. R.F.A.

War Diary of the 56th Battery from the 13th to 18th August 1915.

Hour, Date and Place	Events	Remarks
CAMBRIN 13.8.15. 11.2 am	Shelled enemy mine shaft in BRICKFIELD.	12 rounds
2.35 pm	Shelled enemy sniper's post on N. side of RAILWAY EMBANKMENT.	
CAMBRIN 14.8.15	No firing	
CAMBRIN 15.8.15	No firing	
CAMBRIN 16.8.15	No firing	
CAMBRIN 17.8.15. 9 am	Fired on trenches near N.E. BRICKSTACK in retaliation	
1 pm	Shelled work at Sqd 58. S.E. of GIVENCHY.	
8.40 pm	Shelled dug out in front of enemy BRICKSTACKS	
CAMBRIN 18.8.15 1.40 pm	Fired on post on CANAL BANK in retaliation	
5.15 pm	Fired on MINENWERFER S. of LABASSEE RD.	
5.30 pm	Fired on MINENWERFER limbered up, N.E. BRICKSTACK	

MMOR(?) COX
Major RGA
Commanding 56th Battery RGA
A/c 24.

War Diary of the 56th Battery for the month of August 1915

Hour Date and Place	Event	Remarks
CAMBRIN		
19.8.15	No firing	
CAMBRIN		
20.8.15 10.19 am	Shelled reported post of Minenwerfer N. of LA BASSÉE RD	
1.25 pm	In retaliation to Minenwerfer fired 2 salvos at	
4.30 pm }	cnt reported positions	
4.55 pm	Shelled Minenwerfer N. of N.E. BRICKSTACK.	
5.20 pm	Shelled Minenwerfer (small one) N. of LA BASSÉE RD	A.2.a 39
9.44 pm	Fired on Minenwerfer N. of LA BASSÉE RD	
9.55 pm	Fired on Minenwerfer S. of LA BASSÉE RD.	
CAMBRIN		
21.8.15 3.52 am	Fired on Minenwerfer N. of LA BASSÉE RD	
4.45 pm	Fired on Minenwerfer S. of LA BASSÉE RD (shells ½ min fuse)	
4.45 pm	Fired on Minenwerfer near N.E BRICKSTACK.	
7.20 pm	Retaliated above.	

Major R.F.A.
Commanding 56th Battery, R.F.A.

84

War Diary of the 56th Battery for the month of August 1915

Hour Date and Place	Events	Remarks
CAMBRIN 22.8.15 5.8 am	Fired on MINENWERFER S of LA BASSÉE RD.	
5.12 am	Fired on MINENWERFER N. of LA BASSÉE RD	
8.15 am 1.40 p 1.45 p	Fired on MINENWERFER enfilading South of bridgehead A16 c 4.1.	
2.46 p	Shelled MINENWERFER works between A16.c.9.1 and A22.c.1.10 with unknown observation, no firing again seen	
6.48 p 7.57 p	Fired rapid at same target. Fired on MINENWERFER position in A16 c m support from infantry.	
10.12 p	Fired on MINENWERFER (active) S of LA BASSÉE RD.	

[signature] MAJOR. R.F.A.
COMMANDING 56TH BATTERY. R.F.A.

War Diary of 56th Battery from 11th 9 August 1915   85

Hour Date and Place	Event	Remarks
CAMBRIN 23.8.15 12.5a.m.	Fired on MINENWERFER where Small ? LA BASSEE RD.	
12.16 a.m.	Fired on MINENWERFER position Also on report of proceeding up	
12.37 a.m.	Fired to MINENWERFER position S. of LA BASSEE RD.	
11.13 a.m.	Fired on trench works near NE BRICKSTACK.	
6.20 p.m.	Re-registered N.W. corner of RAILWAY TRIANGLE	
CAMBRIN 24.8.15 1.28 a.m.	Fired on MINENWERFER (active) S. of LA BASSEE RD.	
9.30 a.m.	Fired on trench S. of CANAL in retaliation	
6.55 p.m.	Fired on MINENWERFER N. of LA BASSEE RD.	
CAMBRIN 25.8.15 10:25 p.m.	Fired on MINENWERFER S. of LA BASSEE RD	
CAMBRIN 26.8.15 11 a.m.	Fired on trench on RAILWAY EMBANKMENT in retaliation to shelling by 105 m How.	
9.31 p.m.	Fired on MINENWERFER N. of LA BASSEE RD.	

M.
MAJOR. R.F.A.
COMMANDING 56TH BATTERY. R.F.A.

War Diary 56th Battery for the month of August 1915

Hour, Date and Place	Events	Remarks
CAMBRIN 27·8·15 LAMBRIN	no firing	
28·8·15 1·55a	Fired on trenches behind BRICKSTACKS in which a request of infantry	
CAMBRIN 29·8·15	no firing.	
CAMBRIN 30·8·15	1.12 P.m. Fired 4 rounds at TRENCH MORTAR at request of infantry. Casualties during month. Accidentally injured 1 Ordinary admissions to Hosp 2 Joined from BASE 9 Grs 2 Drs	

Morris
MAJOR. R.F.A.
COMMANDING 56TH BATTERY. R.F.A.

2nd Divisional Artillery.

44th BRIGADE R. F. A.

JANUARY 1 9 1 5

Army Form C. 2118.

WAR DIARY
or
INTELLIGENCE SUMMARY
(Erase heading not required.)

Instructions regarding War Diaries and Intelligence Summaries are contained in F.S. Regs, Part II. and the Staff Manual respectively. Title pages will be prepared in manuscript.

Hour, Date, Place	Summary of Events and Information	Remarks and references to Appendices
1/1/15 LE TOURET	Ordered to shift our horses to W of LOCON. Bde only fired a few rounds. Lieut FETHERSTONHAUGH posted to 60th Battery to date 19/12/14.	
2/1/15 — " —	Quiet day; horses moved back to PARADIS except a few for battery for drawing supplies, & the Bde Hd Qrs which remain at LE TOURET. Very quiet.	
3 & 4/1/15 — " —	Ordered to send three gunners to work trench howitzers and mortars.	
5/1/15 — " —	Quiet. The 60th Batt laid out a wire to an alternative observing station in a house in the RUE DU BOIS. The 47th Batt shot with an aeroplane.	
6/1/15 — " —	Quiet. The 60th Batt arranged a shoot in conjunction with aeroplane but too windy and very wet.	
7/1/15 — " —	Quiet, very wet and stormy.	
8/1/15 — " —	Very wet. Concerted bombardment on enemies trenches at 1.23 pm	
9/1/15 — " —	Fine day. Bombardment at 11 am followed by slow fire until 1.50 pm. Rapid for 1.50 pm till 2 pm then was done with a view to covering an attack on our rgt lt by part of the 1st Div S of GIVENCHY. Our trenches nearly full of water	
10/1/15 — " —	Quiet & wet.	
11 & 12/1/15 — " —		

Army Form C. 2118.

WAR DIARY
or
INTELLIGENCE SUMMARY
(Erase heading not required.)

Instructions regarding War Diaries and Intelligence
Summaries are contained in F. S. Regs., Part II.
and the Staff Manual respectively. Title pages
will be prepared in manuscript.

Hour, Date, Place		Summary of Events and Information	Remarks and references to Appendices
13/1/15	LE TOURET	Quiet. The 60th Batt. turned out at 1.30 a.m. to fire on Germans who were putting up entanglements in front of L10 a R/60.	
14/1/15	"	The 60th Batt. worked with aeroplane. Registered three targets. Later in the day fired on convoy reported by K.R.R.	
15/1/15	"	The 47th Battery moved to a new position in the RUE de L'EPINETTE so as to be in closer touch with the infantry. Two guns left at LE TOURET for night firing. Lt. HUGGINS left on appointment to R.H.A. & went to join U Battery.	
16/1/15	"	Lieut. CUTBUSH posted to 47th Battery. Stormy but quiet.	
17/1/15	"	Quiet, no firing.	
18 & 19/1/15	"	Cold. Snow, but quiet.	
20/1/15	"	Quiet, 60th Battery registered on targets with an aeroplane	
21 to 24/1/15	"	Quiet, very little shooting.	
25/1/15	"	Germans attacked GIVENCHY at 8 a.m. took a trench, but were driven out by a counter attack during the morning.	
26 to 31/1/15	"	All quiet. The 60th Battery on the 30th was shelled by a German battery. Three direct hits on their observing station.	

2nd Divisional Artillery.

44th BRIGADE R. F. A.

FEBRUARY 1 9 1 5

Army Form C. 2118.

WAR DIARY
or
INTELLIGENCE SUMMARY

(Erase heading not required.)

Instructions regarding War Diaries and Intelligence Summaries are contained in F. S. Regs., Part II. and the Staff Manual respectively. Title pages will be prepared in manuscript.

Hour, Date, Place	Summary of Events and Information	Remarks and references to Appendices
1.2.15 Le Touret	Quiet. Aeroplane shoot arranged for 60th Battery stopped by bad weather	
2.2.15	Quiet. No firing.	
3.2.15	60th Battery attempted to range with aeroplane observation but wireless again interfered, then observing station shelled & one direct hit. The 47th Battery went into reserve in billets at HINGES & the 37th Battery took their place	✓ ✓ ✓ ✓
4.2.15	Quiet day	
5.2.15	60th Battery moved to CUINCHY & took over the 40th Battery position registration during afternoon	
6.2.15	60th Battery joined in general bombardment of enemy trenches around Luckfields at 2 pm Infantry advanced at 2.15 with their turn & captured brickstacks. Fire continued right & left during remainder of afternoon to enable infantry to dig themselves in. This battery received a congratulatory message from G.O.C. 4th Guards Brigade on the excellent work done by its artillery	
7.2.15	The Germans opened a heavy bombardment at 4 pm & 60th Battery replied by firing on German trenches. The Germans attempted a counter attack which was stopped dead by artillery fire. This battery again congratulated by G.O.C. 4th Guards Brigade. 47th Battery took over 30th Battery position in MARAIS 1 mile W of GORRE. Brigade HQ's moved to LE QUESNOY.	
8.2.15 LE QUESNOY.	Quiet day.	

Army Form C. 2118.

WAR DIARY
or
INTELLIGENCE SUMMARY.
(Erase heading not required.)

Instructions regarding War Diaries and Intelligence Summaries are contained in F.S. Regs., Part II. and the Staff Manual respectively. Title pages will be prepared in manuscript.

Hour, Date, Place	Summary of Events and Information	Remarks and references to Appendices
9.2.15. LE QUESNOY	2Lr HOLMES attached to 47th battery for instruction. 2Lt BORTHWICK attached to 60th battery for instruction. Quiet	
10&11.2.15	" "	
12.2.15	2Lt MURDOCH attached to 47th battery, 60th battery bombarded trenches at 7.45 am in conjunction with the French.	
13.2.15	2Lt GARNETT attached to 60th battery. Bombardment at 10 am in support of French attack, whole battery fired.	
14.2.15		
15.2.15	Quiet. Lt R.F.T. CALDWELL 47th Battery slightly wounded in the shoulder at GIVENCHY & went to hospital.	
16&17.2.15	2Lt BAXTER attached to 47th Battery from R.A.C. on 17th. Quiet.	
18&19.2.15	Quiet. 58th Battery returned to the Brigade & went into new range at LES HARRISOIRS.	X L I V
20.2.15	47th Battery joined in general bombardment on German trenches @ GIVENCHY at 5 pm. Partner of Royal Berks & S. Staffords attacked at 5.20 & artillery fire turned on to support trenches. Trees up to 5.50 pm to cover their retirement. The attack was completely successful, enemy's wire being cut & their trenches being much damaged.	
21.2.15	London Gazette of 14th Jan 1915 publishes the following men were mentioned: — Lt.-Col D Arbuthnot receives the C.M.G. 47th Battery. 2Lt H.N. HUGGINS. Br- CLARKSON. 60th Battery BQMS THOMPSON " CURRY Lt J.P. KNIGHT Sgt HINES " NEALE R.S.M DRYDEN Cpl ADIE " MORRIS Cpl BUXIE 2Lt HOLMES left 47 Battery on completion of attachment & returns to England	

Forms/C. 2118/10

WAR DIARY
or
INTELLIGENCE SUMMARY.
(Erase heading not required.)

Army Form C. 2118.

Hour, Date, Place	Summary of Events and Information	Remarks and references to Appendices
22.2.15 LE QUESNOY	2/Lt BORTHWICK left 60th Battery on completion of attachment & returned to England. Quiet.	
23.2.15 "	Quiet	
24.2.15 "	Quiet. Dr BARNETT accidentally injured (revolver shot) & went to hospital	
25 & 26.2.15 "	Quiet. No firing	
27.2.15 "	66th Battery relieved by 58th Battery & went into reserve at LES HARRISONS. 58th Battery registered.	
28.2.15 "	Quiet. No firing.	

2nd Divisional Artillery.

44th BRIGADE R. F. A.

MARCH 1915

WAR DIARY
or
INTELLIGENCE SUMMARY

(Erase heading not required.)

Army Form C. 2118.

Instructions regarding War Diaries and Intelligence Summaries are contained in F.S. Regs., Part II. and the Staff Manual respectively. Title pages will be prepared in manuscript.

Hour, Date, Place		Summary of Events and Information	Remarks and references to Appendices
1/3/15	LE QUESNOY	60th Battery placed under orders of O.C 26th Brigade R.F.A. & battery moved to LE TOURET, observation station at BREWERY. Some snow.	
2/3/15 to 9/3/15	—	The battery did nothing during this period except reg'n fire on the German trenches. Reg't S.M. PHILLIPS joined Bde Staff.	
10/3/15	—	All three batteries of the brigade took part in a bombardment at 7.30am of the German trenches at GIVENCHY. (The 60th on Bluff) just N of GIVENCHY afterwards the infantry attacked, the wire was not sufficiently cut & the assault failed. There was a second bombardment at 2 p.m. but infantry did not assault again. The 47th Batt fired 740 rounds by able. Bombardment continued but assault abandoned.	
11/3/15	—	Regimental S.M. T.E WOOD promoted to 2/Lt in R.F.A.	
12/3/15	—	Lieut STILLMAN appointed to R.F.C. During the day the 7th Division broke through enemy's lines at PIETRE and Indian Division took BOIS DU BIEGE.	
13/3/15 to 22/3/15	—	On 17th enemy shelled GIVENCHY heavily, very little damage. 60th Batt occupied a new observation station at LE PLANTIN. On 20th Lieut R.T.L.BUSH joined the 60th Battery, & Lieut C Tidey on the 22nd, the former from Home E+, the latter from 41st (L) Bde A.C.	

Army Form C. 2118.

WAR DIARY
or
INTELLIGENCE SUMMARY

(Erase heading not required.)

Instructions regarding War Diaries and Intelligence Summaries are contained in F. S. Regs., Part II. and the Staff Manual respectively. Title pages will be prepared in manuscript.

Hour, Date, Place	Summary of Events and Information	Remarks and references to Appendices
23/3/15 LE QUESNOY 26/3/15 27/3/15 30/3/15	On 24th 60th Battery moved to 30th Bty position i.e. their originally position at the RUE DE CHEVATTE. Left Section joined 1st Division for temporary attachment from the 58th Battery. Ammunition all spent. During the month all the brigade guns were overhauled at CHOCQUES.	

2nd Divisional Artillery.

44th BRIGADE R. F. A.

~~~~~~~~ APRIL 1 9 1 5

Army Form C. 2118.

WAR DIARY
or
INTELLIGENCE SUMMARY.
(Erase heading not required.)

Instructions regarding War Diaries and Intelligence Summaries are contained in F.S. Regs., Part II. and the Staff Manual respectively. Title pages will be prepared in manuscript.

Hour, Date, Place	Summary of Events and Information	Remarks and references to Appendices
LE QUESNOY 30/4/15.	The Brigade Hd. Qrs & the three batteries remained in the same positions.	
4.4.15.	B.S.M. WALBY.G. 47th Battery promoted 2 Lieut and L/v for the base on 16th April. No 23301 Sgt Turner 56" Battery appt. B.S.M (Class 2 WO) in his place.	
6.4.15.	2Lr JOLLY and 2Lr DEWEY joined 60" Batt for attachment	
7.4.15.	Lieut. R. ALLHUSEN posted to 56th Battery	
8.4.15.	Major B.B. CROZIER and Major H.W. NEWCOME awarded D.S.O's 2Lr TIDY, BAXTER, and DYSON proceeded on 8 day's leave. Q.M.S WILSON. A.O.C Bde Staff appointed temporary aS.M (class 1 W.O).	
19.4.15.	2Lr JOLLY and 2Lr DEWEY returned to England from 60th Batt.	

(30.4.15)

2nd Divisional Artillery.

44th BRIGADE R. F. A.

MAY 1915

44TH Brigade R.F.A.

WAR DIARY
or
INTELLIGENCE SUMMARY.
(Erase heading not required.)

Army Form C. 2118.

44TH Bde. R.F.A.

Hour, Date, Place	Summary of Events and Information	Remarks and references to Appendices
1st MAY 1915.	Hqrs at LE QUESNOY. 4th & 56th in action N. of LA BASSEE CANAL 1 mile W. of FESTUBERT. 56th 4 guns in action TOURBIERES; 2 guns attacked to 56th 60th in action 3/4 mile S. of RICHEBOURG ST VAAST	4th Lt H.J. PARHAM & Colliver attached 15-47th to 60th Batteries from home for 2 weeks.
5/V/15	B.A.C. BETHUNE. 60th divided into two 4 gun Batteries, Captain CARFRAE taking command of 2nd	
7/V/15	Capt. KNYVETT, Lt BAXTER & Centre Section 47th detached to Rue de CAILLOUX to co-operate in attack of 1st DIVISION.	
8/V/15	Col. ARBUTHNOT left to take command of Artillery 28th Div	
9/V/15	60th Co-operated in attack of 1st Div. S. of RICHEBOURG	
	L'AVOUÉ. Infantry could not get in	
12/V/15	Centre Section 47th rejoined Battery.	
	Captain G.C. NEVILE left on posting to 96th Battery.	
15-18/V/15	60th Co-operated in attack by 2nd Div. S. of RICHEBOURG L'AVOUÉ. Observation Station heavily shelled 15th - 17th	
16-17/V/15	47th Supported attack by 7th Division, in co-operation with 2nd & Indian Divisions, on GIVENCHY.	

WAR DIARY
or
INTELLIGENCE SUMMARY.
(Erase heading not required.)

Army Form C. 2118.

Hour, Date, Place	Summary of Events and Information	Remarks and references to Appendices
18/V/15	47TH supported attack of 2ND Division in afternoon	
19/V/15	CAPT. CARFRAE (60TH) wounded	17th Lieut. LYON (56TH) sent to replace Captain CARFRAE.
20/V/15	B.Q.M.S. THOMPSON (47TH) awarded Russian decoration St GEORGE'S CROSS 4TH CLASS.	
22/V/15	60TH. Went into rest at FERFAY. Left section of 56TH reformed Battery. Major H.D.O. WARD on posting from 49TH Battery assumed command of Brigade.	
24/V/15	Capt. C.D.G. LYON posted to 41ST Brigade to take over duties of next higher rank. Lt C.L. ZIEGLER to perform duties of next higher rank vice Capt. CARFRAE.	
25/V/15	60TH. Moved to billets at AMES.	
25-26/V/15	56TH supported operations of 47TH (LONDON) Division against GIVENCHY.	

Army Form C. 2118.

WAR DIARY
or
INTELLIGENCE SUMMARY.
(Erase heading not required.)

Instructions regarding War Diaries and Intelligence Summaries are contained in F.S. Regs., Part II. and the Staff Manual respectively. Title pages will be prepared in manuscript.

Hour, Date, Place	Summary of Events and Information	Remarks and references to Appendices
27/V/15	Inspection of 60th by Major-Gen. Horne Captain T.N. French joined from 77th Brigade R.F.A & took over duties of Adjutant.	
29/V/15	47th went into rest near FERFAY.	
31/V/15	2Lt. Allhusen had high explosive shell burst beside him, not hit but knocked out & deaf & went to Hospital.	

T. French Capt. R.F.A.
Adj. 44th Bde. R.F.A.

2nd Divisional Artillery.

44th BRIGADE R.F.A.

JUNE 1915

Army Form C. 2118.

46TH BRIGADE R.F.A.

WAR DIARY
or
INTELLIGENCE SUMMARY.
(Erase heading not required.)

Instructions regarding War Diaries and Intelligence Summaries are contained in F.S. Regs., Part II. and the Staff Manual respectively. Title pages will be prepared in manuscript.

Hour, Date, Place	Summary of Events and Information	Remarks and references to Appendices
1st June 1915.	H.Q. at LE QUESNOY.	
	47th Battery resting at BELLERY S Kely SE Julions	
	50th " in action at TOURBIERES.	
	60th " Arrived from AMES to COMBRIN.	Major J. N. S. Gardner 157A 53°(2) Joined for att'achment.
	2nd Bde slightly wounded, also Dr Tucker arrived.	
	BDE HEAD BETHUNE	
2nd June 1915	56th Battery — nothing of importance	
	60th Battery — firing intermittent ALLOUAGNIN	
3rd June 1915	Lt Skinner photos to 4 Battery from 47th	
	56th Battery move to LAPUGNOY.	
4th " "	58th Battery fires on enemy standing near	
5th " 5 AM	LA BASSEE Road in extinction	
6th " "	47th made from LAPUGNOY gone into action at VERMELLES at N. Side N. of the WATER TOWER

Army Form C. 2118.

24th Brigade R.F.A.

WAR DIARY
or
INTELLIGENCE SUMMARY.
(Erase heading not required.)

Instructions regarding War Diaries and Intelligence Summaries are contained in F.S. Regs., Part II. and the Staff Manual respectively. Title pages will be prepared in manuscript.

Hour, Date, Place	Summary of Events and Information	Remarks and references to Appendices
7th June 1915	Capt. T.N. French joined 38th from Bde 10 pm Lieut (Acting Major) W.E. Maitland Dougall D.S.O. joined the Bde.	
8th June		
9th " 1–10 h.	38th fired on trenches H.Q. TRIANGLE	
10th " 1–10 h.	38th fired 306 rounds howe cutting E.B. ORCHARD at GIVENCHY	
" 11.37 am –1.0 pm	H.Willcocks H.E. fuze 47th By 6.5 pm. B.R. 2nd By. 38th BG fired 40 rds wire cutting N.E.B. ORCHARD 58th fired to enemy trench in retaliation at GIVENCHY	
11th June	Capt. O.S. Cameron joined as Adjutant. Lt. Maitland Dougall D.S.O. to 136th B.R.A.C.	
" 2–4.30 pm	47th fired 38 rds on breastworks near CUINCHY – results very satisfactory –	
12th June	60th exploded a further 100 lbs in workings just behind enemy's trenches.	

WAR DIARY or INTELLIGENCE SUMMARY

Army Form C. 2118.

(Erase heading not required.)

Hour, Date, Place	Summary of Events and Information	Remarks and references to Appendices
13th June 1915 KEMMEL 3 a.m. CAMBRIN	27th June 31st inducted ourselves very cleverly 10th had a recognition not of a nature.	
14th June 1915 TRENCHES	58th recovered and enlarged NE of CUINCHY.	
15th June 10–11 a.m. 5 p.m.	58th had serious injuries. 93 a dist and shortly intercoms after shortly the infantry halted cleared out of the microwave. 49th third 40 women at trenches N.g. HOLMES stated at BRICKSTACKS	Engt. Sister Nyts 56th.
16th June 4–4.40pm	31st Shelters mainly behind and marks on enemy embankment comulanoing into attack on QUEVERING front.	
18th June 2–3 p.m.	56th shelled front enemy myrtle & registration from Binck. 10th Bde filled shells shows 2 m killed 2 wounded Reliefs of RUCOY & Gillony erases	

4th HB of RFA

WAR DIARY
or
INTELLIGENCE SUMMARY.

Army Form C. 2118.

(Erase heading not required.)

Hour, Date, Place	Summary of Events and Information	Remarks and references to Appendices
20th June 15. 8.30 pm	58th Battery withdrew to BETHUNE.	
	60th " " to BOIS DE BIEZ.	
24th June 1915.	Honours	
	Bd. Gen. Sclater Booth D.S.O. Was mentioned in September 13/4/15	
	Major Pen Newcome DSO " "	
	Lieut C.L. Knyvett " "	
	Bomb. PEMBERTON " "	
	58th Battery	
	Brigr. B.B. Crozier D.S.O. " "	
	60th Battery	
	Brigr. H.T. Mostyn Price " "	
	Bomb. Turner Price " "	
	Brigr. Bundey awarded D.S.O. " "	
28th June 1915.	order required " Pudding Crow.	

Army Form C. 2118.

WAR DIARY
44th 73 one BTA
INTELLIGENCE SUMMARY
(Erase heading not required.)

Instructions regarding War Diaries and Intelligence Summaries are contained in F. S. Regs., Part II. and the Staff Manual respectively. Title pages will be prepared in manuscript.

Hour, Date, Place	Summary of Events and Information	Remarks and references to Appendices

23rd June 1915. 60th Battery transferred to Meerut Division

29th June 1915 12pm 47th —

7.48pm 56th 4 Guns came out of action moved to BETHUNE

Reserves re-occupied position vacated on 20-6-15 —

Both Bns moved to BETHY. BEUURY.

30th June 15 — 47th Remaining 2 Guns came into action

J/7/1
15

J Cameron
Lt. Col. RBA 15th
Arg. 44 H.Bde.15th.

2nd Divisional Artillery.

44th BRIGADE R. F. A.

JULY 1915

Army Form C. 2118.

44th B.R.F.A.
WAR DIARY
or
INTELLIGENCE SUMMARY
(Erase heading not required.)

Instructions regarding War Diaries and Intelligence Summaries are contained in F. S. Regs., Part II. and the Staff Manual respectively. Title pages will be prepared in manuscript.

Hour, Date, Place	Summary of Events and Information	Remarks and references to Appendices
1.7.15.	47th Battery moved from BETHUNE at 8 pm. and came into action 1 mile E. of GORRE, taking over from 35th Batt. R.F.A. 36th Batty at CAMBRIN. Registered South of BETHUNE – LA BASSÉE road.	
2.7.15.	47th Battery registered and occupied new observing station in LE PLANTIN.	
4.7.15.	56th Battery heavily shelled by 4.2" & 5.9" how. for 2 hours. 1 gun (Rt. No. 69) knocked out. Maj. B. CROZIER slightly wounded (on duty).	Cause:- Exposure to enemy aeroplane by Coy. 1/7 Kings Liverpool Regt. Billeted at Gorre.
6.7.15.	Both batteries fired on houses and trenches in enemy lines in retaliation.	
7.7.15.	56th Batty received new gun (No. 47).	
9 & 10/7.15.	55th fired on enemy trenches and a pipe in enemy's trench.	
11.7.15.	2 Lt. H. CUTBUSH received Military Cross.	
12 & 13.7.15.	2 Lts. F.L.V. MILLS, H.E. BARKWORTH, H. CUTBUSH, & BROOKES to be Lieuts. Both batteries retaliated on enemy trenches. 1 Cpl. WARD posted to 38th Bde R.F.A. mining.	
14.7.15.	47th Batty fired 65 rounds into crater exploded by enemy in front E. of GIVENCHY. 56th Batty retaliating.	

/11th BDE RFA.

WAR DIARY
or
INTELLIGENCE SUMMARY
(Erase heading not required.)

Army Form C. 2118.

Hour, Date, Place	Summary of Events and Information	Remarks and references to Appendices
15.7.15.	56th Batty registered points between GIVENCHY and BETHUNE — LA BASSEE road from alternative position N.W. of ANNEQUIN.	
16.7.15. 17.7.15. 18.7.15.	56th Batty fired on trench mortar each day, and on working party N.8. of CANAL. A combined night shoot with 16th & 50th Batteries and infantry N.+ S. of CANAL was carried out successfully against this working party.	
19th 7.15. 20th 7.15.	56th Batty fired on working parties N.8 canal.	
21.7.15.	24th made new platform for single gun near FESTUBERT to fire on main crater E. of GIVENCHY.	
22.7.15	Both batteries fired on enemy trenches by day and night in retaliation. 56th Batty frequently fired on working parties N. of CANAL. (Asst)	
31.7.15.	Capt. O.S. CAMERON posted to 364th Batty 20th Bde RFA.	
24.7.15	Hd Qrs and B.A.C. remained in BETHUNE during this month.	

2.8.15.

F.V. Neville Lt.
O/C 11th Bde RFA.

2nd Divisional Artillery.

44th BRIGADE R. F. A.

AUGUST 1 9 1 5

Army Form C. 2118.

WAR DIARY
or
INTELLIGENCE SUMMARY
(Erase heading not required.)

Instructions regarding War Diaries and Intelligence Summaries are contained in F.S. Regs., Part II. and the Staff Manual respectively. Title pages will be prepared in manuscript.

Hour, Date, Place	Summary of Events and Information	Remarks and references to Appendices
1.8.15. BETHUNE.	Quiet but batteries retaliated back to hostile shelling	
9.8.15	of trench mortars, and exchange between batteries continues whilst.	
10.8.15	Br H. F. WILLCOCKS posted to 44th Bde. Lt F.L.V. MILLS posted to 36th D.V. Lt H LOWE R.V.C. posted to 44th Bde. R.G.A. Lt A. WILKES Acts. posted to 44th Bde. but has not joined on 31.8.15	
11.8.15	Retaliation by hostile batteries in reply to shelling of trench mortars took to-day an active form.	
15.8.15	Lt. COL E. H. HARPUR posted to 44th Bde.	
16.8.15	Major H.W. NEWCOME attached Staff Officer to M.G. R.A. 1st Army, and handed over 47th Bty to Capt. KNYVETT.	
17.8.15	Retaliation on usual strengthening of prominent stations completed.	
19.8.15		
20.8.15	Capt. H. H. JOLL from 17th Battery posted to command 47th Battery.	

Army Form C. 2118.

WAR DIARY
or
INTELLIGENCE SUMMARY

(Erase heading not required.)

Instructions regarding War Diaries and Intelligence Summaries are contained in F. S. Regs., Part II. and the Staff Manual respectively. Title pages will be prepared in manuscript.

Hour, Date, Place	Summary of Events and Information	Remarks and references to Appendices
21. 8. 15. BETHUNE	Enemy trench mortars very active but between intervals - continually.	
31. 8. 15		
9. 8. 15	No action of importance on this front during the week. B.A.C. remaining in BETHUNE. Captain C.D. HOPE accidentally injured and admitted to hospital on 10.8.15 Granted 3 weeks sick leave from 17.8.15.	

E.W.Harperne? Lt Col R.F.A.
Comdg. 44 Bgde R.F.A.

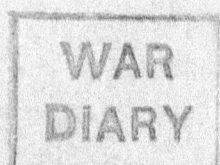

Headquarters,

44th BRIGADE, R.F.A.

(2nd Division)

S E P T E M B E R

1 9 1 5

Army Form C. 2118

WAR DIARY
~~INTELLIGENCE SUMMARY~~
(Erase heading not required.)

Instructions regarding War Diaries and Intelligence Summaries are contained in F. S. Regs., Part II. and the Staff Manual respectively. Title pages will be prepared in manuscript.

Hour, Date, Place	Summary of Events and Information	Remarks and references to Appendices
8 9.15 BETHUNE.	2Lr (Temp) D.J. Anderson R.F.A. Joined + posted to 56 Bry – 47 Bry. "2Lt (S.R.) G.T. Taylor. R.F.A.	E.W.Harper Lieut-Col. R.F.A. Comdg 44th Bde R.F.A.

Army Form C. 2118.

WAR DIARY
or
INTELLIGENCE SUMMARY

(Erase heading not required.)

Instructions regarding War Diaries and Intelligence Summaries are contained in F. S. Regs., Part II. and the Staff Manual respectively. Title pages will be prepared in manuscript.

Hour, Date, Place		Summary of Events and Information	Remarks and references to Appendices
BETHUNE			
1-9-15	BETHUNE	Capt: H.H. JAZZ posted to command 17th Battery R.F.A. Capt: T.N. FRENCH from 56th Batt I.R.F.A. posted to command 47th Batt.T & took over command on 4-9-15	
1-9-15 to 5-9-15	–	} Nothing of importance	
6-9-15 to 19-9-15	–	} A good deal of registration carried out by both batteries. Some retaliation and almost daily firing at MINENWERFER.	
21-9-15	LE PREOL.	Bde H.Q. moved forward to Canal Bank LE PREOL.	
21-9-15 to 25-9-15	–	Both batteries carried out nightly bombardment from 6 p.m. to 6 a.m. on selected points in German line	
25-9-15	–	Both batteries assisted in attack by 2nd Division	
26-9-15	–	Fired on various points in German line as required by infantry	
27-9-15	–	Both batteries at 5 p.m. formed barrage on fortified German points to assist operations by 6th Infantry Brigade.	
28-9-15 to 30-9-15	–	hourly quiet. 56th Battery used special shell on selected points on 27-9-15	
30-9-15	LE QUESNOY.	Bde H.Q. moved to LE QUESNOY	

2nd Divisional Artillery.

44th BRIGADE R. F. A.

OCTOBER 1 9 1 5

Army Form C. 2118.

WAR DIARY
or
INTELLIGENCE SUMMARY

(Erase heading not required.)

Instructions regarding War Diaries and Intelligence Summaries are contained in F. S. Regs., Part II. and the Staff Manual respectively. Title pages will be prepared in manuscript.

Hour, Date, Place	Summary of Events and Information	Remarks and references to Appendices
1.10.15. LE QUESNOY	47th Battery reconnoitred for new position between CANAL and VERMELLES.	
2.10.15. "	47th battery handed over Guns and Gun position to 61st battery, MEERUT Division, and moved to LE QUESNOY.	
3.10.15. "	47th Battery found position E of ANNEQUIN church and started working on new gun pits.	
4.10.15. "	Right section of 47th Bty. moved into new position and registered various points in the morning also with aeroplane observation. In the afternoon 56 B Bty. also registered with aeroplane observation. Remainder of 47th Bty. occupied new position.	
5.10.15. 6.10.15 to 12.10.15 "	Both batteries registered points in neighbourhood of Fosse 8. 56B Bty. retaliated to shelling of HOLLOW by 150mm hows. and frequently to MINENWERFER in BRICKFIELD.	
13.10.15. "	Both batteries cooperated in attack by 46th Division on HOHENZOLLERN REDOUBT. Attack held up after taking Western Face of REDOUBT.	
14.10.15. "	3 men of 47th Bty. wounded by hostile shelling with 105mm. hows. near battery. 56 B Bty. fired on MINENWERFER in BRICKFIELD.	

WAR DIARY
or
INTELLIGENCE SUMMARY

(Erase heading not required.)

Army Form C. 2118.

Hour, Date, Place	Summary of Events and Information	Remarks and references to Appendices
15.10.15 to 18.10.15. LE QUESNOY	56 R Bty. fired daily in retaliation to MINENWERFER in BRICKFIELD	
19.10.15. "	Enemy shelled HOHENZOLLERN REDOUBT heavily in evening. 47 R battery retaliated.	
21.10.15. "	56 R. Battery bombarded strong west of Face 8 at 8.10am for 1 hour according to programme, also retaliated to hostile shelling of trenches S. of CANAL, and dispersed working party. One man was slightly wounded by premature. 47 R Bty. registered with aeroplane observation.	
22.10.15. "	56 R Bty. continued bombardment, retaliated to MINENWERFER in BRICK FIELD, and dispersed working party in TORTOISE.	
23.10.15. "	56 R Bty. continued bombardment at 8 rounds per hour, retaliated to MINENWERFER and heavy shelling. One man slightly wounded by premature.	
24.10.15. BETHUNE	Brigade Hd Qrs. moved to BETHUNE. 56 R Bty. continued bombardment, dispersed working party in PLAIN ALLEY, fired at H Brickstack at request of 6 Inf. Bde., and retaliated to MINENWERFER.	

Army Form C. 2118.

WAR DIARY
or
INTELLIGENCE SUMMARY
(Erase heading not required.)

Instructions regarding War Diaries and Intelligence Summaries are contained in F. S. Regs., Part II. and the Staff Manual respectively. Title pages will be prepared in manuscript.

Hour, Date, Place	Summary of Events and Information	Remarks and references to Appendices
25.10.15. BETHUNE	58 Battery retaliated to hostile shelling, fired at H Brickstack at request of 6 Inf. Bde., and continued bombardment.	
26.10.15 "	58 Battery continued bombardment till 12. noon, fired at H Brickstack at request of 6 Inf. Bde., retaliated to MINENWERFER, and dispersed working party in PLAIN ALLEY.	
27.10.15. to 30.10.15 "	Both batteries registered special points on CANAL banks and to north. 58 Th. Battery fired in retaliation to MINENWERFER and hostile shelling, and fired on house S of Railway Triangle where movement was observed. Enemy guns not more active than usual.	

Army Form C. 2118.

WAR DIARY
INTELLIGENCE SUMMARY
(Erase heading not required.)

Instructions regarding War Diaries and Intelligence Summaries are contained in F. S. Regs., Part II. and the Staff Manual respectively. Title pages will be prepared in manuscript.

Hour, Date, Place	Summary of Events and Information	Remarks and references to Appendices
5.10.15.	Temp. 2nd Lieut. R.Q. THOMAS joined & posted to 47th By from 365th A.C. Temp 2nd Lieut. B.B. MURDOCH posted to 365 Brigade RFA	
14.10.15.	Lieut. H CUTBUSH to hospital, sick	
15.10.15.	Capt. H.F. WILLCOCKS posted to a/d joined 56 th Battery. Lieut H.E. BARKWORTH posted to and joined 44th Bde H.Qrs.	

W.S Sankrybh
Major RFA
a/Adjt. 44 Bde RFA

2nd Divisional Artillery.

44th BRIGADE R. F. A.

NOVEMBER 1915

WAR DIARY / INTELLIGENCE SUMMARY

Army Form C. 2118.

44 Bde R.F.A.

(Erase heading not required.)

Hour, Date, Place	Summary of Events and Information	Remarks and references to Appendices
1.11.15. BETHUNE	No firing.	
2.11.15. "	Sgt. T.H. GODFREE 58 M. Bty. commissioned 2nd Lt.	
3.11.15 to 10.11.15 "	Firing in retaliation to MINENWERFER and howitzer shelling, and at working parties.	
11.11.15. "	58 M. Bty. fired on and stopped field battery active on CANAL bank at A.18.a.0.0.	
12.11.15. "	58 M. Bty. fired on same field battery, and on a working party in the TORTOISE. Lieut. C.L. GREIG posted to 47th Bty. from R.M.A. westward	
13.11.15. "	47th Bty's wagon line moved to new position 1½ miles N.W. of BETHUNE.	
14.11.15. "	11.a.m. 58 M. Bty. shelled battery at A.18.a.0.0 at gun fire for 2 minutes in conjunction with all other batteries of 2nd Division, 6" siege and 3 60 pr. batteries. Retaliation to MINENWERFER. Capt. C.L. KNYVETT left 47th Bty. on posting to 9th Div.	

Army Form C. 2118.

WAR DIARY
or
INTELLIGENCE SUMMARY
(Erase heading not required.)

Hour, Date, Place	Summary of Events and Information	Remarks and references to Appendices
15. 17.15. BETHUNE.	Retaliation to hostile shelling and Minenwerfer.	
16. 12.15. "	56th Bty. fired at working parties entering CANTELEUX ALLEY. Lieut. P.S. FRASER-TYTLER joined 47th Bty. on posting from 4th Bde.	
17. 11.15. "	Usual retaliation.	
18. 11.15. "	No firing.	
19. 11.15. "	56th Bty. fired at working parties and retaliated to Minenwerfer, and at 9.30 p.m. joined in combined bombardment of house and Canal bank at A 16.a.5.1. lasting 10 minutes.	
20. 11.15 } 21. 11.15 } "	Usual retaliation to hostile shelling and Minenwerfer, and firing at working parties.	
22. 11.15. "	47th Bty. were called on to support infantry in mine fighting. About 400x rounds by LA BASSEE – BETHUNE road. 2/Lieut. J.M. SANGAR R.F.R.A. posted to 56th Bty. " A.J. SHIPLEY " " 56th Bty. " T.J.S. HAWTAYNE " " 47th Bty. Capt. DARBY # 2nd Suffolk R.F.A. joined 47th Bty. for instruction Lieut. WOLTON " " 47th " Capt. WARD " " 56th "	

Army Form C. 2118.

WAR DIARY
INTELLIGENCE SUMMARY

(Erase heading not required.)

Instructions regarding War Diaries and Intelligence Summaries are contained in F. S. Regs, Part II. and the Staff Manual respectively. Title pages will be prepared in manuscript.

Hour, Date, Place	Summary of Events and Information	Remarks and references to Appendices
23.11.15. BETHUNE	Naval retaliation to hostile shelling + minenwerfer	
24.11.15. "	56th Bty. displaced enemy in open at A.10.d.7.9 and A.11.a.5.7. Naval retaliation. 2nd Lieut. R.Q. THOMAS. 47th Bty. posted to 36th Bde & joined.	
25.11.15. "	Naval retaliation.	
26.11.15. "	56th Bty. dispersed working parties and enemy in the open. 2nd Lieut. R.T. BAXTER promoted Lieut. a/23/VIII/15.	
27.11.15. "	Naval retaliation and firing at working parties.	
28.11.15 } " 29.11.15 }	Both Batteries took part in bombardment of enemy's front line and mine craters from 200t to 700t S of BETHUNE – LA BASSÉE road. Capt. WARD, Capt. DARBY, & Lt WOLTON left on 28.11.15 Maj PENDELBURY 2nd Suffolk RFA. joined 47 Bty on 29.11 to relieve 58 t Lt. PRETTYMAN.	
30.11.15 "	Enemy artillery much more active. Both batteries retaliated.	

J.K. Harker
Lieut-Col R.F.A.
Cmdt 44th Bde R.F.A.

2nd Divisional Artillery

44th BRIGADE R. F. A.

DECEMBER 1 9 1 5

Army Form C. 2118.

WAR DIARY
or
INTELLIGENCE SUMMARY
(Erase heading not required.)

Hour, Date, Place	Summary of Events and Information	Remarks and references to Appendices
1-12-15 BETHUNE	Retaliation + firing at various enemy working parties and suspected O.Ps.	
7-12-15 "		
7-12-15 "	2 Lieut: H.J.W. KINGSTON posted to and joined B.A.C.	
8-12-15 "	Usual retaliation to Minenwerfers and shelling of our line, and fire on working parties.	
14-12-15 "		
8-12-12-15 "	Capt: E.W. GRIFFITH posted to B.A.C. Both batteries carried out bombardment of enemies 2nd line trenches.	
15-12-15		
16-12-15	Retaliation + shelling of working parties carried out by both batteries + some successful bombardments of M.G. emplacements.	
22-12-15		
23-12-15	Capt: E.W. GRIFFITH joined B.A.C.	
23-12-15	47th Battery bombarded HAISNES at night	

Army Form C. 2118.

44 IBaRDA

WAR DIARY
or
INTELLIGENCE SUMMARY
(Erase heading not required.)

Instructions regarding War Diaries and Intelligence Summaries are contained in F. S. Regs., Part II. and the Staff Manual respectively. Title pages will be prepared in manuscript.

Hour, Date, Place	Summary of Events and Information	Remarks and references to Appendices
24/12/15 25/12/15 BETHUNE	Some pre-arranged bombardments carried out	
26-12-15 to 31-12-15	Usual retaliation etc by both batteries	
28-12-15	47th Battery successfully engaged an enemy sniper's post, obtaining several direct hits.	
	During the month various Officers + men of 33rd Div. were attached to both batteries for instruction.	
	Enemy guns were much more active than in preceding month + observation stations were hit several times.	
	On Dec 14th Wagon line of 47th Battery moved to new position	

DHHarper
Lieut-Col R.F.A.
Comd F 44th D 2nd R.F.A.

Forms/C. 2118/11.

**2ND DIVISION
DIVL ARTILLERY**

44TH BRIGADE R.F.A.
JAN - APL 1916.

Bde broken up in May 1916

2nd Divisional Artillery.

44th BRIGADE R. F. A. ::: JANUARY 1916.

WAR DIARY
or
INTELLIGENCE SUMMARY

Army Form C. 2118.

Hour, Date, Place	Summary of Events and Information	Remarks and references to Appendices
Jan 1st 1916	Both Batteries in same position as last month. 47th Bty Bombarded RAIGNES in retaliation to enemy shelling of FOSSE 9 CORONS. 50th Bty fired on houses near A.22.b.3.2. Reserves on TORTOISE & shelling of SOUTH BANK of TRAIN in retaliation of KINGSCLERE. Fired on enemy Bty at A.21 & 5.8 Houses A22 & 26 in retaliation to enemy shelling HOH. VIEW. Enemy exploded large mine just S of BETHUNE LA BASSEE RD and did no apparent damage to enemy front line trenches at CAMBRIN in reply. Enemy shelled our rear lines. Bty return no casualties injured to Enemy lines. In KEEPS.	
2nd		
3rd 4th & 5th	Usual retaliation fairly quiet.	

Army Form C. 2118.

WAR DIARY
or
INTELLIGENCE SUMMARY

(Erase heading not required.)

Instructions regarding War Diaries and Intelligence Summaries are contained in F. S. Regs., Part II. and the Staff Manual respectively. Title pages will be prepared in manuscript.

Hour, Date, Place	Summary of Events and Information	Remarks and references to Appendices
21st	Post billets letter signatures	
	26th Bty first on duty working party afternoon	
22nd	27th Battery from BELLEVUE S.TRENCH	
23rd	26th " " " INA/BART	
24th to 27th	Preparation & inspection	
	Each Bty carried out registration and fire	
	trials, working from emplacements and	
	communication	
28th	Enemy very active. Enemy attention otherwise	
	Apple Tree & 91st fired a lot in reply	
	Col LE DASSE had with me registered on	
29th	S6 & front on BUF DE MARIE also J also	
	& had all night in army trenches by day	
29 & 31st	Quiet	
	Lt HF BARKWORTH promoted Capt. 17.12.15	
	" " " " posted to W/O orders 11.1.16	
	Mr. chute MW firework Twenty 66 and appointed	
	Capt 11.1.16	
16.1.16	Capt. HF COURAGE RA transport RAC via Capt 2nd Division 6.10 BAC	
	LT-COL HARBOR RA to 167th Bde 33rd Div 28/1/16	
	2LT A.L. WYNNE-WILLIAMS joined 56th Bty 21.1.16	

2nd Divisional Artillery.

44th BRIGADE R. F. A. ::: FEBRUARY 1916.

WAR DIARY
or
INTELLIGENCE SUMMARY 44th Bde R.F.A.

Army Form C. 2118

(Erase heading not required.)

Hour, Date, Place	Summary of Events and Information	Remarks and references to Appendices
1st to 6th Feb 1916	47th Bty in rest at Bty Wagon lines W of BETHUNE during which time their guns were manned by a Bty of 33rd Div	
4th to 16th	56th Bty moved retaliation to registrations	2nd Lt Q.D. CHALMERS
	47th Bty in action as during latter part of joined 47th Bty 16th	
7th to 12th	Jan N of BETHUNE–LABASSEE CANAL	
	56th Bty in rest at Bty Wagon lines LE QUESNOY during which time their guns were manned by a Bty of 33rd Div	
13th	56th Bty returned to their guns.	
	Nothing unusual neither visit.	
15th	One section 47th Bty moved into action	
16th	Bde moved out to rest at NORRENT-FONTES after handing over guns to 38th Division	
17th to 21st	Bde rested	
21st	47th Bty Right Section moved into action Bty	
22nd	47th Bty Centre Section " " "	
	Position just S of FOSSE 9 – LABASSEE Railway about 1000 yards E of ANNEQUIN. Left Section & Wagon Lines in SAILLY-LA BOURSE awaiting building of Pits. Bty relieved 1/II London Bty R.F.A. T.F.	

WAR DIARY or INTELLIGENCE SUMMARY of 44th Bde RFA

Army Form C. 2118

(Erase heading not required.)

Instructions regarding War Diaries and Intelligence Summaries are contained in F.S. Regs., Part II. and the Staff Manual respectively. Title pages will be prepared in manuscript.

Hour, Date, Place	Summary of Events and Information	Remarks and references to Appendices
22nd Cont'd	56th Bty moved into action at PHILOSOPHE in relief of 1/10 London Bty R.F.A. T.F.	
23rd & 24th	Bty registered. Bde Hqrs moved to NOYELLES	
25th & 26th	47th Bty Handed over to A/65 Bty R.F.A. 12th Division. Two Sections moved to MARLES LES MINES. 56th Handed over to D/65 Bty R.F.A. 12th Division. Left Section moved to MARLES LES MINES. Bde. Hqrs moved to HERRIN	
27th	47th Bty Moved into action E of BULLY-GRENAY. Moved into empty pits. 56th Left 2 Centre Sections joined up at HERRIN. 2nd Division commenced relieving 18th French Division in view of German offensive against VERDUN which commenced on 20th.	W. Stubbs Lt Col 44th Bde
28th	47th Preparing Position. 56th In rest at HERRIN	LT COL T.L.S OFF RFA joining from 45th Bty to commence the Bde
29th	47th Bty Position heavily shelled 8.45 – 9.45 a.m. 10 c.m. & 1.20 to 1.40 p.m. with 15 c.m. One gun disabled. Casualties Nil. Reinforcements 20 Other Ranks 1 Officer	

2nd Divisional Artillery.

44th BRIGADE R. F. A. ::: MARCH 1916.

Army Form C. 2118.

WAR DIARY
or
INTELLIGENCE SUMMARY

44th Bde : RFA

March 1916 (Erase heading not required.)

Instructions regarding War Diaries and Intelligence Summaries are contained in F. S. Regs., Part II. and the Staff Manual respectively. Title pages will be prepared in manuscript.

Hour, Date, Place	Summary of Events and Information	Remarks and references to Appendices
March 1st	Moved Bty position 300 yards to rear in BULLY GRENAY. 57th Bty.	
2nd	57th moved into action in BOIS NOULETTE and commenced preparing new position.	
3rd to 12th	Btys registered and worked on improving positions. Bde HQrs at AIX NOULETTE commanding SOUCHEZ GROUP consisting of 50th 9th 17th (19th 20th) Batteries (London Terr.)	
12th	Lt Brookes left 50th Bty for England as Temp. Capt.	
16th	Maj T.N. French left 47th Bty on posting to R.H.A.	
22 & 23rd	Division relieved by 23rd Division.	
	Bde HQrs relieved by 102 Bde.	
	Bde moved into Fifteenths rest area. 47th Bty to AUCHEL 50th and BAC to FOSSE CLARENCE, HQrs & CALONNE-RICOUART	
23rd	Capt J. Atkinson left 50th Bty on posting to 47th Bty	
25th	Lt G. Gardner joined 50th as act-Capt. from 70 Bde	
27th	47th Bty moved to new billets at GRICOURT	
28th – 31st	Bde is resting and training.	

MWL [initials] 1/4/16

2nd Divisional Artillery.

44th BRIGADE R. F. A. ::: APRIL 1916.

Army Form C. 2118.

WAR DIARY
or
INTELLIGENCE SUMMARY

(Erase heading not required.)

44th Bde R.F.A.

April 1916

Instructions regarding War Diaries and Intelligence Summaries are contained in F. S. Regs., Part II. and the Staff Manual respectively. Title pages will be prepared in manuscript.

Hour, Date, Place	Summary of Events and Information	Remarks and references to Appendices
1st to 18th	The Brigade was in rest. 47th Bty at GRICOURT, 36th and BAC at FOSSE CLARENCE. Bde Hqrs at COLONNE-RICOURT.	
16th	The following Officers joined the 44th Bde. 2nd Lt W. G. Brown from D.A.C. 15th Bty from Gillingham Woolwich 47th " (On 9th Sic dicision from RA Reserve LISTERES) " The Division went into the line in relief of the 23rd Div.	7½ "
19th	The Bde formed 3, 4 gun batteries temporarily whilst in action. The controls by - commanded by Capt Frank Tyler composed of right-section of nil Bty. 47th Bty in action at Bois de NOULETTE (position made by 35th Cast time we were)	47" " 15 " "
	Contents Bty " " " " BULLY GRENAY "	
	Bde Hqrs on command of SOUCHEZ GROUP at AIX NOULETTE.	
	B.A.C. at CITÉ DE LIATOY near BARLIN.	
20th to 28th	There was no change. Germans used fairly active and made several raids and gas attacks to our flanks but none on our front.	
28th	Bde Hqrs handed SOUCHEZ GROUP over to 41st Bde and went to RACQUENCOURT	W. Nuttall Lt Col Comdg 44th Bde RFA 1.5.16
29th to 30th	No change.	

www.ingramcontent.com/pod-product-compliance
Lightning Source LLC
Chambersburg PA
CBHW080818010526
44111CB00015B/2576